T0215473

Communications in Computer and Information Science 651

Commenced Publication in 2007
Founding and Former Series Editors:
Alfredo Cuzzocrea, Dominik Ślęzak, and Xiaokang Yang

More information about this series at http://www.springer.com/series/7899

Lynn Batten · Gang Li (Eds.)

Applications and Techniques in Information Security

6th International Conference, ATIS 2016
Cairns, QLD, Australia, October 26–28, 2016
Proceedings

 Springer

Editors
Lynn Batten
School of Information Technology
Deakin University
Geelong
Australia

Gang Li
School of Information Technology
Deakin University
Geelong
Australia

ISSN 1865-0929   ISSN 1865-0937   (electronic)
Communications in Computer and Information Science
ISBN 978-981-10-2740-6   ISBN 978-981-10-2741-3   (eBook)
DOI 10.1007/978-981-10-2741-3

Library of Congress Control Number: 2016953327

Printed on acid-free paper

This Springer imprint is published by Springer Nature
The registered company is Springer Nature Singapore Pte Ltd.
The registered company address is: 152 Beach Road, #22-06/08 Gateway East, Singapore 189721, Singapore

Preface

The International Conference on Applications and Techniques in Information Security (ATIS) has been held annually since 2010. This year, the seventh in the series was held at Central Queensland University, Cairns, Australia, during October 26–28, 2016. ATIS 2016 focuses on all aspects of techniques and applications in information security research, and provides a valuable connection between the theoretical and the implementation communities attracting participants from industry, academia, and government organizations.

The selection process this year was competitive, each submitted paper was reviewed by three members of the Program Committee. Following this independent review, there were discussions among reviewers and chairs. A total of ten papers were selected as full papers, and another three papers were selected as short papers.

We would like to thank everyone who participated in the development of the ATIS 2016 program. In particular, we would give special thanks to the Program Committee, for their diligence and concern for the quality of the program, and also with their detailed feedback to the authors. The general organization of the conference also relied on the efforts of ATIS 2016 Organizing Committee. We especially thank Biplob Ray, Judy Chow, and Gina Jing for the general administrative issues, the registration process, and the maintaining of the conference website.

Finally and most importantly, we thank all the authors, who are the primary reason why ATIS 2016 is so exciting, and why it is the premier forum for presentation and discussion of innovative ideas, research results, applications, and experience from around the world as well as for highlight activities in the related areas. Because of your great work, ATIS 2016 was a great success.

September 2016

Lynn Batten
Gang Li

Organization

ATIS 2016 was organized by the School of Engineering and Technology, Central Queensland University (Australia), and the School of Information Technology, Deakin University (Australia).

ATIS 2016 Steering Committee

Steering Committee

Lynn Batten (Chair)	Deakin University, Australia
Heejo Lee	Korea University, Korea
Gang Li (Secretary)	Deakin University, Australia
Jiqiang Liu	Beijing Jiaotong University, China
Tsutomu Matsumoto	Yokohama National University, Japan
Wenjia Niu	Chinese Academy of Sciences, China
Yuliang Zheng	University of Alabama at Birmingham, USA

ATIS 2016 Organizing Committee

Program Co-chairs

Lynn Batten	Deakin University, Australia
Gang Li	Deakin University, Australia

Conference Advisor

William Guo	Central Queensland University, Australia

Organizing Committee

Biplob Ray (Chair)	Central Queensland University, Australia
Rudd Rankine	Central Queensland University, Australia
Nur Hussan	Central Queensland University, Australia
Joy Jenkins	Central Queensland University, Australia
Gina Jing (Secretary)	Central Queensland University, Australia
Jamie Shield	Central Queensland University, Australia

ATIS 2016 Program Committee

Mamoun Alazab	Macquarie University, Australia
Moutaz Alazab	Melbourne Institute of Technology, Australia
Edilson Arenas	Central Queensland University, Australia
Leijla Batina	Radboud University, The Netherlands
Liang Chang	University of Manchester, UK
Guoyong Cai	Guilin University of Electronic Technology, China
Morshed Choudhury	Deakin University, Australia

Xuejie Ding	Chinese Academy of Sciences, China
Jiaxin Han	Xi'an Shiyou University, China
Nur Hussan	Central Queensland University, Australia
Meena Jha	Central Queensland University, Australia
Rafiqul Islam	Charles Sturt University, Australia
Kwangjo Kim	KAIST, Korea
Jie Kong	Xi'an Shiyou University, China
Heejo Lee	Korea University, Korea
Qingyun Liu	Chinese Academy of Sciences, China
Yufeng Lin	Central Queensland University, Australia
Jiqiang Liu	Beijing Jiaotong University, China
Wei Ma	Chinese Academy of Sciences, China
Lei Pan	Deakin University, Australia
Na Pang	Chinese Academy of Sciences, China
Rudd Rankin	Central Queensland University, Australia
Biplob Ray	Central Queensland University, Australia
Wei Ren	China University of Geosciences, China
Zhongzhi Shi	Chinese Academy of Sciences, China
Tony de Souza-Daw	Melbourne Polytechnic, Australia
Lisa Soon	Central Queensland University, Australia
Jamie Shield	Central Queensland University, Australia
Jinqiao Shi	Chinese Academy of Sciences, China
Dirk Thatmann	Technische Universitaet Berlin, Germany
Steve Versteeg	CA, Australia
Matthew Warren	Deakin University, Australia
Xiaofeng Wang	Siemens Research, China
Hongtao Wang	Chinese Academy of Sciences, China
Ping Xiong	Zhongnan University of Economic, China
Gang Xiong	Chinese Academy of Sciences, China
Rui Xue	Chinese Academy of Sciences, China
Fei Yan	Wuhan University, China
Ziqi Yan	Beijing Jiaotong University, China
Feng Yi	Chinese Academy of Sciences, China
Xun Yi	RMIT University, Australia
John Yearwood	Deakin University, Australia
Chengde Zhang	Southwest Jiaotong University, China
Yuan Zhang	Nanjing University, China
Dali Zhu	Chinese Academy of Sciences, China
Liehuang Zhu	Beijing Institute of Technology, China
Tianqing Zhu	Deakin University, Australia
Tingshao Zhu	Chinese Academy of Sciences, China
Yujia Zhu	Chinese Academy of Sciences, China

Sponsoring Institutions

Central Queensland University, Australia
Deakin University, Australia

Invited Speeches

Countermeasures Against Implementation Attacks on Private and Public-Key Cryptosystems

Paolo Maistri

Centre National De Ra Recherche Scientifique, Paris, France
paolo.maistri@imag.fr

Abstract. Implementing a secure system is much more complex than providing a theoretically secure algorithm. Careless implementations can be easily vulnerable to a large spectrum of passive and/or active attacks. In this talk, we will present the most important attacks and a (non- exhaustive) list of possible countermeasures that will make the attacker's job a bit harder. Both symmetric and asymmetric cryptography will be presented, with application examples to the Advanced Encryption Standard and Elliptic Curve Cryptosystems.

Keywords: Implementation attacks · Cryptography

Current and Emerging Issues in Privacy and Data Security in Queensland, Australia and Internationally

Philip Green

Office of the Information Commissioner, Brisbane City, QLD, Australia
Philip.Green@oic.qld.gov.au

Abstract. The increasing pace of technology and the explosion in production and collection of data has created serious challenges for privacy and data protection. Australia's privacy legislation dates back to 1988 and is largely based on international human rights protections that pre date this legislation. Where hacktivists or sophisticated hackers can mount attacks in a matter of days or weeks, government legislators and regulators and procurement processes can often take years to respond. Queensland's legislation is currently under review but even since 2009 has not kept up with the technological advances to date nor is it equipped to deal with the challenges of the future. The Panama leak has been used to argue that a kind of Moore's law applies to the magnitude of data breaches. Governments around the world have taken note and there is international debate on where lines should be drawn and the balance been privacy and security should be struck. Increasingly jurisdictions are investigating mandatory data breach notification and debating proportionality in terms of counter terrorism, privacy and other civil rights and ethical issues. Business and Government are looking for productivity gains and customer focused solutions to be had from big data and data analytics. Queensland's Privacy Commissioner will discuss emerging issues in privacy and data protection in Australia, the Queensland State and Internationally. In an increasingly connected and wired world, the challenges cannot be ignored and the stakes are high. Data security becomes of life threatening proportions in a virtual operating theatre or in a world of autonomous vehicles which is rapidly approaching.

Keywords: Data protection · Privacy

Contents

Data Privacy

Attacks on Data Security Systems

A New Sign-Change Attack
on the Montgomery Ladders

Lynn Margaret Batten[⊠] and Mohammed Khalil Amain

Deakin University, Burwood, Australia
{lmbatten, mkamain}@deakin.edu.au

Abstract. In the 1980s, Peter Montgomery developed a powerful, fast algorithm for calculating multiples of field elements. Over subsequent years, the algorithm was adapted to work in arbitrary abelian groups. By the year 2000, it had been developed further to resist standard power and timing attacks and became known as the 'Montgomery ladder'. In the literature, the focus of this algorithm has been to compute from most to least significant bit, known as the 'left-to-right' version. In this paper, we first resurrect the corresponding 'right-to-left' version of the Montgomery powering ladder and then demonstrate a new attack on both versions in the context of elliptic curves.

Keywords: Montgomery ladder · Elliptic Curve · ECDLP · Sign change attack

1 Introduction

In the papers [1, 2], Peter Montgomery introduced ideas for speeding known methods of factorization; the focus was on efficiency. His principal context was finite fields with a multiplicative operation, but he also considered the elliptic curve case with an additive operation in the later paper. Since those papers appeared, a number of authors have developed from them efficient algorithms for point addition in the elliptic curve case, and these have been determined to be resistant to a number of modern day side channel attacks. What has come to be known as the 'Montgomery powering ladder' has been studied extensively by Joye and Yen in [3] and by Joye in [4]. In particular, in Sect. 4.1 of [3], both 'left-to-right' and 'right-to-left' versions of Montgomery's algorithm are presented in Fig. 6, the former starting with the most significant bit and the latter with the least significant bit of the exponent. The authors note that these algorithms are highly regular in the sense that when any bit of the exponent is being processed, the two operations of multiplying and squaring are used together, which prevents a power or timing analysis to distinguish between such operations. However, the authors of [3] also note that the algorithms of their Fig. 6 contain 'dummy' operations when a bit of the exponent is 0, making them susceptible to 'safe-error' attacks. The authors then modify the left-to-right version in their Fig. 7 which makes no use of dummy operations. This last algorithm is what is typically now known as the 'Montgomery powering ladder' (e.g. [5–7]). Our aim in the current paper is to first resurrect the corresponding dummy-free right-to-left version of the Montgomery powering ladder and then to demonstrate a new attack on both versions.

© Springer Nature Singapore Pte Ltd. 2016
L. Batten and G. Li (Eds.): ATIS 2016, CCIS 651, pp. 3–14, 2016.
DOI: 10.1007/978-981-10-2741-3_1

In Sect. 2, we describe briefly the types of attacks against scalar multiplication elliptic curve algorithms, with a focus on the Montgomery powering ladders. Section 3 provides the necessary background on Weierstraß elliptic curves and also the special 'Montgomery elliptic curves'. Section 4 describes both versions of the Montgomery powering ladders as used in this paper. Sects. 5 and 6 are the main focus of the paper, describing our attack in detail, followed by examples computed with Maple software [8]. Section 7 briefly summarizes our work.

2 Physical Attacks on Elliptic Curves

For any positive integer k and point P on the elliptic curve E, by kP we mean P added to itself k times. The underlying security of the use of elliptic curves in cryptography is based on the difficulty, believed to be mathematically NP-hard [9], of finding the scalar multiple k when P and Q = kP are known. This is referred to as The Discrete Logarithm Problem for elliptic curves (ECDLP).

Because attacking the mathematical structure in order to recover the secret k is believed to be extremely difficult, a number of alternative types of attacks on the implementation of the scalar multiple algorithm have been developed over many years. Common so-called 'side channel attacks' in the literature are based on power, electromagnetic reading and timing, which are aimed at distinguishing between operations while the algorithm is performed. In all cases, there is an assumption that the attacker has sufficient access to the device to be able to perform the attack. Good review articles on these attacks are available; for example [5, 10].

In this paper, our interest is in a second important type of attack, called a 'fault attack', introduced in the late 1990s [11] and classified by the literature into safe error, weak curve-based and sign change attacks. The first of these induce temporary faults into cryptographic computations with the aim of leaking key bits as shown in Joye and Yen in [11, 12] and in [3]. The second type moves computations from a strong elliptic curve onto a weak elliptic curve. The third type works directly on the original curve and introduces sign changes to points used in the computation.

Algorithms in which the computations made take the same amount of time are referred to as *regular*. Such algorithms are resistant to (simple) power, timing, and safe error attacks [4].

In the present paper we focus on the regular point addition algorithms due to Montgomery which are benchmarks for algorithms based on the common 'double and add' method for elliptic curves [5]. There are two versions, one using the bits of the scalar multiple from most to least significant bit and the other in the opposite direction. Algorithms 1A, 1B (a minor efficiency improvement on 1A) and 3 of later sections demonstrate these two directions; regularity is evident by the fact that in all three algorithms, an addition is always followed by a doubling. The authors of [3] give a comprehensive analysis of our target algorithms, focusing on the 'left to right' version which they refer to as the 'Montgomery powering ladder' (their Fig. 7), and discuss a range of attacks against which it is resistant; they argue that because of its speed and secure implementation it is highly suitable for use on constrained devices. When the powering ladder is used on the special class of Montgomery curves described in Eq. (5)

of Sect. 3 along with the addition operations described in Eqs. (6) and (7), it is resistant against weak curve-based attacks [5].

In this paper, we implement a sign change attack on both left-to-right and right-to-left versions of the Montgomery powering ladder. Like all physical attacks, we assume that we can access the device, and in our case, we require the ability to write to, read and erase from Erasable Programmable Read-Only Memory (EPROM). How this is done practically (especially in an IoT context) can be viewed on the YouTube video at https://www.youtube.com/watch?v=vUDP1XTmF9A. Our attack has some features of the work of Yen and Joye in [11] where that paper gives a detailed theoretical description of the placement of faulty bits in registers during the computations of an exponentiation algorithm.

The next section describes two types of elliptic curve equations, one a completely general situation over a field of any characteristic referred to as the Weierstraß elliptic curve, the other, due to Montgomery and designed specifically for speed and efficiency with use of the powering ladder.

3 Weierstraß and Montgomery Elliptic Curves – Background

Elliptic curves form the basis of an efficient cryptosystem which is often chosen for implementation on small devices, such as those which would be used to authenticate messages in an IoT scenario. The general affine version of the elliptic curve equation, as taken from the monograph [13] by Blake, Seroussi and Smart, is known as the Weierstraß elliptic curve equation and is given by:

$$y^2 + a_1 xy + a_2 y = x^3 + a_3 x^2 + a_4 x + a_5 \tag{1}$$

where the constants a_i are from a fixed finite field GF(q) of any characteristic ≥ 2, and q is a prime power. (We have taken the liberty of labelling the coefficients in a slightly different way than that of Eq. (3.3) in [13].) Using E to refer to such a curve, we then use the notation $E(F_q)$ to indicate that the coefficients are from GF(q).

The points of such a curve, along with an additional 'point at infinity', which acts as the identity and for which we use the symbol O, form an abelian group under an operation '+' on the points defined algebraically by the Eqs. (3) and (4) given below [13; Chap. 3]. This '+' operation can be defined regardless of the characteristic of the field. Points on the curve are represented as affine pairs (x, y) where each of x and y come from GF(q) and satisfy the Eq. (1).

For any point P = (x, y) on E, the negative of P is defined to be the point

$$- P = (x, -y - a_1 x - a_2). \tag{2}$$

As mentioned on p. 33 of [13], this definition applies for all finite field characteristics. We define P + (– P) to be O.

In order to define the addition of two points (other than the pair P and –P) on E, we introduce some further notation to simplify the formulas. Let $P1 = (x_1, y_1)$ and $P2 = (x_2, y_2)$ be distinct points on E. In case P1 = P2 or P1 $\neq$ P2, coefficients α and β

can be defined as described in [13] allowing us to derive the sum of P1 and P2 using the same equations. In fact, letting P1 + P2 = (x_3, y_3), then the coordinates of this sum in both cases above are given by:

$$x_3 = \alpha^2 + a_1\alpha - a_3 - x_1 - x_2, \tag{3}$$

and

$$y_3 = -(\alpha + a_1)x_3 - \beta - a_2. \tag{4}$$

In the late 1980s, Montgomery developed a revised form of (1) in order to speed up elliptic curve factorization methods [2]. The general version of these Montgomery curves, for prime order fields of characteristic > 3, in affine form is given by:

$$By^2 = x^3 + Ax^2 + x \tag{5}$$

where A and B are elements of the underlying field.

As pointed out by Hamburg in [14], over fields of prime characteristic congruent to 3 modulo 4, the curve in (5) is equivalent to one with B = 1, whereas this is not the case for fields of prime characteristic congruent to 1 modulo 4.

Computations on an elliptic curve can be performed in affine or in projective coordinates. However, the authors of [15] advise that not transferring back to affine coordinates before output provides an adversary with the opportunity of capturing some side-channel information from the projection as has been shown in [16]. In the present paper, we will stay with affine point representation.

Based on the Eq. (5), the x-coordinate values are computed as follows [2] for 2(x, y):

$$x_{2P} = \left[(x^2 - A)^2 - 8Bx\right] / [4(x^3 + Ax + B)] \tag{6}$$

for P1 = (x_1, y_1) and P2 = (x_2, y_2) with $x_1 \neq x_2$, letting x_R be the x-coordinate of the sum and $x_{R'}$ be the x-coordinate of the difference P1 − P2:

$$x_R = [2(x_1 + x_2)(x_1x_2 + A) + 4B]/(x_1 - x_2)^2 - x_{R'}. \tag{7}$$

We refer to Eqs. (6) and (7) as the *Montgomery point addition* formulas.

While Montgomery curves proved efficient for use in elliptic curve factorisation methods, especially in conjunction with the Montgomery ladders [14], the curves have been found to be too specialised for general use in most international standards used today, including ANSI, IEEE and SEC (e.g. [17]). The efficiency benefit of Eqs. (6) and (7) is that only the x-coordinate of points is used at each stage; however, the major drawback with using (7) is that it requires that we be able to produce a difference of two points. Izu, Möller and Takagi comment on this issue in [18] and in [17], where the doubling and addition operations are separated. Efficiency is achieved by writing the multiplier k as a sum of powers of 2 and producing repeated doublings of the point using (6) until sufficiently many have been acquired. At this stage, however, in order to produce the value for Q = kP, point additions of random points must be made, and thus the need for point differences becomes problematic. The authors of [18] deal with this situation by use of a 'YRecovering' algorithm given in Appendix A.5 of their paper. Alternatively, Eqs. (3) and (4) can be used throughout instead of (6) and (7), and this is our choice.

None-the-less, the 'right-to-left' and 'left-to-right' algorithms produced by Montgomery for point additions (actually first proposed in the context of RSA), and made explicit on p. 7 of [3], are still much in demand for point doubling which is the major phase of the fast exponentiation procedure in point scalar multiplication especially over curves with form (5).

In our case, we focus on an attack in which many additions, which are not doublings are required. We therefore use the addition formulas of (3) and (4); an additional benefit for us is that these provide both coordinates of the sum which we can then compare with our target point.

4 The Montgomery Ladder – Background

The Montgomery powering ladder, introduced in [2] to assist in speeding up elliptic curve factorization methods, has been analysed in many papers in the last twenty years and is still used as one of the benchmarks of elliptic curve computations of point multiples (e.g. [5]). While it was initially introduced for use with the Montgomery curve equations, the authors of [3, 19] explain how it can be adapted to work with any abelian group, and so to any elliptic curve group represented by the form (1). In fact, it is currently one of the three most commonly used standards for elliptic curve scalar multiplication [6], the others being the Coron 'Add-and-double always' algorithm which is Algorithm 1' of [20], and the Add-Always scalar multiplication method of Joye [4; Algorithm 3]. In all three algorithms, the computations made take the same amount of time, without the use of dummy operations, giving them the attribute 'regular'. Despite that, all are vulnerable to some recent attacks.

Any algorithm for point scalar addition inputs a secret multiplier in bit format; the algorithm may then begin with either the most significant bit or the least significant bit. Left-to-right versions have some advantages; one being that the first bit can be assumed to be 1, and so the algorithm can actually begin with the second bit.

The aim of this paper is to attack the ECDLP for both right-to-left and left-to-right versions of the Montgomery powering ladder; we deal with the left-to-right version in Sect. 5 and the right-to-left version in Sect. 6. When using bits of k from left-to-right, we can always assume that the first bit is 1. In this case, there are two ways to establish the algorithm computing multiples of P: either begin from the left-most bit, or begin from the second bit from the left. For small values of k, the latter method saves one round in the loop and so is more efficient than the former method; however, for very large values of k, there is little saving in efficiency between the two methods. In the next sections, we present the Montgomery algorithms corresponding to each method and explain the minor differences in our attack on them.

5 Our Attack on the Left-to-Right Montgomery Algorithm

Algorithm 1A (taken from [3; Fig. 7] where it is presented in multiplicative form) describes the Montgomery powering ladder with left-to-right scalar multiplication beginning the point additions from the left-most bit, while Algorithm 1B (taken from [5; Algorithm 1]) describes the Montgomery powering ladder with left-to-right scalar multiplication beginning the point additions from the second bit from the left. We attack both.

Algorithm 1A Montgomery powering ladder, left-to-right scalar multiplication

INPUT: $k = (k_t, k_{t-1}, \ldots, k_1)_2$, $P \in E(F_q)$.
 OUTPUT: $k*P$
 1. $R(0) \longleftarrow O$, $R(1) \longleftarrow P$
 2. For i from t down to 1 do
      2.1 $R(\neg k_i) \longleftarrow R(0)+R(1)$
      2.2 $R(k_i) \longleftarrow 2R(k_i)$
 End for
 3. Return $(R(0))$

The input of both algorithms is a t-bit secret key $k = (k_t, k_{t-1}, \ldots, k_1)$ in binary form, a known base point P, which belongs to the known curve $E(F_q)$ over the field GF(q). The output is the known point $Q = k*P$. However, Algorithm 1B assumes that $k_t = 1$ and does not use this bit. Both algorithms initiate $R(0)$ as an intermediate variable used to store the scalar additions of P; the first algorithm begins with the identity O while the second begins with the point P. Note that after the step with i = t in Algorithm 1A, we are at the same position as in line 2 in Algorithm 1B because $k_t = 1$.

Algorithm 1B Montgomery powering ladder, left-to-right scalar multiplication

INPUT: $k = (1, k_{t-1}, \ldots, k_1)_2$, $P \in E(F_q)$, where $k_t = 1$.
 OUTPUT: $k*P$
 1. $R(0) \longleftarrow P$, $R(1) \longleftarrow 2P$
 2. For i from t-1 down to 1 do
      2.1 $R(\neg k_i) \longleftarrow R(0)+R(1)$
      2.2 $R(k_i) \longleftarrow 2R(k_i)$
 End for
 3. Return $(R(0))$

The addition operation used is that of scalar addition and can use Eqs. (3) and (4) or (6) and (7). In our examples in this section and the next, we use addition point formulas (3) and (4).

Our Attack on the Montgomery Ladders of Algorithms 1A and 1B

We assume that each algorithm is stored in EPROM on a chip to which we have access and on which we can induce faults during the processing of the algorithm. While the curve, field, and points P and Q are public knowledge and available on the chip; we do not know k nor the value of t, but do know that the bits of k are stored in registers on the chip and were used in processing the output Q. When we access the chip's EPROM, we assume that the bits of k used (in the case of Algorithm 1A, these are k_t, k_{t-1}, ..., k_1 and in the case of Algorithm 1B, these are k_{t-1}, k_{t-2}, ..., k_1) are accessible in order from left to right. We assume that we can access the chip immediately after the addition algorithm has been run and that the bits of k are still stored in the registers.

Our attack makes changes to produce algorithms which capture the binary values of k and our approach is based on ideas concerning the 'safe error attack' on elliptic curve crypto-systems described in [11] in which the attacker injects a fault into the intermediate calculation values of multiples of P, and from this, deduces a bit value of the secret k. As usual, we assume that the attacker has the necessary access to the hardware on which the algorithm runs.

Algorithm 2. Negative base point attack on Montgomery powering ladder left-to-right scalar multiplication

INPUT: The elliptic curve E, its field F_q, points P and Q on E (F_q).
Access to Algorithm 1 on hardware containing the stored (in left to right order) bits of the (secret) value k where Q = kP.
OUTPUT: k in binary form.
1. R(0) ⟵ P, R(1) ⟵ 2P, e ⟵ 2
COMMENT: assign first pointer label e ⟵ 2 and through the loop store the bits of k in order in the (t-1)-tuple d.
2. X ⟵ – P.
COMMENT: Inject error by using X instead of P in addition operations
3. While R (0) ≠ Q do
  3.1 Z ⟵ R(0)
  3.2 N ⟵ R(0) + X
  3.3 If k_e=1 then
    R($\neg k_e$) ⟵ R(0) +X
    End if
  3.4 If R($\neg k_e$) = N then
    d_e ⟵ 1
COMMENT: Eliminate the error in R($\neg k_i$) by replacing fault value by a correct value stored in Z
    R($\neg k_e$) ⟵ Z
    Else
    d_e ⟵ 0
    End If
  3.5 R($\neg k_e$) ⟵ R(0) + R(1)
  3.6 R(k_e) ⟵ 2R(k_e)
  3.7 Print d_e
  3.8 e ⟵ e+1
End While loop
4. set t ⟵ e–1
5. k = (1, d_2, d_3 ... d_{t-1}, d_t)

Our attack is described in Algorithm 2 and based on Algorithm 1B. We assume that pointers point to the bits k_{t-1}, ... k_2, k_1 stored in this order in memory, which we can then access in order labelling the pointers as we go beginning with 2 and increasing through point additions until we arrive at Q, at which point we can determine the length of k. Along the way, the captured bits of k are stored in values d_2, d_3 ... d_{t-1}, d_t. The attack is based on the introduction of a significant error, using $- P$ instead of P at some points in the point addition process. In order to avoid confusion, we set $- P$ to be the value X, and to avoid forensic discovery of this error, we correct it at line 3.4.

The same attack works against Algorithm 1A with the minor changes of setting R (0) to O, R(1) to P and e to 1.

Example of our Attack on the Montgomery Ladder of Algorithm 1B

We implement our attack in software using Intel (R) Core (TM) i7-4500 CPU 2.4 GHZ with 8 GB RAM as a hardware platform and Windows 7 as the operating system. Maple 18 [8] was chosen as the software platform as it contains a cryptography package designed for elliptic curve arithmetic operations.

Here, we demonstrate the attack on a Weierstraß curve, using point addition formulas (3) and (4) in the computations, so that both coordinates are evaluated in each step.

We use the curve $y^2 = x^3 + x + (3w + 3)$ over GF (5^2) where w is a solution of the irreducible polynomial $x^2 + 4x + 2$ over GF(5), and so $w^2 = w+3$. We choose the point P = (0, 2w + 1), value k = 6 and using Algorithm 1B, compute Q = (2w + 2, 3). Based on the general Weierstraß equation (1), the coefficients are: $a_1 = 0$, $a_2 = 0$, $a_3 = 0$, $a_4 = 1$, $a_5 = 3w + 3$. We also need –P which, from Eq. (2), is (0, 3w + 4).

Maple will not directly compute elliptic curve points for GF (5^2) using the inbuilt commands. We therefore used as many of the Maple commands as we could and did the remaining work by hand.

Because k is 110 in binary form, Algorithm 1B will run through two complete iterations, in each of which it will produce a bit of k. It will stop at the beginning of the third iteration after checking that R(0) has reached Q. The steps are given below.

Step 1
>R(0) = P=[0, 2w + 1]
>R(1) = 2P = [3w + 4, 3w + 2]
> e = 2;
Step 2
X = – P = [0, 3w + 4];
Step 3
Iteration 1
Since R(0) $\neq$ Q, continue
Z = R(0) = [0, 2w + 1]
N = R(0) + X=P + (–P) = O
Since $k_2 = 1$ then R($\neg k_2$) = R(0) + X = P + (–P) = O
Since R($\neg k_2$) = R(0) = N we set $d_2 = 1$ and 'eliminate error': R($\neg k_2$) by
R($\neg k_2$) = Z = P = [0, 2w + 1]
R($\neg k_2$) = R(0) = R(0) + R(1) = P+2P = 3P = [4w + 3, 4w + 3]
R(k_2) = R(1) = 2R(k_2) = 2R(1) = 4P = [2w, w + 3]
Set e = e + 1 = 3 updating the pointer

Iteration 2

Since $R(0) \neq Q$, continue

$Z = R(0) = 3P = [4w + 3, 4w + 3]$

$N = R(0) + X = 3P + (-P) = 2P = [3w + 4, 3w + 2]$

Since $k_3 = 0$ then no value is added to X and stored in $R(\neg k_3)$

Since $R(\neg k_3) = R(1) \neq N$ we set $d_3 = 0$ and no error occurs in $R(\neg k_3)$

$R(\neg k_3) = R(1) = R(0) + R(1) = 3P + 4P = 7P = [2w, 4w + 2]$

$R(k_3) = R(0) = 2R(k_3) = 2R(0) = 6P = [2w + 2, 3]$

Set $e = e + 1 = 4$ updating the pointer

Iteration 3

Since $R(0) = Q = 6P = [2w + 2, 3]$ then the iterations end.

Set $t = e - 1 = 3$

We output the final value of k as the components of the triple $(1, d_2, d_3)$ which is 110.

6 Our Attack on the Right-to-Left Montgomery Algorithm

While there appears to be no algorithm in the literature cited as being the right-to-left equivalent of Algorithm 1A, we take the right-to-left version of the EC equivalent of Fig. 6(b) of [3] which we modify to be suitable for elliptic curves. The details are shown in Algorithm 3. Because the algorithm begins from the right, it must start with the least significant bit.

Algorithm 3 initiates $R(0)$ as an intermediate variable used to store the additions of P, beginning with the identity point. $R(1)$ is initiated to P. Then the algorithm enters a for loop from 1 up to t. In each iteration, $R(1)$ is stored in the dummy variable G and when the loop ends, the value in $R(0)$ will be the final result of k*P. As in the previous section, addition is based on Eqs. (3) and (4).

Algorithm 3. Montgomery powering ladder, right-to-left scalar multiplication
INPUT: $k = (k_t, k_{t-1}, \ldots, k_1)_2$, $P \in E(F_q)$
OUTPUT: $Q = k*P$
1. $R(0) \longleftarrow O$
2. $R(1) \longleftarrow P$
3. For i from 1 up to t do
3.1 $G \longleftarrow R(1)$
3.2 $b \longleftarrow 1 - k_i$
3.3 $R(b) \longleftarrow R(0) + R(1)$
3.4 $R(1) \longleftarrow G$
3.5 $R(1) \longleftarrow 2R(1)$
End for
4. Return $R(0)$

Our Attack on the Montgomery Ladder of Algorithm 3

Regarding access to memory and which values are known or unknown, we make the same assumptions here as for the attack on Algorithms 1A and 1B. The attack is shown in Algorithm 4.

In this attack, the pointer is first set to the right-most bit (labelled 1) and moves left until the value of the storage $R(0)$ reaches Q. At this stage, we capture the value of t and can output all t bits of k.

Example of our Attack on the Montgomery Ladder of Algorithm 3

We use the same experimental environment and addition operations as for the attack of the previous section.

The chosen curve is of Montgomery type:

$y^2 = x^3 + 35605593463286537234197408466 4\, x^2 + x$ with $P = (737747, 724721)$, $Q = kP = (3812234234350108026693041842 79,\ 32418667974535034980321800 28$ 49) where $k = 8957$ and the prime field is $GF(1083948976932424618521046268491)$.

We use point addition formulas (3) and (4) in the computations. We do not give the Maple code here for lack of space, but the steps are similar to those in our example for Algorithm 2. Steps 1 and 2 set up R(0), R(1) and X; in Step 3, the error is introduced and b is used as a variable storing a bit. The correct value of the current multiple of P is always stored in R(0). The loop continues until R(0) = Q.

Algorithm 4. Negative base point attack on Montgomery powering ladder right-to-left scalar multiplication

INPUT: The elliptic curve E, field F_q over which it is defined, points P and Q on $E(F_q)$.
Access to Algorithm 3 on hardware containing the stored (in right to left order) bits of the (secret) value k where Q=kP.
OUTPUT: k in binary form.
1. R(0) ⟵ O, R(1) ⟵ P, e ⟵ 1
COMMENT: assign pointer label e ⟵ 1, through the loop store the bits of k in order in the d_e.
2. X= – P.
COMMENT: Inject error by using X instead of P in addition operations
3. While R(0) ≠ Q do
3.1 E ⟵ R(0)
3.2 G ⟵ R(1)
3.3 b ⟵ 1– k_e
3.4 N ⟵ R(0) + X
3.5 If b=0 then
    R(b) ⟵ R(0) + X
    End If
3.6 If R(b) = N then
    { d_e ⟵ 1
COMMENT: Eliminate the error in R(¬ k_e) by replacing fault value by a correct value stored in E
    R(b)=E}
    Else
      d_e ⟵ 0
    End If
3.7 R(b) ⟵ R(0) +R(1)
3.8 R(1) ⟵ G
3.9 R(1) ⟵ 2R(1)
3.10 Print d_e
3.11 e ⟵ e+1
End While loop
4. set t ⟵ e-1
5. k= $(d_t, d_{t-1}, \ldots, d_2, d_1)$

7 Summary Discussion

This paper has focused on the Montgomery powering ladder, which has been of great interest in several contexts since the middle of the 1980s. The left-to-right version, Algorithms 1A and 1B as presented here, has proved to be resistant to a number of traditional attacks on such algorithms. Until today, not much emphasis has been placed on the comparable right-to-left version; however, in this paper, we present this as Algorithm 3, and point out that this version is as resistant to attack as its counterpart.

The emphasis of our paper is a sign-change attack against both of these algorithms. The attack assumes that we have access to a device on which the algorithms ran and can therefore capture the key bits stored in the registers. Blömer et al. [21] suggested a countermeasure against sign change attacks based on an 'after-the-fact' check for errors; however, this does not prevent our attacks as we eliminate errors as we go.

References

1. Montgomery, P.L.: Modular multiplication without trial division. Math. Comput. **44**, 519–521 (1985)
2. Montgomery, P.L.: Speeding the Pollard and elliptic curve methods of factorization. Math. Comput. **48**, 243–264 (1987)
3. Joye, M., Yen, S.-M.: The Montgomery powering ladder. In: Walter, C.D., Koc, C.K., Paar, C. (eds.) CHES 2002. LNCS, vol. 2779, pp. 291–302. Springer, Heidelberg (2002)
4. Joye, M.: Highly regular right-to-left algorithms for scalar multiplication. In: Paillier, P., Verbauwhede, I. (eds.) CHES 2007. LNCS, vol. 4727, pp. 135–147. Springer, Heidelberg (2007)
5. Fan, J., Verbauwhede, I.: An updated survey on secure ECC implementations: attacks, countermeasures and cost. In: Cramer, R. (ed.) Cryphtography and Security: From Theory to Applications. LNCS, vol. 7194, pp. 265–282. Springer, Heidelberg (2012)
6. Feix, B., Roussellet, M., Venelli, A.: Side-channel analysis on blinded regular scalar multiplications. In: Meier, W., Mukhopadhyay, D. (eds.) Progress in Cryptology–INDOCRYPT 2014. LNCS, vol. 8885, pp. 3–20. Springer, Heidelberg (2014)
7. Li, L., Li, S.: High-performance pipelined architecture of elliptic curve scalar multiplication over GF (2 ^{m}). IEEE Trans. Very Large Scale Integr. Syst. **24**, 1223–1232 (2016)
8. Maplesoft 2015, 'User Manual'. http://www.maplesoft.com/documentation_center/
9. Galbraith, S., Gaudry, P.: Recent progress on the elliptic curve discrete logarithm problem. Number 1022 in the IACR eprint Archive (2015). (https://eprint.iacr.org/2015/1022.pdf)
10. Fan, J., Guo, X., De Mulder, E., Schaumont, P., Preneel, B., Verbauwhede, I.: State-of-the-art of secure ECC implementations: a survey on known side-channel attacks and countermeasures. In: 2010 IEEE International Symposium on Hardware-Oriented Security and Trust (HOST), pp. 76–87. IEEE Press, New York (2010)
11. Yen, S.M., Joye, M.: Checking before output may not be enough against fault-based cryptanalysis. IEEE Trans. Comput. **49**, 967–970 (2000)
12. Yen, S.-M., Ko, L.-C., Moon, S.-J., Ha, J.C.: Relative doubling attack against montgomery ladder. In: Won, D.H., Kim, S. (eds.) ICISC 2005. LNCS, vol. 3935, pp. 117–128. Springer, Heidelberg (2006)

13. Blake, I.F., Seroussi, G., Smart, N.: Elliptic curves in cryptography. London Mathematical Society Lecture Notes, vol. 265. Cambridge University Press, Cambridge (1999)
14. Hamburg, M.: Decaf: Eliminating cofactors through point compression. In: Gennaro, R., Robshaw, M. (eds.) CRYPTO 2015. LNCS, vol. 9216, pp. 705–723. Springer, Heidelberg (2015)
15. Karaklaji, D.K., Fan, J., Schmidt, J.R.M., Verbauwhede, I.: Low-cost fault detection method for ECC using Montgomery powering ladder. In: Proceedings of Design, Automation & Test in Europe Conference & Exhibition (DATE), pp. 1–6. IEEE Computer Society (2011)
16. Naccache, D., Smart, N.P., Stern, J.: Projective coordinates leak. In: Cachin, C., Camenisch, J.L. (eds.) EUROCRYPT 2004. LNCS, vol. 3027, pp. 257–267. Springer, Heidelberg (2004)
17. Izu, T., Takagi, T.: A fast parallel elliptic curve multiplication resistant against side channel attacks. In: Naccache, D., Paillier, P. (eds.) PKC 2002. LNCS, vol. 2274, pp. 280–296. Springer, Heidelberg (2002)
18. Izu, T., Möller, B., Takagi, T.: Improved elliptic curve multiplication methods resistant against side channel attacks. In: Menezes, A., Sarkar, P. (eds.) INDOCRYPT 2002. LNCS, vol. 2551, pp. 296–313. Springer, Heidelberg (2002)
19. Brier, E., Joye, M.: Weierstraß elliptic curves and side-channel attacks. In: Paillier, P., Naccache, D. (eds.) PKC 2002. LNCS, vol. 2274, pp. 335–345. Springer, Berlin, Heidelberg (2002)
20. Coron, J.-S.: Resistance against differential power analysis for elliptic curve cryptosystems. In: Koç, Ç.K., Paar, C. (eds.) CHES 1999. LNCS, vol. 1717, pp. 292–302. Springer, Heidelberg (1999)
21. Blömer, J., Otto, M., Seifert, J.-P.: Sign change fault attacks on elliptic curve cryptosystems. In: Breveglieri, L., Koren, I., Naccache, D., Seifert, J.-P. (eds.) FDTC 2006. LNCS, vol. 4236, pp. 36–52. Springer, Heidelberg (2006)

Investigating Cube Attacks on the Authenticated Encryption Stream Cipher ACORN

Md Iftekhar Salam[1]($\boxtimes$), Harry Bartlett[1], Ed Dawson[1], Josef Pieprzyk[1,2],
Leonie Simpson[1], and Kenneth Koon-Ho Wong[1]

[1] Science and Engineering Faculty, Queensland University of Technology,
Brisbane, QLD 4000, Australia
{m.salam,h.bartlett,e.dawson,josef.pieprzyk,
lr.simpson,kk.wong}@qut.edu.au
[2] Institute of Computer Science, Polish Academy of Sciences, Warsaw, Poland

Abstract. The cube attack is an algebraic attack that allows an adversary to extract low degree polynomial equations from the targeted cryptographic primitive. This work applies the cube attack to a reduced round version of ACORN, a candidate cipher design in the CAESAR cryptographic competition. The cube attack on 477 initialization rounds of ACORN can recover the 128 bit key with a total attack complexity of about 2^{35}. We have also shown that linear equations relating the initial state of the full version of ACORN can be easily generated which can lead to state recovery attack with an attack complexity of about $2^{72.8}$.

Keywords: CAESAR · Authenticated Encryption · Cube attack · ACORN

1 Introduction

The cube attack is an algebraic cryptanalysis method introduced by Dinur and Shamir at EUROCRYPT 2009 [1]. The attack is applicable to a wide variety of symmetric ciphers. In this paper, we analyze the applicability of the cube attack to the authenticated encryption (AE) stream cipher ACORN.

ACORNv1 [2] is a binary feedback shift register based AE stream cipher submitted to the Competition for Authenticated Encryption: Security, Applicability, and Robustness (CAESAR) [3] in May 2014. ACORNv1 is one of the cipher proposals selected for the second round of CAESAR. In September 2015, a tweaked version named ACORNv2 [4] was included in the second-round submission of the CAESAR competition.

Both versions of ACORN use a 128-bit secret key and a 128-bit initialization vector. The cipher provides authentication and encryption functionality for the input message. Encryption is performed by XOR-ing the plaintext message bitstream with the binary keystream output by the keystream generation function.

© Springer Nature Singapore Pte Ltd. 2016
L. Batten and G. Li (Eds.): ATIS 2016, CCIS 651, pp. 15–26, 2016.
DOI: 10.1007/978-981-10-2741-3_2

Message authentication is provided by a 128-bit tag computed from the plaintext message, secret key and the initialization vector. The cipher also provides authentication but not encryption for associated data (AD) if required.

2 ACORN Specification

ACORN uses a 128-bit key, $K \in \{0,1\}^{128}$ and a 128-bit initialization vector, $V \in \{0,1\}^{128}$. The cipher takes a plaintext message $P \in \{0,1\}^*$ of arbitrary length l_p within the range $0 \leq l_p \leq 2^{64}$. The input to the cipher may also include associated data $D \in \{0,1\}^*$, again of arbitrary length l_d within the range $0 \leq l_d \leq 2^{64}$. The associated data does not require confidentiality and so is not encrypted, but an integrity mechanism is applied. The output of ACORN consists of ciphertext $C \in \{0,1\}^{l_p}$ and an authentication tag $T \in \{0,1\}^{64 \leq l_{tag} \leq 128}$, where l_{tag} denotes the size of the tag. The designer of the cipher strongly recommends the use of a 128-bit tag. The structure of ACORN is based on six binary linear feedback shift registers (LFSRs) of lengths 61, 46, 47, 39, 37 and 59, respectively, and an additional 4 bit register. This gives the cipher a total internal state, $S = \{s_0, \cdots, s_{292}\}$ of 293 bits.

Operations performed in the ACORN stream cipher can be divided into four phases: Initialization, Encryption, Tag Generation and Decryption & Tag Verification. The differences between ACORNv1 and ACORNv2 occur mainly in the initialization phase and in the varying feedback functions used in the specific rounds of different phases. For the rest of the paper, unless specifically mentioned, ACORN will refer to both versions: ACORNv1 and ACORNv2. Figure 1 shows the generic diagram of ACORN encryption and decryption procedure.

ACORN uses three functions: an output keystream generation function, f_z, a nonlinear feedback function, f, and a state update function. ACORN state update function uses the output of the nonlinear feedback function and the input message, M to update internal state of the LFSRs. Depending on the phase the cipher is in, the input message M can denote either the key, initialization vector, padding vectors, associated data or plaintext. All of the register stages in the internal state are updated linearly except for the last register stage, s_{292}. The last register stage, s_{292}, is updated by combining the output of the nonlinear feedback function f with the input message M. Different variants of the feedback function f are used in different phases of the cipher. The output keystream generation function, f_z takes input from several register stages and generates a single keystream bit output at each round of the encryption/decryption phase and during the final l_{tag} rounds of the tag generation phase.

During the initialization phase, ACORN takes as its input message, M, a sequence formed by the concatenation of the key, initialization vector, padding bits and associated data. Note that, in the original description of ACORN the designer considered only loading of the key, initialization vector and the padding bits as part of the initialization phase. However, we consider the associated data loading process as part of the initialization phase, because no keystream bits are output until after that process is complete. The initialization phases

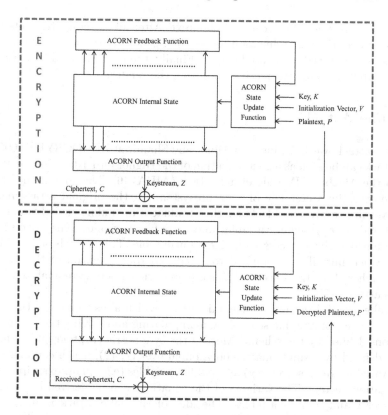

Fig. 1. Generic Diagram of ACORN

in ACORNv1 and ACORNv2 differ with respect to the feedback function used during the different rounds of the cipher, and also in the selection of the padding bits. For ACORNv1, the padding bits are constant whereas in ACORNv2 the padding bits are derived from the key bits. Both versions of ACORN have an initialization phase of $l_d + 2048$ rounds.

The encryption procedure is same for both ACORNv1 and ACORNv2. The cipher takes the plaintext, P, as the input message, M, and computes the output ciphertext, C, by XOR-ing the output keystream Z and plaintext P.

After all the plaintext bits have been processed, the keystream generator goes through a 1024 round finalization process. During these 1024 rounds, the input message M is a 1024-bit padding vector consisting of one bit with value 1 followed by 1023 bits of value 0. The difference in the finalization phase of ACORNv1 and ACORNv2 is the feedback function used during the different rounds. During the last l_{tag} rounds of the finalization phase, the output bits Z are computed and used as the tag.

The decryption procedure is the same as the encryption phase except that at each round the decrypted plaintext P' is computed by XOR-ing the ciphertext bit C with the corresponding keystream Z and this bit is fed back in to the internal state instead of the original plaintext. After all the ciphertext bits have been processed, the tag verification process first generates the tag using the same tag generation procedure as used earlier. Finally, the tag is verified by matching the generated tag with the received tag from the sender.

3 Cube Attack

The cube attack was introduced by Dinur and Shamir at EUROCRYPT 2009 [1]. The attack can be seen as a generalization of the Higher Order Differential attack [5] and the Algebraic IV differential attack (AIDA) [6]. The goal of the attack is to recover the secret key of a cryptosystem. In the original attack model, the adversary is given a blackbox that evaluates an unknown polynomial, Q constructed over l_k secret variables and l_v public variables. The adversary is also assumed to have access to a single output bit. This is a chosen plaintext attack which initially was applied to a reduced round version of the Trivium stream cipher [1,7]. Later, several other symmetric ciphers were analyzed based on this attack [8–10].

A cube attack is a kind of algebraic attack which aims to recover the secret variable of a cryptographic scheme by manipulating and solving the polynomial equations defined by the scheme. Most of the symmetric cryptographic schemes can be defined by a single master polynomial over $GF(2)$, which contains some secret variables (e.g., secret key) and public variables (e.g., plaintext, ciphertext, initialization vector). The variants of the equations can be derived by changing these secret and public variables. The idea of the cube attack is to generate sufficient number of closely related low degree equations by manipulating the public variables. An adversary can then solve the generated low degree equations to recover the secret variables of the cryptosystem. The low degree equations are derived by evaluating the master polynomial over all the possible values of some specific public variables and then summing the resultant equations. This is called the cube attack since we sum over all the possible values of the n-dimensional Boolean cube. The observation found here is that, if an appropriate cube was chosen then summing over all the possible values of the cube will eliminate all the higher degree terms from the resultant equation. In general, the cube attack is performed in two phases: Preprocessing phase and Online phase.

3.1 Preprocessing Phase

In the preprocessing phase the adversary has access to both the public and secret variables. The goal of this phase is to construct linear equations in terms of the secret variables by using suitably chosen cubes. Let the blackbox polynomial, $Q(K, V)$ be constructed over the set of l_k secret variables in K and l_v public variables in V. Let $K = \{k_0, \cdots, k_{l_k-1}\}$ denote the set of the secret variables and $V = \{v_0, \cdots, v_{l_v-1}\}$ denote the set of the public variables of the cryptosystem. The adversary manipulates these secret and public variables to construct a linear variant of the blackbox polynomial, Q.

In the preprocessing phase, the adversary selects a cube of size l_c by randomly choosing l_c of the public variables $v_i \in V$. This selected subset of the public variables is known as the cube. The blackbox polynomial is evaluated and summed over all the possible values of this cube to determine if there exist any linear equation for that selection of the cube. The rest of the values of the public variables are usually set to zero. Let Q_c denote the equation obtained after summing over all the possible values of the cube.

At first, a linearity test is performed to verify that the equation obtained for the chosen cube is linear. This can be done by using the BLR test [11], which chooses two random input vectors $x, y \in \{0, 1\}^{l_k}$ and then verifies that $Q[0] + Q[x] + Q[y] = Q[x + y]$. This is a probabilistic test which indicates Q_c is non-linear if the test fails. For randomly chosen x, y, the BLR test can detect non-linearity in Q_c with a probability of 0.5. Therefore, if Q_c passes the BLR test j times, then the probability of it being non-linear is 2^{-j}.

The adversary finds out the linear relation if the chosen cube passes the linearity test. To find out the linear coefficients of the secret variable k_i for a particular cube, the adversary sets k_i to 1 and all the other secret variables are set to zero. The public variables are set to zero everywhere except the l_c cube bits. Summing over all the possible values of the cube bits will give one bit of output which is the linear coefficient of k_i. The constant (either 0 or 1) in the linear equation for any cube is computed by summing over all the possible values of the cube with input values of zero everywhere except the chosen cube. This procedure is done to find out all the linear coefficient of the secret variables. The left hand side of the linear expression is then reconstructed once all the coefficients for the particular cube have been found. In the preprocessing phase, the adversary performs the procedure for different combinations of cubes and tries to find out sufficient number of cubes which output a linear equation. Note that not all choices of the cube will result in a linear equation.

3.2 Online Phase

In the online phase the adversary has access to the public variables and the cubes obtained during the preprocessing phase, to try to recover the secret variables. An adversary evaluates and sums the output of the master polynomial over all possible values of a cube to determine the right hand side of the corresponding linear equation. The resultant equations then can be solved by Gaussian elimination to recover the secret variables. Algorithm 1 provides a pseudo-code for the generic cube attack.

4   Cube Attack on ACORN

This section provides a description of the application of the cube attack to the authenticated encryption stream cipher ACORN. The attack can be performed either in the initialization phase, encryption phase or in the decryption phase. ACORN does not take any external input during the tag generation phase and

---

Algorithm 1. Algorithm for Cube Attack

Inputs: Output kesytream bits, Number of linearity test, Initial cube size, Number of cubes tested

Output: Secret variables of the cryptosystem

Preprocessing Phase

Select a random cube: Estimate the degree, d of the polynomial, choose a initial cube size $l_c \leq d - 1$ and select a subset of l_c public variables v_i

Do the linearity test and construct the linear equation

for Number of Cubes Tested **do**

    for Number of linearity test **do**

        if nonlinear **then**

            if Cubes Tested < Number of Cubes Tested **then**

                Select another cube of size l_c and do the linearity test

            else

                Increase the number of cube variables l_c

            end if

        else

            Compute the coefficients of the secret variables by summing over all the possible values of the cube

            if all the coefficients are zero **then**

                Select another subset of l_c public variables

            else

                Output the coefficients and construct the linear equation

            end if

        end if

    end for

end for

Do the preprocessing phase till sufficient number of linear equations are generated

Online Phase

Find the right hand side of the linear equations:

for Each possible cube found in prepreocessing phase **do**

    Compute the output bit

    Sum all the output bits for all the possible values of the cube

end for

Solve the linear equations to recover the secret variables

---

therefore a cube attack is not applicable in this phase. In the following, we discuss the applicability of the cube attack to the initialization and encryption phases of ACORN.

4.1   Cube Attack During the Initialization Phase

In the initialization phase the key, initialization vector and associated data are loaded in to the internal state of ACORN. In general, the cube can be selected either from the input key, the initialization vector or the input associated data set. However, an adversary needs to have the ability to manipulate the key bits if the cube bits are chosen from the input key. On the other hand, the attack scenario falls under the nonce-reuse scenario when the cube bits are chosen from the associated data set. This is since multiple associated data will be authenticated using the same key and initialization vector, if we choose to select the cube bits from the associated data set. The designer of ACORN does not claim any security when the same initialization vector is used with a given (the same) key to encrypt or authenticate multiple sets of data.

We consider the scenario where the cube is chosen from the initialization vector set. This requires the preprocessing phase to identify suitable cube bits chosen from the input initialization vector, which generate linear equations in terms of the key bits. Each of the linear equations is computed by summing the output function of ACORN for all the possible values of the corresponding cube. Therefore in the online phase, an adversary first needs to compute the right hand side of these equations for the corresponding cube. This follows the chosen plaintext model, where an adversary encrypts the plaintext with the key and chosen initialization vectors (varying the cube bits obtained from the preprocessing phase) and sums the output bits over n-dimensional Boolean cube to compute the right hand side of the corresponding equation. The secret key can be recovered by solving these equations if sufficient number of equations are generated. The attack requires an output bit from the ACORN output function for $n_c \times 2^{l_c}$ chosen initialization vectors where n_c and l_c represent the total number and the length of the cubes, respectively. So, the complexity of finding the right hand side of the linear equations during the online phase of the attack is no more than $n_c \times 2^{l_c}$. This will be followed by solving the equations using Gaussian elimination, which will require approximately n_c^3 operations when $n_c = 128$. Thus the total complexity of the attack is about $n_c \times 2^{l_c} + n_c^3$. If the equations generated are insufficient, i.e., $n_c < 128$, an adversary can achieve partial key recovery by solving the equations and the rest of the key bits can be found by exhaustive search.

4.2   Cube Attack During the Encryption Phase

In the encryption phase, plaintext bits are loaded in to the internal state of ACORN. Therefore plaintext can be considered as the public variables in this phase and cubes can be chosen from the input plaintext set. In this case, during the preprocessing phase an adversary manipulates the plaintext bits to generate linear equations in terms of the state bits. The linear equations are computed by summing the output function of ACORN for all the possible values of the corresponding cube. In the online phase, the adversary first needs to find the right hand side of these equations. This is a chosen plaintext attack, where an adversary encrypts the chosen plaintext (varying the cube bits obtained from the preprocessing phase) with the same key and initialization vector and sums the output bits over n-dimensional Boolean cube to compute the right hand side of the corresponding equation. Finally the initial state of the cipher can be recovered by solving the generated equations if sufficient equations are generated, i.e., $n_c = 293$. The attack requires the output bit from the ACORN output function for $n_c \times 2^{l_c}$ chosen plaintext vectors. Following the similar computation as shown in the previous section, the total attack complexity of the state recovery attack requires about $n_c \times 2^{l_c} + n_c^3$ operations.

Unlike the initialization phase, the encryption phase of ACORN does not need to go through a large number of rounds before producing the output bits. So the degree of the output polynomial is expected to be low if an adversary searches for the cube bits from the plaintext variables. Note that cube attack is more effective on low degree polynomials since a lower degree polynomial will require a smaller cube size. For ACORN an adversary can manipulate the plaintext bits to generate linear equation from the 58th round of the encryption phase when the first plaintext bit p_0 reaches to the output keystream generation function f_z. The degree of the output polynomial of ACORN at the 58th round of encryption phase is only 3. Therefore, at that point of the encryption phase an adversary needs a cube size of 2 at most. This makes it trivial to find linear relations in terms of the state bits.

Note that this attack falls under the nonce-reuse scenario. This means an adversary chooses different set of cubes from the plaintext variables and evaluate the output function of ACORN with a fixed key and initialization vector. As mentioned earlier, the designer of ACORN does not claim any security when the same initialization vector is used with the same key to encrypt or authenticate multiple sets of data.

5   Experimental Results

Our experimental analysis of the cube attack on ACORN is conducted using Sage version 6.4.1 [12] on a standard 3.4 GHz Intel Core i7 PC with 16 GB memory. Experiments are performed on both the initialization and encryption phases of ACORN to identify suitable cubes. The following sections discuss the application of the cube attack to these two different phases of ACORN.

5.1   Cube Attack Using the Initialization Vector

The initialization of ACORN has a large number of rounds: $l_d + 2048$ rounds. This has a minimum value of 2048 when there are no associated data inputs, i.e., $l_d = 0$. The degree of the output function of ACORN grows with the increase in the number of rounds and is expected to be quite high when the full 2048 rounds are used. So, the size of the cube is also expected to be high if we choose to find a cube after 2048 rounds. This requires a significant amount of computational time. We therefore tested the cube attack on reduced round versions of ACORN.

For a reduced round version of ACORNv1, with initialization phase of 500 rounds, we have a total of 21 linear equations in terms of the secret key bits. These equations are derived during the preprocessing phase of the cube attack. For this 8000 random cubes of size 2 were tested; however, none of these cubes passed the linearity test. So we increased the cube size and checked if there exist linear equations when the cube size is increased. No suitable cubes were found for a cube size of 3 and 4 after searching over 1000 random cubes. For a cube size of

5, 1000 randomly chosen cubes were tested among which 20 passed the linearity test, but for most of these cubes the linear coefficient of the secret variable was found to be 0, i.e., the cube summation results only in a constant. Only 3 cubes $\{v_{120}, v_{124}, v_{93}, v_7, v_{63}\}$, $\{v_{31}, v_{124}, v_{115}, v_{18}, v_{122}\}$, $\{v_{39}, v_{51}, v_{124}, v_{76}, v_{115}\}$ were found which give linear coefficients in terms of the secret variable. These cubes were obtained by running the preprocessing phase for about a week.

Note that there are possibly more cubes of size 5 after 500 initialization round, however to find more cubes an adversary needs to increase the cube search space. Instead of increasing the search space, we used the following method to obtain new cubes from the randomly chosen cubes. For a given randomly chosen cube, increase both the cube indices and the number of rounds by one. Choose the new cube as a valid one if it satisfies the linearity test. This reduces the time complexity in the preprocessing phase since the adversary does not need to search for a suitable random cube from a total possible search space of $\binom{128}{5}$. With this technique, we were able to find total 12 cubes of size 5 which gives 12 linear equations in terms of the secret key bits. Further experiments are performed by choosing the cubes from a smaller subset of the previously found cubes, i.e., the cubes of size 5 were selected from the subset of the cube indices $\{120, 124, 93, 7, 63, 31, 115, 18, 122, 39, 51, 76\}$. This technique gave us two more new cubes: $\{v_{39}, v_{93}, v_{31}, v_{124}, v_{122}\}$, $\{v_{120}, v_{51}, v_{124}, v_7, v_{63}\}$ at round 500 and an additional cube at round 503: $\{v_{42}, v_{125}, v_{21}, v_{127}, v_{118}\}$. Using these cubes, combined with the previously mentioned technique, we were able to find 9 more cubes which result in distinct linear equations. In total 21 linear equations are found after the 500 initialization round of ACORNv1. Therefore for ACORNv1 with 500 initialization rounds, adversary can guess 107 key bits and the remaining 21 bits can be found by solving these linear equations. This is dominated by the exhaustive search. In the following we discuss about reducing the dominance of the exhaustive search by reducing the initialization round further.

Observing the linear equations generated for round 500, we have found that the equations consist only of the first 99 variables of the key. Therefore, an adversary needs 99 independent linear equations to find out these 99 key bits. To reduce the dominance of the exhaustive search we have further examined on generating more linear relations by reducing the number of rounds and the cube indices. The new cube is considered valid if it still satisfies the linearity test. The experiment is repeated by reducing the number of rounds and the cube indices, till 99 or more cubes are found. These equations were found after reducing the round of ACORN initialization phase from 500 to 477.

During the online phase of the attack, an adversary first needs to find the right hand side of these linear equations. An adversary encrypts the plaintext with the key and chosen initialization vectors (varying the cube bits) and sums the respective output bits over the n-dimensional Boolean cube to compute the right hand side of the corresponding equation. This requires a total $99 \times 2^5 \approx 2^{11.6}$ chosen initialization vectors. Therefore, an adversary can expect to recover the key bits with complexity less than exhaustive search, if the initialization phase of ACORN is reduced to 477.

We implemented the attack to verify the online phase of the cube attack on the 477 initialization round version of ACORNv1. We started by computing the right hand side of each equation by summing the output bits for all the possible values of the corresponding cube. This requires access to $2^{11.6}$ specific output bits. The equations are then solved once the right hand side of all the equations are computed. We found that the solution was not unique for some of the key bits. Some of the solutions for the secret key bits are found to be dependent on the key bits: $k_{91}, k_{94}, k_{95}, k_{96}, k_{97}, k_{98}$. This is because some of the computed equations are linearly dependent. Guessing these six key bits correctly results in a unique solution which provides the key bits for $k_0, \cdots, k_{90}, k_{92}, k_{93}$. We also need to guess the rest of the 29 key bits to recover the whole key. Therefore, the attack require to guess total $29 + 6 = 35$ of the key bits. The linear equations can be solved using row reduction and back substitution, and the resulting solutions must then be checked with each of the 2^{29} possibilities for the remaining key bits. So, in practice the total attack complexity is about $2^{11.6} + 93^3 + 6 \times 93 \times 2^6 + 2^6 \times 2^{29} \approx 2^{35}$.

We have also performed the experiments for the reduced round variant of ACORNv2. For this experiment, we tested the same cubes that were found for ACORNv2 (as above). Interestingly we noticed that the same cube sets result in linear equations for ACORNv2 as well. This was also verified by running the online phase of the attack to recover the key bits.

5.2   Cube Attack Using Plaintext

This section discusses the application of the cube attack to the encryption phase of ACORN. Unlike the initialization phase, the degree of the output polynomial during the encryption phase is expected to be comparatively low. Therefore cube attack using the plaintext can be applied to the full version of ACORN. In the following, we describe the cube attack to the encryption phase of ACORN.

For searching suitable cubes we first represented the internal state, S of ACORN symbolically and checked the output function Z while loading each bit of plaintext P. At each round of the plaintext loading we looked into the symbolic output function to determine whether it becomes linear when differentiating it with respect to a subset of plaintext variables. Any such set of plaintext, if it exists, is equivalent to the set of cubes in the cube attack. For the first 57 round of the plaintext loading phase no such set were found because the plaintext bit does not reach the output function till the 58th round. At the 58th round of the plaintext loading, we found that differentiating the output equation Z^{58} with respect to plaintext p_0 results in a linear equation. That also means that if we do a cube attack numerically, then summing the output polynomial Z^{58} over the cube p_0 will result a linear equation. However, when running the experiments symbolically, the software runs out of resource after a few number of rounds. The symbolic computation with Sage was able to successfully compute the output function until 148th round of the plaintext loading phase. This method gave us 103 linear equations with 293 unknowns. This is not sufficient to reduce the complexity below the exhaustive search of 2^{128}.

To find more cubes that produce linear equations we performed the experiment numerically. We started with the cubes $\{p_0\}$, $\{p_0, p_7\}$ and $\{p_0, p_{21}\}$ for round 58, 107 and 121, respectively, which are found using the symbolic computation. We then used the following method to obtain a new cube: Increase the cube indices and the number of round by one and choose the new cube as a valid one if it satisfies the linearity test. 100 linearity tests were performed for each of the cube. With this technique, we have obtained 245 linear equations with 293 variables. Among the 245 cubes for these equations, 42 are of size 1 and the rest are of size 2.

In the online phase of the attack an adversary needs to compute the right hand side of these equations and then solve the equations to recover the state bits. An adversary first encrypts the chosen plaintexts (varying the cube bits) with the same key and initialization vector and sums the respective output bits over the n-dimensional Boolean cube to compute the right hand side of the corresponding equation. This requires about $42 \times 2^1 + 203 \times 2^2 \approx 2^{9.81}$ chosen plaintext bits to find the right hand side of these 245 equations.

To verify the online phase of the attack, we implemented the attack by solving these linear equations. We first computed the right hand side of each equation by summing the output bits for all the possible values of the corresponding cube. This requires an adversary to have access to $2^{9.81}$ specific output bits. We then represented these linear equations by a matrix and found that the rank of the matrix is 234. Applying Gaussian elimination to the underdetermined system yields a row reduced matrix that can be used with each guess of the 59 underdetermined variables to calculate the remaining 234 variables. This process enables us to recover all the state bits. Therefore in practice the total attack complexity is about $2^{9.81} + 234^3 + 59 \times 234 \times 2^{59} \approx 2^{72.8}$.

6   Conclusion

We applied the cube attack to the reduced round version of ACORN. Our analysis shows that cube attack can recover the secret key with a complexity of 2^{35} when the number of initialization rounds is reduced to 477. We have also tested and verified the attack by recovering the actual key bits for a randomly chosen key. The attack can be possibly extended to higher number of initialization rounds, but it will require a larger cube size which requires a search over very large cube spaces. It is difficult to evaluate the performance of the cube attack for larger versions of ACORN without knowing the suitable choices of the cube. Due to the high time complexity of searching larger cubes, our experiments were conducted only for smaller cube sizes. Also, note that the cubes identified for the 477 initialization rounds are only of size 5, whereas the degree of the output function after 477 round is expected to be much higher than 5. This suggests that the key and the initialization vector are not mixed properly yet after the 477 rounds; however, it would be interesting to check if this behaviour continues for higher rounds of the initialization phase as well. Currently, the cube attack seems to be impractical for the full round version of ACORN.

We have also shown that it is trivial to recover the state bits of the full round version of ACORN with complexity less than exhaustive search, if the same key and initialization vector is used to encrypt or authenticate multiple sets of input plaintext. This does not threaten the security of ACORN if it is used as the designers suggested.

Acknowledgements. Md Iftekhar Salam was supported by the QUT Postgraduate Research Award (QUTPRA), QUT Higher Degree Research Tuition Fee Sponsorship and QUT Excellence Top Up Scholarship. Josef Pieprzyk was supported by the Polish National Science Center Grant DEC-2014/15/B/ST6/05130.

References

1. Dinur, I., Shamir, A.: Cube attacks on tweakable black box polynomials. In: Joux, A. (ed.) EUROCRYPT 2009. LNCS, vol. 5479, pp. 278–299. Springer, Heidelberg (2009). doi:10.1007/978-3-642-01001-9_16
2. Wu, H., ACORN: A Lightweight Authenticated Cipher (v1). CAESAR Competition. http://competitions.cr.yp.to/round1/acornv1.pdf. Accessed 29 May 2015
3. CAESAR: Competition for Authenticated Encryption: Security, Applicability, and Robustness. http://competitions.cr.yp.to/index.html. Accessed 10 Sep 2015
4. Wu, H., ACORN: A Lightweight Authenticated Cipher (v2). CAESAR Competition. http://competitions.cr.yp.to/round2/acornv2.pdf. Accessed 10 Sep 2015
5. Lai, X.: Higher order derivatives, differential cryptanalysis. In: Blahut, R.E., Costello, D.J., Maurer, U., Mittelholzer, T. (eds.) Communications, Cryptography: Two Sides of One Tapestry. The Springer International Series in Engineering and Computer Science, vol. 276, pp. 227–233. Springer, US (1994)
6. Vielhaber, M., Breaking One. Fivium by AIDA an Algebraic IV Differential Attack. IACR ePrint Archive 2007/413. https://eprint.iacr.org/2007/413.pdf. Accessed 28 May 2016
7. Cannière, C.: TRIVIUM: a stream cipher construction inspired by block cipher design principles. In: Katsikas, S.K., López, J., Backes, M., Gritzalis, S., Preneel, B. (eds.) ISC 2006. LNCS, vol. 4176, pp. 171–186. Springer, Heidelberg (2006). doi:10.1007/11836810_13
8. Mroczkowski, P. and Szmidt, J., The Cube Attack on Courtois Toy Cipher. IACR ePrint Archive 2009/497. https://eprint.iacr.org/2009/497.pdf. Accessed 17 June 2016
9. Dinur, I., Shamir, A.: Breaking grain-128 with dynamic cube attacks. In: Joux, A. (ed.) FSE 2011. LNCS, vol. 6733, pp. 167–187. Springer, Heidelberg (2011). doi:10.1007/978-3-642-21702-9_10
10. Sarkar, S., Maitra, S., Baksi, A.: Observing biases in the state: case studies with Trivium and Trivia-SC. Des. Codes Crypt. 1–25 (2016)
11. Blum, M., Luby, M., Rubinfeld, R.: Self-testing/correcting with applications to numerical problems. J. Comput. Syst. Sci. **47**, 579–595 (1993)
12. Stein, W., et al.: Sage Mathematics Software (Version 6.4.1), The Sage Development Team (2015). http://www.sagemath.org

Detection of Attacks
on Data Security Systems

Investigating Security Vulnerabilities in Modern Vehicle Systems

Xi Zheng[1(✉)], Lei Pan[1], Hongxu Chen[2], and Peiyin Wang[1]

[1] Deakin University, Geelong, VIC 3220, Australia
{xi.zheng,l.pan,peiyinw}@deakin.edu.au
[2] State Key Laboratory of Automotive Safety and Energy,
Tsinghua University, Beijing, China
herschel.chen@gmail.com

Abstract. Modern vehicle systems have evolved from an isolated control system into an interconnected architecture combining software, hardware, and data. Such architecture is specialized into vehicle infotainment system (e.g., SYNC of Ford, iDrive of BMW and MMI of Audi), Vehicle to Vehicle (V2V), Vehicle to Infrastructure (V2I), and vehicle social system which connects to social media networks. These systems hold private and sensitive information such as travel plans, social network messages, login credentials to bank accounts, and so on, which is a lucrative target for malicious attackers. Unfortunately, existing research overlooks the security issues with respect to this highly integrated system. This paper presents security issues across various systems related to modern vehicles through a a holistic and systematic view. We analyze each system components with respect to published attacks in details and present a synthesized body of knowledge. We identify the growing trend where security attacks are launched from the cyber space to vehicle control system via smartphones and vehicle networks. In the foreseeable future, we expect more security attacks both in numbers and in complexity. Knowing this will arise the awareness of vehicle system security and help engineers to build security solutions.

Keywords: Evaluation of security · Authentication and authorization · Distributed systems security · Privacy protection · Smartphone security · Modern vehicle system · Security · Privacy · Reliability

1 Introduction

Nowadays, automobile manufacturers integrate car control system (e.g., CAN bus) with mobile applications, which in turn evolves into a multi-function vehicle system named vehicle infotainment system. Vehicle infotainment system differs from traditional vehicle system which typically has audio playing function with several buttons. Vehicle infotainment system provides more interaction between drivers/passengers and vehicle systems, which allows drivers to monitor their cars and to achieve advanced functions such as making hand-free calls, sending

© Springer Nature Singapore Pte Ltd. 2016
L. Batten and G. Li (Eds.): ATIS 2016, CCIS 651, pp. 29–40, 2016.
DOI: 10.1007/978-981-10-2741-3_3

voice messages, establishing Bluetooth connection and so on. To utilize the information outside a vehicle, Vehicle to Vehicle (V2V) and Vehicle to Infrastructure (V2I) system enables the communications and interaction among nearby vehicles or road infrastructures. The V2V system aims to share the information related to traffic information and accident warning among nearby vehicles or road infrastructures, to improve the road and drivers' safety. Based on V2V and V2I, the concept of social networking was brought into the area of the vehicle system. Drivers can share their experiences and useful information to other drivers via the Internet not only restricted to nearby vehicles. Hence, Vehicle to Social (V2S) system is the future trend of current modern vehicle systems.

The introduction of these new systems inside vehicles increases the level of security risks. For example, some latest vehicles can be hacked within 360 s [38]; actuators of the modern vehicles can be remotely controlled; terrorists can potentially hack into V2V and V2I to cause chaotic traffic accidents (e.g., to hack into an autonomous intersection system [7]), stealing privacy information from any driver. Many research work have been done for modern vehicle systems to cover the design, control, and automation of vehicles [8,12,20,30,39], or to cover vulnerability issues in a specific system (e.g., control system [31], vehicle to vehicle communication [37], vehicle networks [14], in-car wireless network [17]).

However, there is a significant gap in the current research. On one hand, researchers are not fully aware of the security impact of introducing the new features. Thus, no comprehensive analysis is yet provided to cover these features. On the other hand, car manufacturers are not aware of what security vulnerabilities possible in those features they have introduced or going to introduce to the modern vehicle systems which researchers have potential to help. Therefore, this paper first analyses these modern vehicle systems, and then discusses the vulnerabilities in these systems and proposes potential solutions. Overall, this paper makes the following two research contributions:

- We analyze features of modern vehicle systems.
- We analyze open problems and challenges for these modern vehicle systems in terms of security and reliability.

The rest of paper is organized as follows. Section 2 introduces the features of modern vehicle systems. The security challenges associated with these features are presented in Sect. 3. In Sect. 4, we summarize some related works. And we conclude this paper in Sect. 5.

2   Background

2.1   Vehicle Network Control System

The vehicle network control system connects all components of vehicle, where Controller Area Network (CAN) [9] is widely used in most vehicles. According to [9], CAN provides two layers of the Open Systems Interconnection (OSI): the physical layer and the data link layer. CAN protocol gains its popularity because of its open design and good performance in data transmission. However, CAN also has obvious limitations: big and variable pulse, lack of clock synchronization, finite speed-distance ratio, inflexible design, data conformance problem, finite error control, and limited support for fault tolerance [9].

2.2 Vehicle Infotainment System

Vehicle infotainment system provides user-friendly functions, such as hand-free call, checking SMS, controlling audio player, mobile device support, and other accessories which can improve drivers' experience. A comprehensive vehicle info-tainment system provides some safety and security functions, such as to monitor vehicle status (i.e. tire pressure, and road condition using 360-degree camera). Meanwhile, vehicle infotainment system also serves passengers, a rear seat info-tainment system is usually provided on some luxury vehicles, such as Mercedes-Benz S-series, BMW 7 series, and Audi A8 series etc. The rear seat infotainment system has the same function with drivers' one. It controls audio/video player, checks vehicle running status, controls navigation, and browses web contents [28].

In the current vehicle market, almost each automobile manufacturer has its own vehicle infotainment system, such as SYNC of Ford, iDrive of BMW, and MMI of Audi. In recent years, some players in the software industry also try to access the area of vehicle infotainment system and become an emerging member, such as NVIDIA and Apple.

Moreover, drivers now prefer to tap their smartphone to control this system [11]. Tesla [36] launched Model S in 2012, which is the first premium electric sedan. And there is a 17-inch display touch screen installed into Model S, which offers the largest display touch screen among selling vehicles. This touch screen is powered by NVIDIA's Tegra [35], it has climate control, navigation, and display vehicle information. The driver can download the "Tesla Motors"application via Google Play and App Store, which can monitor and control their car with their mobile device remotely. When the user finishes download and installation, they can use their'My Tesla' account to log in and access this application. This application provides several functions: keyless driving, range status, climate control, and GPS location. After successfully installing and connect with their Tesla Model S, the vehicle owner can unlock and drive their car without the key, they also can check current range and charge status. In addition, the car owner can use this application to turn on the climate control system and vent sunroof remotely. The vehicle's parked location will be provided when car owner forget where did they park.

SYNC is used on Ford, Lincoln, Mercury, and Flex models, which is developed based on Microsoft Auto platform. SYNC can also handle most media players in the current market: iPod (Apple), Zune (Microsoft), and MP3 files which are stored in the USB or SD card [34]. The latest version (version 3) of SYNC also has the system update service over Wi-Fi, enhanced voice recognition, high-speed performance, and Apples Siri [3] seamless integration.

Apple launched its in-vehicle infotainment system called CarPlay [2], which is based on Blackberry's QNX platform. This system allows iPhone user to use maps, send messages, listen to music, and make calls. Apple listed several committed partnerships, including Mercedes-Benz, Ferrari, Volvo, PORSCHE, GMC, and Volkswagen. In addition, CarPlay is compatible with all iPhone models after iPhone 5.

2.3 Vehicle to Vehicle (V2V) and Vehicle to Infrastructure System (V2I)

The setup of Vehicle to Vehicle (V2V) and Vehicle to Infrastructure (V2I) enables communications between vehicles and infrastructure so that useful road information and emergency messages can be exchanged. These systems aim to reduce the rate of accidents, and increase the safety of the road users. To achieve efficient communications among vehicles and infrastructures, Vehicular Ad Hoc Networks (VANETs) is introduced as the base for V2V and V2I systems [13].

However, VANETs are facing some technical challenges and socio-economic challenges, among which bandwidth and dynamic network topology received a lot of attention. For instance, when the communication starts, can the underlying network hold huge information during traffic peak hours? Meanwhile, how modern vehicle system interact with infrastructure while vehicle itself is moving at a fast speed? What useful information can be shared by infrastructure to the vehicle system to maintain an optimum level of performance?

In [33], an architecture of Vehicular Communications (VC) is presented, which includes inter-vehicle communications (IVC), hybrid-vehicle communications (HVC), and roadside-vehicle communications (RVC). Meanwhile, inter-vehicle communications (IVC) is divided into two types of system: the single-hop system and the multi-hop system.

Nowadays, Vehicle to Vehicle communication system is usually used to provide some warning messages or notifications, such as Cooperation Collision Warning to avoid accident. In [41], it shows that the emerging wireless technologies were used for Dedicated Short Range Communications (DSRC) [6]. In [6], it is shown that 60 % of collision can be avoided by using some warning mechanisms. As the analysis of collision warning, a V2V application should be developed to support the system operation.

There are two approaches for developing the V2V applications — passive or active.

- The passive approach needs all the vehicles nearby to communicate using the same application. Then important information can be updated and exchanged at real time among the vehicles nearby. When the traffic congestion happened, the network however might suffer from communication saturation due to huge amount of data communicated.
- In comparison, the active approach will select the vehicle, which might face emergency situation, to send an Emergency Warning Messages (EWMs). The active approach can avoid network saturation in peak hour.

In order to decrease congestion time and air pollution level, V2I system can be seen as a possible solution to this environmental issue. In [21], V2I system can provide some audio messages of traffic to the vehicle system, which can help to improve driving performance with a smooth speed. Meanwhile, V2I system can also be used to notify emergency situations to drivers. For example, sometimes drivers cannot react to the change of traffic lights during the daytime when they approach intersections due to sun glare. Now drivers can receive an audio message from roadside infrastructure to notify the change of traffic light. Another application of V2I in people daily trip is that it can notify ahead road work. When drivers drive with a high speed, they cannot realize the speed limit and reduce their speed to the speed limit required for the ahead road work. Therefore, V2I system can be used to send audio messages to drivers and notify the information of ahead road work zone. A roadside infrastructure system will help the driver to avoid accidents happened. Meanwhile, In [21], it points out V2I system can also reduce vehicle emissions due to improved driving efficiency. When V2I system is used, most of car emissions, including nitrogen dioxide, hydrocarbons, carbon monoxide, carbon dioxide, have been reduced with smallest reduction in carbon dioxide emission (around 7 %) and biggest reduction in carbon monoxide (around 32 %).

In [13], it shows that there are safety-related applications of Vehicle Safety Communication (VSC): signal violation warning, curve speed warning, emergency electronic brake light, pre-crash sensing, cooperative forward collision warning, left turn assistant, lane-change warning and stop sign movement assistant.

2.4 Vehicle Social System

The automobile manufacturers and software providers are not confined to V2V and V2I systems, they have started to shift the focus towards the communications between vehicles and social medias.

With network widely used in people's daily life, people can obtain more information from the internet. People also can share their experience and information anytime and anywhere. For the vehicle social system, drivers can share their experiences and useful information to other drivers via the internet. It is not only restricted to communicate and interaction among nearby vehicles. Therefore, Vehicle to Social (V2S) system is going to play a major role in the future vehicle systems. The following graph is a prototype of Vehicle Social Networks (VSNs). There are some communications and interactions between vehicles and signal towers, mobile devices and signal tower, and people and signal tower.

In [23], with the development of online social networks, a new type of ad hoc networks was introduced called Vehicular Social Networks (VSNs). VSNs can be used to implement Intelligent Transportation System (ITS). VSNs aims to improve the road and drivers' safety, as well as to reduce the traffic congestion. In [23], a new system prototype was implemented, which called SocialDrive and the concept and architecture of SocialDrive were also provided in the case study. In [32], an advanced social network prototype was presented, where real-time road conditions are shared via cloud.

SocialDrive is a novel prototype of vehicle social system, it provide data sharing and data receiving function. SocialDrive aims to publish the dynamic data and information to other vehicles, meanwhile, receive messages from other vehicles. In their study, an example of SocialDrive is provided: There are five hypothetical vehicles on the road. If the first and last vehicle want to share data, but the distance is not enough so that the data can only be received by the third vehicle. SocialDrive can gather these data and make the third vehicle as a center to share different data to other vehicles.

3 Analysis of Possible Security Attacks

3.1 Vehicle Network Control System Attacks

Many protocols are adopted to implement the vehicle network. According to [19], all vehicles sold in the United State are required to implement the Controller Area Network (CAN) bus (ISO 11898) for diagnostics. Meanwhile, CAN is facing security challenges due to broadcast nature, vulnerability to denial of service attack, no authenticator fields, weak access control, and Electronic Control Units (ECUs) firmware updates and open diagnostic control [19].

In [5], many essential components of modern vehicles, including gearbox, climate control, ignition system, and electrical window control, are now controlled by ECUs as embedded systems. ECU is one of the most important parts of a vehicle, and there are about 90 ECUs in the luxury-class vehicles [5]. Due to the huge number of ECUs installed on the vehicle, ECUs are also facing security issues: modifying code, reverse engineering, fuzzing attack, and phlashing attack. For instance, the attacker can modify the programming code during design and implementation processing. The data is the target for the attackers to achieve the purpose of corruption or degradation of hardware performance, and destroy of information.

In [15], the electronic window lift system can be attacked by the attacker via CAN bus. The attackers can use real hardware to attack the electronic window lift system, thus, to attack the anti-theft system and airbag system's warning lights on the dashboard.

In [25], a vehicle virus was created which can capture the messages delivered by CAN bus. Upon successful capture of door locking messages, this virus can lock the vehicle's doors remotely. As a connection media to all vehicle components, security issues in CAN bus bring huge risks to drivers' safety and privacy. Hackers can hack the networked control system and control vehicle easily. The hackers can configure the setting, modify the code, implant virus and malware. Therefore, it is of vital importance to address these security issues during the development and implementation process.

3.2 Vehicle to Vehicle and Vehicle to Infrastructure System Attacks

As previously mentioned in Sect. 2, VANETs is used to enhance drivers' safety (i.e., collision warning, Blind Spot Information System (BLIS)) and comfort (i.e., locating gas station, tollway and parking payment, and internet access). Intelligent Transportation Systems is used to reduce traffic congestion, and both road and vehicle safety are also improved.

The main vulnerabilities of dense VANETs are caused by the lack of fixed infrastructure to protect the security and privacy in the application of wireless networks and application of Medium Access Control (MAC) 802.11 layer [5,16,18]. It directly implies eavesdropping attacks.

In current society, Vehicle to Vehicle (V2V) system can be used to send messages among the vehicles. V2V system should be designed with high reliability and low delay when the messages are sent. Because drivers need the sufficient amount of time to react to the emergency situations. In order to ensure the high reliability and low delay, simple mechanisms without high level security protection are used in the V2V system such as Medium Access Control (MAC) and 802.11a radio. In [40], the reliability of receiving messages in VANETs can be greatly affected due to issues in transmission collision and transmission power in the wireless ad hoc network.

In general, VANETs threats can be summarized into three aspects: confidentiality, authenticity, and availability.

- Threats of confidentiality mainly refer to that the communications among vehicles have been eavesdropped, which lead to important information of vehicles illegally collected without permission. For instance through eavesdropping processing, attackers can collect the privacy information to know the location of driver.
- For threats to authenticity, there are several types of attack for Vehicular Ad Hoc Network (VANET): Sybil attack, bogus information, man in the middle attack (MiMA), Global Positioning System (GPS) spoofing, and replay attack.
  1. Sybil attack means that attackers forged a large number of fake vehicle identities in VANET, this will cause a vehicle in the same VANET to believe the presence of multiple vehicles in the network simultaneously. Sybil attack has a great influence, a hacker gaining access to VANET using Sybil attack may also be able to declare there is no vehicle at one particular position currently. However, the fact is that there is a vehicle at that location, which would cause crash and accident. As a result of Sybil attack, it will disrupt the normal order of the network, as well as disrupt the real-life order, which would threaten the safety of the driver and the road [4,26].
  2. Bogus information attack means that attacker accesses network and sends wrong messages to the vehicle which uses V2V and V2I system. For example, the attacker invades the roadside infrastructure and sends bogus information "slow down" to the yellow car, and sends "the way is clear" to the blue car. In a normal situation, the driver trusts this information, then the attacker most likely succeed in cause the planned accident as the driver would not have enough time to react to it.
  3. In [1], Man in the Middle Attack (MiMA) means that a malicious vehicle eavesdrops on the communication messages in VANET, and injects some wrong information, which can mislead other vehicles in the network.

4. Global Positioning System (GPS) spoofing means that an attacker could modify some of the data to make a wrong GPS data, which misleads drivers and let them think they are in different locations.
5. For replay attack, the attackers reinject the packets which were created before inside the network. Since VANETs essentially need a real-time operating system to support it, the replay attack will upset the networks' order thus to achieve the purpose of affect the network.

- Many threats affect availability: denial of service attack, malware, spamming, black hole attack, and broadcast tampering [1,5,18,27,29].
    1. Denial of service (DoS) attacks is an attack which uses network protocol vulnerabilities or uses some illegal means to attack the network. DoS usually creates unprecedented/unexpected fake communication loads for VANETs in a short time to render VANETs impossible to provide normal services thus to achieve the purpose of crashing VANETs.
    2. Malware is an attack, which usually originates from vehicles' inside. It might undermine vehicle infotainment systems, ECUs or other mission critical components inside a vehicle causing critical outages.
    3. Spamming may make the network transmission speed slower than before. Meanwhile, the spam messages are difficult to control due to lack of centralized management and infrastructure support.
    4. Black hole attack is caused by malicious nodes. The malicious nodes can send false information to mislead the network connecting with the vehicle. When the connection is established, the malicious nodes can drop some transmission data, thus resulting in packet loss and transfer failure.
    5. Broadcast Tampering is an attack which generates false traffic messages into VANETs and causing significant outages.

3.3   Vehicle Social System Attacks

In the foreseeable future, vehicles will be able to connect to the cloud client via the wireless network or the mobile phone network 3G/4G. According to [10], many vehicle manufacturers including Ford, Nissan, and Toyota have begun to design and develop the vehicle social system (vehicle to cloud). Especially, Microsoft will provide their Azure cloud platform to Toyota which used to provide a cloud solution [10]. This kind of communication can provide vehicle tracking, remotely assistance and emergency relief to the drivers.

As explained in Sect. 2, Vehicle Social System is going to lead the future of vehicle systems. In [10], it is shown that many vehicle manufacturers (i.e., Ford, Nissan, and Toyota) have begun to design and develop the vehicle social system (vehicle to cloud). Especially, Toyota already built a partnership with Microsoft. Microsoft will provide their Azure cloud platform to Toyota which used to provide a telematics cloud solution. This kind of communication can provide vehicle tracking, remotely assistance and emergency relief to the drivers.

However, since drivers can start to share information and experience to cloud client, their privacy information are at risk. For instance, vehicle social system relies on mobile devices and thus so long as attackers can hack into mobile devices, they can track drivers' location, and steal their personal information.

Moreover, the vehicle to cloud communication is also facing the following challenges: communication latency, gateway, data processing, fleet management, and security [10].

In [10], it is shown the Vehicle Social System is facing the research challenges with communication latency, gateway design, data processing, fleet management, and security. Among these challenges, security and privacy issues are mission critical. Since Vehicle Social Systems, for the first time in this scale in vehicle's history, integrates vehicle systems with other non-vehicle systems to form a big social system, attackers can steal personal information and launch security attacks more easier than ever. Therefore, a wide variety of security and privacy issues must be improved. According to [10], it is necessary to integrate data security and privacy features, and create a cryptography technique which follows certain standards and design efficiency.

4 Related Work

According to the trend of modern vehicle system's development, there are several kinds of modern vehicle systems, such as vehicle networked control system, vehicle infotainment system, vehicle to vehicle (V2V) and vehicle to infrastructure (V2I) system, and vehicle social system. Most recent attacks focus on the inter-vehicle systems.

Luo and Hubaux [22] stated that inter-vehicle communication (IVC) is an important part of Intelligent Transportation System (ITS) and IVC provide communications between driver and driver, or vehicle and vehicle, which can improve the road safety and driving efficiency. Meanwhile, this study simulated the real situation and procided the result of simulation, especially compare between Control Access CDMA (CA-CDMA) and IEEE 802.11. This study covered various aspects of IVC system, which is the strength of the work. But that, unfortunately, this study did not provide any possible solutions of security issues, which is a limitation.

According to Hartenstein and Laberteaux [13], vehicle to vehicle (V2V) and vehicle to infrastructure (V2I) is based on wireless network to build and they contain in vehicular ad hoc networks (VANETs). In addition, the authors provided the main challenge of VANETs, which divided into two parts: technical challenges and socio-economic challenges, such as bandwidth, dynamic network topology and roadside infrastructure etc. The strength of the work is that detailed explanation and introduction were provided in this study, especially the main challenges of VANETs.

Sichitiu and Kihl [33] pointed out inter-vehicle communication (IVC) system can improve the road safety, driving efficiency and comfort of drivers and passengers. Meanwhile, the author showed that the main difference between single-hop system and multi-hop system. Moreover, the author provided the architecture of Vehicular Communications (VC), which include inter-vehicle communications

(IVC), hybrid-vehicle communications (HVC) and roadside-vehicle communications (RVC). The strength of the work is that this survey is a basic study of IVC system. However, the limitation and possible solutions were not presented in this survey, which is the weakness of this work.

Moharrum and Al-Daraiseh [24] pointed out vehicular ad-hoc networks (VANETs) are wireless communication system, which can provide safety and efficient road services to drivers and passengers. In addition, some recent security issues in VANETs were presented in this survey. Meanwhile, several types of attacks and attackers were provided in [24]. The strength of the work is that some solutions which based on current techniques were provided in this study. Another strength is that the authors also pointed out some future challenges and security issues, which still in VANETs.

Most of existing research overlook the applications and inter-connectivity of cyber and physical systems. Due to such limited scope, many attacks across cyber-physical layers are overlooked. Thus, this paper highlights such attacks and arises the awareness of researchers in the field.

5 Conclusions

In conclusion, this paper exposes the fact that security attacks across cyber-physical layers post serious threats to the modern vehicle systems and the users of the system.

We analyze the five different types of modern vehicle systems and the associated security attacks in details. We also list the published attacks which successfully took control of the vehicle or at least the key features related to driving. Some attacks severely endanger the security and safety of the vehicle users; some attacks breach the user's privacy; other attacks may impact both security and privacy. Furthermore, these attacks can be launched from the well researched mobile platforms which lowers the cost of successful attacks and increases the difficulty of securing all vehicles connected to a network. Situations can be worse if there exists a high level of connection such as at the social level, where private travel information can be leaked or misused by malicious attackers.

References

1. Al-Kahtani, M.S.: Survey on security attacks in vehicular ad hoc networks (vanets). In Proceedings of ICSPCS, pp. 1–9. IEEE (2012)
2. Apple. CarPlay (2016). http://www.apple.com/au/ios/carplay/?cid=wwa-au-kwg-features. Accessed 5 April 2016
3. Apple. Siri (2016). http://www.apple.com/au/ios/siri/. Accessed 5 April 2016
4. Boneh, D., Franklin, M.: Identity-based encryption from the weil pairing. In: Kilian, J. (ed.) CRYPTO 2001. LNCS, vol. 2139, pp. 213–229. Springer, Heidelberg (2001). doi:10.1007/3-540-44647-8_13
5. Brooks, R.R., Sander, S., Deng, J., Taiber, J.: Automobile security concerns. Veh. Technol. Mag. 4(2), 52–64 (2009)

6. Delgrossi, L., Zhang, T.: Dedicated short-range communications. In: Vehicle Safety Communications: Protocols, Security, and Privacy, pp. 44–51 (2009)
7. Dresner, K., Stone, P.: A multiagent approach to autonomous intersection management. J. Artif. Intell. Res. **31**, 591–656 (2008)
8. Ehsani, M., Gao, Y., Emadi, A.: Modern Electric, Hybrid Electric, and Fuel Cell Vehicles: Fundamentals, Theory, and Design. CRC Press (2009)
9. Etschberger, K.: Controller Area Network: Basics, Protocols, Chips and Applications. IXXAT Press, Weingarten (2001)
10. Faezipour, M., Nourani, M., Saeed, A., Addepalli, S.: Progress and challenges in intelligent vehicle area networks. Commun. ACM **55**(2), 90–100 (2012)
11. Greengard, S.: Automotive systems get smarter. Commun. ACM **58**(10), 18–20 (2015)
12. Gusikhin, O., Filev, D., Rychtyckyj, N.: Intelligent vehicle systems: applications and new trends. In: Cetto, J.A., Ferrier, J.-L., Costa dias Pereira, J.M., Filipe, J. (eds.) Informatics in Control Automation and Robotics. LNEE, vol. 15, pp. 3–14. Springer, Heidelberg (2008)
13. Hartenstein, H., Laberteaux, K.P.: A tutorial survey on vehicular ad hoc networks. Commun. Mag. **46**(6), 164–171 (2008)
14. Hoh, B., Gruteser, M., Xiong, H., Alrabady, A.: Enhancing security and privacy in traffic-monitoring systems. Pervasive Comput. **5**(4), 38–46 (2006)
15. Hoppe, T., Dittman, J.: Sniffing/replay attacks on can buses: a simulated attack on the electric window lift classified using an adapted cert taxonomy. In: Proceedings of WESS, pp. 1–6 (2007)
16. Isaac, J.T., Camara, J.S., Zeadally, S., Marquez, J.T.: A secure vehicle-to-roadside communication payment protocol in vehicular ad hoc networks. Comput. Commun. **31**(10), 2478–2484 (2008)
17. Miller, R., Rouf, I., Mustafa, H., Taylor, T., Oh, S., Xu, W., Gruteser, M., Trappe, W., Seskar, I.: Security and privacy vulnerabilities of in-car wireless networks: a tire pressure monitoring system case study. In: 19th USENIX Security Symposium, pp. 11–13 (2010)
18. Jungels, D., Raya, M., Aad, I., Hubaux, J.P.: Certificate revocation in vehicular ad hoc networks. Technical LCA-Report-2006-006, LCA (2006)
19. Koscher, K., Czeskis, A., Roesner, F., Patel, S., Kohno, T., Checkoway, S., McCoy, D., Kantor, B., Anderson, D., Shacham, D., et al.: Experimental security analysis of a modern automobile. In: IEEE Symposium on Security and Privacy, pp. 447–462. IEEE (2010)
20. Le-Anh, T., De Koster, M.: A review of design and control of automated guided vehicle systems. Eur. J. Oper. Res. **171**(1), 1–23 (2006)
21. Li, Q.: Impacts of vehicle to infrastructure communication technologies on vehicle emissions. Environ. Sci. Technol. **1**, 326 (2014)
22. Luo, J., Hubaux, J.-P.: A survey of inter-vehicle communication. Technical report (2004)
23. Maaroufi, S., Pierre, S.: Vehicular social systems: an overview and a performance case study. In: Proceedings of the Fourth ACM International Symposium on Development and Analysis of Intelligent Vehicular Networks and Applications, pp. 17–24. ACM (2014)
24. Moharrum, M.A., Al-Daraiseh, A.A.: Toward secure vehicular ad-hoc networks: a survey. IETE Techn. Rev. **29**(1), 80–89 (2012)
25. Nilsson, D.K., Larson, U.E.: Simulated attacks on can buses: vehicle virus. In: Proceedings of AsiaCSN, pp. 66–72 (2008)

26. Park, S., Aslam, B., Turgut, D., Zou, C.C.: Defense against sybil attack in vehicular ad hoc network based on roadside unit support. In: Proceedings of MILCOM, pp. 1–7. IEEE (2009)
27. Pawar, T., Manekar, A.: Security threats and its solution for vehicular ad hoc network: a review. Int. J. Electron. Commun. Soft Comput. Sci. Eng. **3**(7), 17 (2014)
28. PRNewswire. PRNewswire (2016). http://goo.gl/ZET6NO. Accessed 5 April 2016
29. Razzaque, M., Salehi, A., Cheraghi, S.M.: Security and privacy in vehicular ad-hoc networks: survey and the road ahead. In: Khan, S., Pathan, A.-S.K. (eds.) Wireless Networks and Security. SCT, pp. 107–132. Springer, Heidelberg (2013)
30. Sangiovanni-Vincentelli, A., Natale, M.: Embedded system design for automotive applications. Computer **40**(10), 42–51 (2007)
31. Schuette, H., Waeltermann, P.: Hardware-in-the-loop testing of vehicle dynamics controllers-a technical survey. Technical report, SAE Technical Paper (2005)
32. Sha, W., Kwak, D., Nath, B., Iftode, L.: Social vehicle navigation: integrating shared driving experience into vehicle navigation. In: Proceedings of the 14th Workshop on Mobile Computing Systems and Applications, p. 16. ACM (2013)
33. Sichitiu, M.L., Kihl, M.: Inter-vehicle communication systems: a survey. Commun. Surv. Tutorials **10**(2), 88–105 (2008)
34. Tashev, I., Seltzer, M., Ju, Y.C., Wang, Y.Y., Acero, A.: Commute UX: voice enabled in-car infotainment system. In: Mobile HCI, vol. 9 (2009)
35. Tegra. Tegra (2016). http://www.nvidia.com/object/tegra.html. Accessed 5 April 2016
36. Tesla. Tesla (2016). https://www.teslamotors.com/en_AU/. Accessed 5 April 2016
37. Toth, P., Vigo, D.: Vehicle Routing: Problems, Methods, and Applications, vol. 18. SIAM, Philadelphia (2014)
38. Verdult, R., Garcia, F.D., Balasch, J.: Gone in 360 seconds: Hijacking with hitag2. In: Proceedings of USENIX Security, pp. 237–252 (2012)
39. Vis, I.F.: Survey of research in the design and control of automated guided vehicle systems. Eur. J. Oper. Res. **170**(3), 677–709 (2006)
40. Xu, Q., Mak, T., Ko, J., Sengupta, R.: Vehicle-to-vehicle safety messaging in DSRC. In: Proceedings of the 1st ACM International Workshop on Vehicular Ad Hoc Networks, pp. 19–28. ACM (2004)
41. Yang, X., Liu, J., Vaidya, N.H., Zhao, F.: A vehicle-to-vehicle communication protocol for cooperative collision warning. In: Proceedings of MOBIQUITOUS, pp. 114–123. IEEE (2004)

Tweaking Generic OTR to Avoid Forgery Attacks

Hassan Qahur Al Mahri[✉], Leonie Simpson, Harry Bartlett, Ed Dawson, and Kenneth Koon-Ho Wong

Queensland University of Technology, George St, Brisbane 4000, Australia
hassan.mahri@hdr.qut.edu.au,
{lr.simpson,h.bartlett,e.dawson,kk.wong}@qut.edu.au

Abstract. This paper considers the security of the Offset Two-Round (OTR) authenticated encryption mode [9] with respect to forgery attacks. The current version of OTR gives a security proof for specific choices of the block size (n) and the primitive polynomial used to construct the finite field $\mathbb{F}_{2^n}$. Although the OTR construction is generic, the security proof is not. For every choice of finite field the distinctness of masking coefficients must be verified to ensure security. In this paper, we show that some primitive polynomials result in collisions among the masking coefficients used in the current instantiation, from which forgeries can be constructed. We propose a new way to instantiate OTR so that the masking coefficients are distinct in every finite field $\mathbb{F}_{2^n}$, thus generalising OTR without reducing the security of OTR.

Keywords: Authenticated Encryption · OTR · Confidentiality · Integrity · Forgery attack · Tweakable block cipher · Symmetric encryption · AEAD

1 Introduction

Block ciphers are fundamental cryptographic primitives used in many encryption algorithms and message authentication codes. A conventional block cipher encryption algorithm E accepts two inputs: a secret and random k-bit key K and an n-bit input string M. The output is an n-bit string C, so the block cipher is represented as a map $E : \mathcal{K} \times \{0,1\}^n \rightarrow \{0,1\}^n$ where $\mathcal{K}$ is the key space.

To process large amounts of data, the message is divided into blocks of size n, and a block cipher has to be used in an appropriate mode of operation. Various block cipher modes of operation have been suggested, either to provide confidentiality or integrity assurance, or to provide both confidentiality and integrity assurance in a single design in a notion called Authenticated Encryption (AE). In Authenticated Encryption with Associated Data (AEAD), some portions of the message (the associated data) do not require confidentiality but still require integrity assurance.

L. Batten and G. Li (Eds.): ATIS 2016, CCIS 651, pp. 41–53, 2016.
DOI: 10.1007/978-981-10-2741-3_4

Tweakable block ciphers. Liskov, Rivest and Wagner [7] introduced another notion of block ciphers called tweakable block ciphers $\widehat{E}$. These ciphers take three inputs: key K, input message M and tweak T. Tweakable block ciphers can be represented as a map $\widehat{E} : \mathcal{K} \times \mathcal{T} \times \{0,1\}^n \rightarrow \{0,1\}^n$ where $\mathcal{T}$ is the tweak space. The purpose of the tweak is to differentiate messages and it should be easier to change the tweak rather than changing the key. Liskov, Rivest and Wagner suggest two approaches for constructing tweakable block ciphers that are provably secure as long as the underlying block cipher is secure. These constructions can be represented as $E(\Delta_h \oplus E(M_i))$ and $E(M_i \oplus \Delta_h) \oplus \Delta_h$ where Δ_h is a universal hash function operating as the tweak. However, these constructions need two keys that should be independent of each other.

Doubling masking technique. Halevi and Rogaway [5] proposed a tweakable block cipher mode of operation called EME that provides only confidentiality. This mode uses the doubling masking technique, where a secret masking value is used in processing each block. This secret value is initially obtained as $L = 2E(0^n)$, and then each time a different value is needed the previous value of L is doubled. This results in a series of masking values: $2L, 2^2L, 2^3L, \ldots, 2^mL$. The multiplication is performed in the finite field $\mathbb{F}_{2^n}$ by multiplying two input polynomials and finding the reminder modulo a primitive polynomial.

The doubling masking technique is very fast and efficient. In hardware implementation, the doubling is equivalent to a conditional of either a shift or shift and XOR operations. When $n = 128$ and the finite field $\mathbb{F}_{2^{128}}$ is constructed using the commonly used primitive polynomial $f(x) = x^{128} + x^7 + x^2 + x + 1$, the doubling is as follows:

$$2L = \begin{cases} L \ll 1 & \text{if MSB}(L) = 0 \\ (L \ll 1) \oplus 0^{120}10000111 & \text{if MSB}(L) = 1 \end{cases} \tag{1}$$

where $\ll$ is a 1-bit logical left shift operation and MSB stands for the most significant bit.

XE and XEX ciphers. Using the sequence of masking values $2L, 2^2L, \ldots, 2^mL$, Rogaway [11] describes two new approaches for tweakable block ciphers. These are known as XE and XEX ciphers, and are represented as $\widehat{E} : E(M_i \oplus 2^{i-1}L)$ or $\widehat{E} : E(M_i \oplus 2^{i-1}L) \oplus 2^{i-1}L$ respectively. Rogaway proves that these designs are secure up to the birthday bound for a certain range of i values. These designs use a single key for both the block encryption operation and to initialise the sequence of masking values used as the tweaks.

When a new value is needed which is outside the range of masking values $2L$, $2^2L, \ldots, 2^mL$, a value $2^{huge}L$ is used such that *huge* is much greater than m. For the primitive polynomial $f(x) = x^{128} + x^7 + x^2 + x + 1$, Rogaway chooses 2^{huge} as 3 and shows that this is far away from the offsets $2L, 2^2L, \ldots, 2^mL$. In addition, 3 is easy to calculate as $3 = 2 \oplus 1$; therefore, $3L$ can be XOR-ed with the checksum of plaintext blocks to obtain the authentication tag as in OCB1 [11].

Note however that 3 might not be equivalent to 2^{huge} when a different primitive polynomial is used. Collisions between the masks $3L$ and $2^j L$ can be found in such cases and lead to simple forgery attacks. Because of this, the choice of values for 2^{huge} must be investigated for every choice of finite field and its distinctness from the series of masking values must be verified.

OTR mode. Several block cipher modes of operation that have been proposed for AEAD use the doubling masking technique as in XE and XEX ciphers. One such mode is Offset Two-Round (OTR) [9] proposed by Minematsu and defined for any block size n. A version of OTR mode called AES-OTR [8] was submitted to the CAESAR competition [2]. The security proof of OTR requires that all input masks are distinct; however, the masks used in OTR and AES-OTR have only been proved to be distinct for a specific choice of n and the primitive polynomial defining the finite field.

Our contribution. Firstly, we show that the current instantiation of OTR uses masking coefficients that are not always distinct in fields based on other primitive polynomials, including when $n \neq 128$. We show that using the current instantiation with other primitive polynomials can result in non-distinct masking values that can be exploited in forgery attacks against the scheme. This is a problem with most modes that use the doubling masking technique.

Secondly, we propose an alternative set of masking coefficients so that OTR can use the same set of coefficients for any block size n and any primitive polynomial, without affecting the security provided by this scheme. That is, our work generalises the OTR mode using the technique of doubling masking, and removes the requirement for the user to perform huge prior calculations in order to ensure that the masks do not overlap.

Note that this work does not imply that OTR mode or AES-OTR are insecure. Note that this solution may also apply to other similar block cipher modes that use the doubling masking technique, such as OCB1 [11], ELmD [4] and AES-COPA [1].

2 Basic Notations

For simplicity and consistency, we follow the notation used in the original OTR document [10].

$\{0,1\}^*$: the set of all finite-length binary strings
ε : the empty string
K : k-bit key used for the block cipher and tweak initialisation
n : the block length of the block cipher
N : the nonce that is changed for each message
m : the number of blocks in the plaintext message
l : the number of chunks of two blocks in the plaintext message
$M[2i-1]$: the odd block in the ith chunk of the plaintext message
$M[2i]$: the even block in the ith chunk of the plaintext message
$C[2i-1]$: the odd block in the ith chunk of the corresponding ciphertext message
$C[2i]$: the even block in the ith chunk of the corresponding ciphertext message
A : the associated data that need only authentication
$|X|$: the length of the string X in bits
$X\|Y$: the concatenation of the strings X and Y
$|X|_a$: $\max\{\lceil|X|/a\rceil, 1\}$
$\xleftarrow{n} X$: returns $(X[1], X[2], \ldots, X[x])$ where $x = |X|_n$, $|X[i]| = n$ for $i < x$ and
          $|X[x]| \le n$
$\underline{X}$: the 10^* padding written as $X\|10^{n-|X|-1}$
$\mathbf{msb}_c(X)$: the first c bits of X provided that $|X| \ge c$
E : the block cipher encryption function under the key K
TA : the authentication tag obtained from associated data
TE : the authentication tag obtained from plaintext message
T : the τ-bit final authentication tag of OTR scheme.

3   OTR Description

Offset Two-round (OTR) is an authenticated encryption block cipher mode that is online, one-pass and each segment of two consecutive blocks can be processed in parallel. OTR mode has a similar structure to OCB mode [11], but OTR uses only the forward function of the block cipher for both encryption and decryption algorithms. The OTR operation is illustrated in Table 1 and Fig. 1.

The OTR algorithm accepts the following inputs: Key $K \in \{0,1\}^k$, Nonce $N \in \{0,1\}^j$ for $1 \le j \le n-1$, Associated Data $A \in \{0,1\}^*$ and Plaintext $M \in \{0,1\}^*$ and has the following outputs: Ciphertext $C \in \{0,1\}^*$ and Tag $T \in \{0,1\}^\tau$. The OTR encryption algorithm consists of two algorithms known as cores: an encryption core EF_E and authentication core AF_E. The OTR encryption core divides a plaintext message M into chunks, each containing two plaintext blocks. Then, each chunk is encrypted using two different masks. These two masks are doubled to obtain other two masks for the next chunk and so on.

The authentication core can process the associated data in either of the two ways: parallel or serial. OTR uses a variant of the PMAC1 scheme [11] to authenticate associated data in parallel, and uses a variant of the OMAC mode [6] to authenticate associated data serially.

The authentication tag T in OTR is generated in two different ways. For parallel associated data, a dedicated mask (depending on the last chunk) is XOR-ed with the checksum of plaintext blocks and the result is encrypted to

Table 1. OTR algorithm [9].

Algorithm 1: OTR Encryption Core	Algorithm 2: OTR Decryption Core
1. $\Sigma \leftarrow 0^n$	1. $\Sigma \leftarrow 0^n$
2. $L \leftarrow E(\underline{N})$	2. $L \leftarrow E(\underline{N})$
3. $(M[1], \ldots, M[m]) \xleftarrow{n} M$, $l = \lceil m/2 \rceil$	3. $(C[1], \ldots, C[m]) \xleftarrow{n} C$, $l = \lceil m/2 \rceil$
4. **for** $i = 1$ **to** $l - 1$ **do**	4. **for** $i = 1$ **to** $l - 1$ **do**
5. $C[2i-1] \leftarrow E(2^{i-1}L \oplus M[2i-1]) \oplus M[2i]$	5. $M[2i-1] \leftarrow E(2^{i-1}3L \oplus C[2i-1]) \oplus C[2i]$
6. $C[2i] \leftarrow E(2^{i-1}3L \oplus C[2i-1]) \oplus M[2i-1]$	6. $M[2i] \leftarrow E(2^{i-1}L \oplus M[2i-1]) \oplus C[2i-1]$
7. $\Sigma \leftarrow \Sigma \oplus M[2i]$	7. $\Sigma \leftarrow \Sigma \oplus M[2i]$
8. **if** m **is even**	8. **if** m **is even**
9. $Z \leftarrow E(2^{l-1}L \oplus M[m-1])$	9. $M[2m-1] \leftarrow E(2^{l-1}3L \oplus C[m]) \oplus C[m-1]$
10. $C[m] \leftarrow \mathrm{msb}_{|M[m]|}(Z) \oplus M[m]$	10. $Z \leftarrow E(2^{l-1}L \oplus M[m-1])$
11. $C[2m-1] \leftarrow E(2^{l-1}3L \oplus \underline{C[m]}) \oplus M[m-1]$	11. $M[m] \leftarrow \mathrm{msb}_{|M[m]|}(Z) \oplus C[m]$
12. $\Sigma \leftarrow \Sigma \oplus Z \oplus \underline{C[m]}$	12. $\Sigma \leftarrow \Sigma \oplus Z \oplus \underline{C[m]}$
13. **if** m **is odd**	13. **if** m **is odd**
14. $C[m] \leftarrow \mathrm{msb}_{|M[m]|}(E(2^{l-1}L)) \oplus M[m]$	14. $M[m] \leftarrow \mathrm{msb}_{|M[m]|}(E(2^{l-1}L)) \oplus C[m]$
15. $\Sigma \leftarrow \Sigma \oplus \underline{M[m]}$	15. $\Sigma \leftarrow \Sigma \oplus \underline{M[m]}$
16. **if** m **is even and** $|M[m]| \neq n$	16. **if** m **is even and** $|M[m]| \neq n$
17. $TE \leftarrow E(2^{l-1}3^3L \oplus \Sigma)$	17. $TE \leftarrow E(2^{l-1}3^3L \oplus \Sigma)$
18. **if** m **is even and** $|M[m]| = n$	18. **if** m **is even and** $|M[m]| = n$
19. $TE \leftarrow E(7.3.2^{l-1}L \oplus \Sigma)$	19. $TE \leftarrow E(7.3.2^{l-1}L \oplus \Sigma)$
20. **if** m **is odd and** $|M[m]| \neq n$	20. **if** m **is odd and** $|M[m]| \neq n$
21. $TE \leftarrow E(2^{l-1}3^2L \oplus \Sigma)$	21. $TE \leftarrow E(2^{l-1}3^2L \oplus \Sigma)$
22. **if** m **is odd and** $|M[m]| = n$	22. **if** m **is odd and** $|M[m]| = n$
23. $TE \leftarrow E(7.2^{l-1}L \oplus \Sigma)$	23. $TE \leftarrow E(7.2^{l-1}L \oplus \Sigma)$
24. $C \leftarrow (C[1], \ldots, C[m])$	24. $M \leftarrow (M[1], \ldots, M[m])$
25. **return** (C, TE)	25. **return** (M, TE)
Algorithm 3: OTR Authentication with Parallel A	**Algorithm 4**: OTR Authentication with Serial A
1. $\Xi \leftarrow 0^n$	1. $\Xi \leftarrow 0^n$
2. $Q \leftarrow E(0)$	2. $Q \leftarrow E(0)$
3. $(A[1], \ldots, A[a]) \xleftarrow{n} A$	3. $(A[1], \ldots, A[a]) \xleftarrow{n} A$
4. **for** $i = 1$ **to** $a - 1$ **do**	4. **for** $i = 1$ **to** $l - 1$ **do**
5. $\Xi \leftarrow \Xi \oplus E(Q \oplus A[i])$	5. $\Xi \leftarrow E(\Xi \oplus A[i])$
6. $Q \leftarrow 2Q$	
7. $\Xi \leftarrow \Xi \oplus A[a]$	6. $\Xi \leftarrow \Xi \oplus \underline{A[a]}$
8. **if** $|M[m]| \neq n$ **then** $TA \leftarrow E(3Q \oplus \Xi)$	7. **if** $|M[m]| \neq n$ **then** $TA \leftarrow E(2Q \oplus \Xi)$
9. **else** $TA \leftarrow E(3^2Q \oplus \Xi)$	8. **else** $TA \leftarrow E(4Q \oplus \Xi)$
10. **return** TA	9. **return** TA

obtain TE. The final tag T is obtained by XOR-ing TE with the resultant tag TA of authenticating the associated data. ($T = TE \oplus TA$.) For serial associated data, the associated data tag TA is used with the Nonce to obtain the secret tweak L. In this case, the plaintext tag TE will be the final tag T.

4   The Current Instantiation of OTR Mode

Initially, OTR was designed using different instantiation values for the masking coefficients. A proof that OTR is secure for the instantiation when $n = 128$ and using the primitive polynomial $f(x) = x^{128} + x^7 + x^2 + x + 1$ is given in [10].

As a general scheme, OTR is designed to work with any block size n and any finite field $\mathbb{F}_{2^n}$. However, to obtain security assurance for a different finite

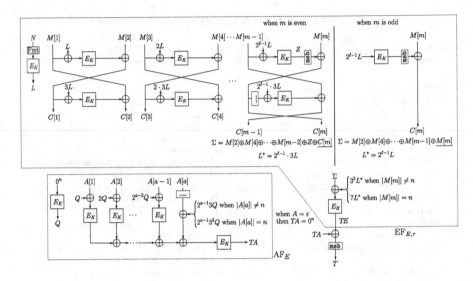

Fig. 1. OTR encryption operation with parallel associated data [9].

field, the user has to prove that the chosen masks for that instantiation of OTR are distinct and do not overlap. This requires discrete log computations. Using discrete log computation, Rogaway proves in [11] that certain sets of masks are distinct from each other and provide unique representation. He considers very specific choices: when $n = 128$ or $n = 64$ and when the finite field is based on certain commonly used primitive polynomials.

Bost and Sanders [3] showed trivial collisions between the OTR input masks can be found when special forms of primitive polynomial are used. These collisions can be exploited in practical forgery attacks. They suggested the use of different masking coefficients chosen from the set given by Rogaway in [11]. Accordingly, Minematsu updated the OTR instantiation coefficients [9] and noted that care must be taken in specifying the masking coefficients for other choices of n and of primitive polynomials defining $\mathbb{F}_{2^n}$.

For generic instantiations of OTR using block sizes and primitive polynomials other than those already examined, there is a risk that a user may not select suitable masking coefficients for the instantiation. This open problem motivates us seek a more robust definition of OTR in which the masking coefficients are distinct for any choice of finite field. Note that this will be applicable to OTR and also to any design which uses the doubling masking technique.

In our analysis, we take a similar approach to Bost and Sanders' work [3]. We consider two special forms of primitive polynomial, different to those discussed in [3], and which lead to a collision for the currently used masking coefficients.
Case 1: Primitive polynomial of the form $f(x) = x^n + x + 1$.

Many primitive polynomials can be found in this trinomial form $f(x) = x^n + x + 1$ [12]. In this case, x^n will be equal to $x + 1$. That is, 3 will be equivalent to

2^n and it is not 2^{huge} as the current instantiation assumes. Therefore, a collision can be found between $3L$ and $2^n L$ as long as $l > n$.

Case 2: Primitive polynomial of the form $f(x) = x^n + x^2 + 1$.

This is another form of trinomial, and in this case, x^n will be equal to $x^2 + 1$. That is, 5 (which is equal to 3^2 in $\mathbb{F}_{2^n}$) will be equivalent to 2^n. In OTR, 3^2 is used when the last block $M[m]$ is not a full block ($|M[m]| \neq n$).

5   Proposed Attacks

In this section, we show how collisions between the masks can be exploited to breach the integrity assurance of OTR. We consider the two cases from Sect. 4 separately. Our analysis assumes a man-in-the-middle attack model where the attacker is able to intercept and alter messages before sending them on to the intended recipient. We assume that the attacker knows both the plaintext message and its corresponding ciphertext using a single query of the OTR oracle.

Suppose that a plaintext message M is as follows:

$$M = (M[1], M[2], \ldots, M[m])$$

such that the number of blocks $m = |M|_n$ is odd and the number of chunks of two blocks $l > n + 1$ where $l = \lceil m/2 \rceil$. This message is encrypted using OTR and results in the ciphertext C:

$$C = (C[1], C[2] \ldots, C[m]).$$

5.1   Case 1 Collisions

In this case, as noted in Sect. 4, $3L = 2^n L$. Suppose that the last block is a full block ($|M[m]| = n$). A forged ciphertext message C^* can be constructed as follows:

$$\begin{aligned}
C^*[1] &= M[2(n + 1) - 1] \\
C^*[2] &= M[1] \oplus M[2(n + 1)] \oplus C[2(n + 1) - 1] \\
&= M[1] \oplus E(M[2(n + 1) - 1] \oplus 2^n L) \\
C^*[i] &= C[i], \quad 3 \leq i < m \\
C^*[m] &= C[m] \oplus C[1] \oplus M[2(n + 1) - 1]
\end{aligned}$$

Decrypting C^* will give the same value for all plaintext blocks except for $M^*[2]$ and $M^*[m]$ as follows:

$$\begin{aligned}
M^*[1] &= E(C^*[1] \oplus 3L) \oplus C^*[2] \\
&= E(M[2(n + 1) - 1] \oplus 3L) \oplus M[1] \oplus E(M[2(n + 1) - 1] \oplus 2^n L) \\
&= M[1] \\
M^*[2] &= E(M^*[1] \oplus L) \oplus C^*[1] = E(M[1] \oplus L) \oplus M[2(n + 1) - 1]
\end{aligned}$$

$$M^\star[m] = E(2^{l-1}L) \oplus C^\star[m]$$
$$= E(2^{l-1}L) \oplus C[m] \oplus C[1] \oplus M[2(n+1)-1]$$
$$= M[m] \oplus C[1] \oplus M[2(n+1)-1]$$

Let Σ' be the checksum of all even plaintext blocks of message M except $M[2]$ and the last block $M[m]$. That is,

$$\Sigma' = \Sigma \oplus M[2] \oplus M[m]$$

Therefore, the checksum of plaintext blocks for the forged message is:

$$\Sigma^\star = \Sigma' \oplus M^\star[2] \oplus M^\star[m]$$
$$= \Sigma' \oplus E(M[1] \oplus L) \oplus M[2(n+1)-1] \oplus M[m] \oplus C[1] \oplus M[2(n+1)-1]$$
$$= \Sigma' \oplus E(M[1] \oplus L) \oplus C[1] \oplus M[m]$$
$$= \Sigma' \oplus M[2] \oplus M[m]$$
$$= \Sigma$$

Both C and the forged message $C^\star$ produce the same checksum value. Thus, $C^\star$ will produce the same tag T as C, and will be accepted as genuine.

5.2   Case 2 Collisions

For this case, suppose that the message M has also the following features: $|M[m]| \neq n$, $M[1] = 0^n$ and $M[2(n+1)-1] = (\{1,0\}^j \,\|\, 10^\star)$ for $1 \le j < n$. If M is encrypted using OTR the pair (C, TE) is obtained. From this pair, an attacker can calculate $E(L) = C[1] \oplus M[2]$. A new pair $(C^\star, TE^\star)$ can be constructed from this such that $C^\star = C^\star[1] = \mathbf{msb}_j(M[2(n+1)-1] \oplus E(L))$ and the tag $TE^\star = C[2(n+1)-1] \oplus M[2(n+1)]$.

Decrypting the forged pair $(C^\star, TE^\star)$ will give:

$$M^\star[1] = \mathbf{msb}_j(E(L)) \oplus C^\star[1]$$
$$= \mathbf{msb}_j(E(L)) \oplus \mathbf{msb}_j(M[2(n+1)-1] \oplus E(L))$$
$$= \mathbf{msb}_j(M[2(n+1)-1])$$
$$\Sigma^\star = \underline{M^\star[1]} = M[2(n+1)-1]$$

Therefore, the tag TE' of the received ciphertext will be:

$$TE' = E(\Sigma^\star \oplus 3^2 L)$$
$$= E(M[2(n+1)-1] \oplus 3^2 L)$$
$$= E(M[2(n+1)-1] \oplus 2^n L)$$
$$= C[2(n+1)-1] \oplus M[2(n+1)]$$
$$= TE^\star$$

Thus, the forged pair $(C^\star, TE^\star)$ will be considered as a valid message. This clearly demonstrates the integrity assurance mechanism is flawed.

6 Proposed Solution

In Sect. 5 we demonstrated that, for certain forms of primitive polynomial, collisions occur between masking values which can be exploited in forgery attacks. This implies that the current choice of masking coefficients cannot be used in a generic construction of OTR. For every choice of finite field the distinctness of the masking values must be verified to ensure the design is secure against forgery attacks.

In this section we propose two minor modifications to OTR which guarantee that the masking coefficients are distinct for any choice of finite field. This makes the generic OTR scheme more robust since it reduces the chance of security compromise as a result of incorrect user choices. Our modifications preserve the main features of OTR mode and still use the powerful doubling masking method.

Note from Table 1 that OTR uses one of four special masks in generating the authentication tag TE from the checksum Σ of the plaintext blocks, with the choice of mask depending on two message features: whether the number of blocks m is even or odd; and whether the last block is a full block ($|M[m]| = n$) or not. To provide resistance against forgery attacks, it is important that when the multipliers of $2^{l-1}L$ in these masks are considered as powers of 2, the differences between the indexes of any pair of multipliers must be much greater than the maximum possible length (number of blocks) of any plaintext message. This will prevent an attacker forcing collisions between masks by changing the message length (inserting or deleting blocks). We suggest the following design changes to avoid collisions between masks without having to find multipliers at such large distances from one another.

Proposed instantiation of encryption/decryption core. We propose two minor modifications, as shown in Table 2 and Fig. 2, to provide a generic version of OTR. Firstly, we set the masking values for odd blocks to start from 2^3L, the masking values for even blocks to start from $2^{-3}L$ and define the four masks to be XOR-ed with the checksum of plaintext blocks as follows:

- 2^2L when m is even and $|M[m]| \neq n$
- $2L$ when m is even and $|M[m]| = n$
- $2^{-2}L$ when m is odd and $|M[m]| \neq n$
- $2^{-1}L$ when m is odd and $|M[m]| = n$

These choices ensure that the masks will not collide regardless of the primitive polynomial being used. The values $2^{-1}L$ and $2^{-2}L$ can easily be obtained from L with the right shift operation instead of the left shift used in the current scheme.

Secondly, we slightly redesign the last step in the process used to compute the tag, separating the XOR of checksum Σ and the number of chunks l in the plaintext message. This will prevent an attacker exploiting the tag computation by compensating between these two variables. In our proposal, changing either variable Σ or l will not have a clear effect on the other. The cost of this change is one extra block cipher call. However, this extra block cipher call makes the generic OTR design more robust.

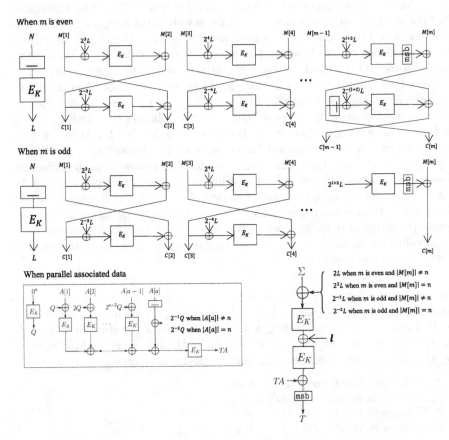

Fig. 2. Proposed OTR encryption diagram with parallel associated data.

Table 2. Proposed OTR algorithm.

Algorithm 5: OTR Encryption	**Algorithm 6**: OTR Decryption
1. $\Sigma \leftarrow 0^n$	1. $\Sigma \leftarrow 0^n$
2. $L \leftarrow E(\underline{N})$	2. $L \leftarrow E(\underline{N})$
3. $(M[1], \ldots, M[m]) \xleftarrow{n} M,\ l = \lceil m/2 \rceil$	3. $(C[1], \ldots, C[m]) \xleftarrow{n} C,\ l = \lceil m/2 \rceil$
4. **for** $i = 1$ **to** $l-1$ **do**	4. **for** $i = 1$ **to** $l-1$ **do**
5. $C[2i-1] \leftarrow E(2^{i+2}L \oplus M[2i-1]) \oplus M[2i]$	5. $M[2i-1] \leftarrow E(2^{-(i+2)}L \oplus C[2i-1]) \oplus C[2i]$
6. $C[2i] \leftarrow E(2^{-(i+2)}L \oplus C[2i-1]) \oplus M[2i-1]$	6. $M[2i] \leftarrow E(2^{i+2}L \oplus M[2i-1]) \oplus C[2i-1]$
7. $\Sigma \leftarrow \Sigma \oplus M[2i]$	7. $\Sigma \leftarrow \Sigma \oplus M[2i]$
8. **if** m **is even**	8. **if** m **is even**
9. $Z \leftarrow E(2^{l+2}L \oplus M[m-1])$	9. $M[2m-1] \leftarrow E(2^{-(l+2)}L \oplus \underline{C[m]}) \oplus C[m-1]$
10. $C[m] \leftarrow \mathrm{msb}_{|M[m]|}(Z) \oplus M[m]$	10. $Z \leftarrow E(2^{l+2}L \oplus M[m-1])$
11. $C[2m-1] \leftarrow E(2^{-(l+2)}L \oplus \underline{C[m]}) \oplus M[m-1]$	11. $M[m] \leftarrow \mathrm{msb}_{|M[m]|}(Z) \oplus C[m]$
12. $\Sigma \leftarrow \Sigma \oplus Z \oplus C[m]$	12. $\Sigma \leftarrow \Sigma \oplus Z \oplus \underline{C[m]}$
13. **if** m **is odd**	13. **if** m **is odd**
14. $C[m] \leftarrow \mathrm{msb}_{|M[m]|}(E(2^{l+2}L)) \oplus M[m]$	14. $M[m] \leftarrow \mathrm{msb}_{|M[m]|}(E(2^{l+2}L)) \oplus C[m]$
15. $\Sigma \leftarrow \Sigma \oplus \underline{M[m]}$	15. $\Sigma \leftarrow \Sigma \oplus \underline{M[m]}$
16. **if** m **is even and** $|M[m]| \neq n$	16. **if** m **is even and** $|M[m]| \neq n$
17. $W \leftarrow E(2L \oplus \Sigma)$	17. $W \leftarrow E(2L \oplus \Sigma)$
18. **if** m **is even and** $|M[m]| = n$	18. **if** m **is even and** $|M[m]| = n$
19. $W \leftarrow E(2^2L \oplus \Sigma)$	19. $W \leftarrow E(2^2L \oplus \Sigma)$
20. **if** m **is odd and** $|M[m]| \neq n$	20. **if** m **is odd and** $|M[m]| \neq n$
21. $W \leftarrow E(2^{-1}L \oplus \Sigma)$	21. $W \leftarrow E(2^{-1}L \oplus \Sigma)$
22. **if** m **is odd and** $|M[m]| = n$	22. **if** m **is odd and** $|M[m]| = n$
23. $W \leftarrow E(2^{-2}L \oplus \Sigma)$	23. $W \leftarrow E(2^{-2}L \oplus \Sigma)$
24. $TE \leftarrow E(W \oplus l)$	24. $TE \leftarrow E(W \oplus l)$
25. $C \leftarrow (C[1], \ldots, C[m])$	25. $M \leftarrow (M[1], \ldots, M[m])$
26. **return** (C, TE)	26. **return** (M, TE)
Algorithm 7: OTR Authentication with Parallel A	**Algorithm 8**: OTR Authentication with Serial A
1. $\Xi \leftarrow 0^n$	1. $\Xi \leftarrow 0^n$
2. $Q \leftarrow E(0)$	2. $Q \leftarrow E(0)$
3. $(A[1], \ldots, A[a]) \xleftarrow{n} A$	3. $(A[1], \ldots, A[a]) \xleftarrow{n} A$
4. **for** $i = 1$ **to** $a-1$ **do**	4. **for** $i = 1$ **to** $l-1$ **do**
5. $\Xi \leftarrow \Xi \oplus E(Q \oplus A[i])$	5. $\Xi \leftarrow E(\Xi \oplus A[i])$
6. $Q \leftarrow 2Q$	
7. $\Xi \leftarrow \Xi \oplus A[a]$	6. $\Xi \leftarrow \Xi \oplus A[a]$
8. **if** $|M[m]| \neq n$ **then** $TA \leftarrow E(2^{-1}Q \oplus \Xi)$	7. **if** $|M[m]| \neq n$ **then** $TA \leftarrow E(2Q \oplus \Xi)$
9. **else** $TA \leftarrow E(2^{-2}Q \oplus \Xi)$	8. **else** $TA \leftarrow E(4Q \oplus \Xi)$
10. **return** TA	9. **return** TA

proposed instantiation of authentication core. As noted is Sect. 3, the authentication core can process the associated data in two modes: serial or parallel. For serial associated data, the same design will be used as it uses only two masks: $2Q$ and 2^2Q. These masks are distinct regardless of the primitive polynomial used. For parallel associated data, we only change the masks used with the last block $A[a]$. OTR (Fig. 1) uses the masks $2^{a-1}3L$ and $2^{a-1}3^2L$ when $|A[a]| \neq n$ and $|A[a]| = n$ respectively. However, there is no need for these two masks to be very far away from each other, as changing the number of blocks a in the associated data will directly affect the accumulated tag TA. Thus, the two masks we suggest for the last block are $2^{-1}L$ and $2^{-2}L$ when $|A[a]| \neq n$ and $|A[a]| = n$ respectively.

Note that the base of all new masks suggested for OTR is 2. This guarantees that the masks will not overlap, and enables us to use the same masks for all choices of n and all choices of the primitive polynomials used to define the finite field $\mathbb{F}_{2^n}$.

7   Security Bounds for OTR Using the New Masking Coefficients

This section discusses the impact of changing the input masks on the security bounds of OTR. Firstly, all of proposed masks for OTR have the form 2^j. Since 2 is the generator of the finite field $\mathbb{F}_{2^n}$ and the order of this field is $2^n - 1$, this assures that $2^j = 2^{j'}$ iff $j = j'$ for any $j \leq 2^n - 1$. Therefore, these masks will not collide for any collection of blocks with a length less than $(2^{n-1} - 3)$, which is well beyond the message length restriction of $2^{n/2}$ blocks imposed by the designer of OTR. Thus, the collision attacks discussed in Sect. 5 are now precluded.

Secondly, the security proofs of OTR [9] assume that all tweakable block cipher calls in each of the two rounds have distinct masks. As shown in the above paragraph, the proposed masks are guaranteed to be different from each other; thus, the same security bounds for OTR still hold.

Finally, our proposed modification to OTR adds one extra block cipher call, as shown in Fig. 2. This step is required in order to avoid using a mask with a base other than 2. The probability that an attacker can guess the tag successfully is still $1/2^\tau$ where is τ the tag length. Therefore, the security of OTR will not be degraded with the new instantiation method.

8   Conclusion

OTR is a block cipher mode of operation for AEAD that uses a doubling masking technique. OTR is designed to be applicable for any block size n but currently requires a suitable choice to be made for the finite field $\mathbb{F}_{2^n}$ used for doubling the mask values. The security of OTR against forgery attacks depends on the distinctness of the masking values. This has only been proved for specific choices of primitive polynomial in the particular cases of $n = 64$ and $n = 128$.

In this paper, we show that the masks used in the current instantiation of OTR are not distinct for certain choices of finite field. Using these choices, we demonstrate practical forgery attacks against OTR. Thus, the generic form of the OTR design is not secure.

We propose two minor modifications to OTR to make the generic version of this scheme more robust. We do this by specifying a set of masks that are distinct in every finite field $\mathbb{F}_{2^n}$. This enables OTR to work with any finite field without invalidating the security claimed. Note that this work does not imply that the versions of OTR described in [8,9] are insecure.

Acknowledgements. Hassan Al Mahri would like to acknowledge the scholarship for this research from the government of the Sultanate of Oman.

References

1. Andreeva, E., Bogdanov, A., Luykx, A., Mennink, B., Tischhauser, E., Yasuda, K.: AES-COPA (2014). http://competitions.cr.yp.to/caesar-submissions.html
2. Bernstein, D.: Cryptographic Competitions: CAESAR (2014). http://competitions.cr.yp.to/caesar-call.html
3. Bost, R., Sanders, O.: Trick or Tweak: On the (In)security of OTR's Tweaks. Cryptology ePrint Archive, Report 2016/234 (2016). http://eprint.iacr.org/
4. Datta, N., Nandi, M.: ElmD (2014). http://competitions.cr.yp.to/caesar-submissions.html
5. Halevi, S., Rogaway, P.: A parallelizable enciphering mode. In: Okamoto, T. (ed.) CT-RSA 2004. LNCS, vol. 2964, pp. 292–304. Springer, Heidelberg (2004). doi:10.1007/978-3-540-24660-2_23
6. Iwata, T., Kurosawa, K.: OMAC: one-key CBC MAC. In: Johansson, T. (ed.) FSE 2003. LNCS, vol. 2887, pp. 129–153. Springer, Heidelberg (2003). doi:10.1007/978-3-540-39887-5_11
7. Liskov, M., Rivest, R.L., Wagner, D.: Tweakable block ciphers. In: Yung, M. (ed.) CRYPTO 2002. LNCS, vol. 2442, pp. 31–46. Springer, Heidelberg (2002). doi:10.1007/3-540-45708-9_3
8. Minematsu, K.: AES-OTR (2014). http://competitions.cr.yp.to/caesar-submissions.html
9. Minematsu, K.: Parallelizable Rate-1 Authenticated Encryption from Pseudorandom Functions. Cryptology ePrint Archive, Report 2013/628 (2013). http://eprint.iacr.org/
10. Minematsu, K.: Parallelizable rate-1 authenticated encryption from pseudorandom functions. In: Nguyen, P.Q., Oswald, E. (eds.) EUROCRYPT 2014. LNCS, vol. 8441, pp. 275–292. Springer, Heidelberg (2014). doi:10.1007/978-3-642-55220-5_16
11. Rogaway, P.: Efficient instantiations of tweakable blockciphers and refinements to modes OCB and PMAC. In: Lee, P.J. (ed.) ASIACRYPT 2004. LNCS, vol. 3329, pp. 16–31. Springer, Heidelberg (2004). doi:10.1007/978-3-540-30539-2_2
12. Seroussi, G.: Table of Low-Weight Binary Irreducible Polynomials. Computer Systems Laboratory, Report HPL-98-135 (1998). http://www.hpl.hp.com/techreports/98/HPL-98-135.pdf?jumpid=reg_R1002_USEN

Recent Cyber Security Attacks and Their Mitigation Approaches – An Overview

Abdullahi Chowdhury[✉]

Faculty of Science and Technology,
Federation University Australia, Ballarat, Australia
Abdullahi.chowdhury@federation.edu.au

Abstract. The advent of digital media, Internet, web and online social media has drawn the attention of relevant research community significantly and created many new research challenges on cyber security. People, organisations and governments around the world are losing a huge amount of money because of having cyber-attacks. For this reason, cyber security has become one of the most difficult and significant problems across the world. Currently, cyber security researchers of both industries and academic institutes are analysing existing cyber-attacks happening across the world and are developing different types of techniques to protect the systems against potential cyber-threats and attacks. This paper discusses the recent cyber security-attacks and the economic loss resulted from the growing cyber-attacks. This paper also analyses the increasing exploitation of a computer system, which has created more opportunities for the current cyber-crimes. Protective mechanisms and relevant laws are being implemented to reduce cyber- crimes around the world. Contemporary and important mitigation approaches for cyber-crimes have also been articulated in this paper.

Keywords: Cyber-attacks · Impact of cyber-attacks · Cyber-crimes · Cyber security

1 Introduction

Nowadays people are getting more dependent on computer and information technologies. Individuals, industries and government sectors utilise online or offline technologies to store and use normal day to day data that is highly critical and confidential. Many of these data (e.g., financial and personal information) attract cyber criminals to break the computer system for damaging these data and the network infrastructure or seeking knowledge from these data. It has already been reported in the literature and online sources that many kinds of cyber-attacks such as email bombing, information or the data theft, Denial of Service (DoS) attacks, Trojan attacks, and hacking the data or the system were happened in the past. The numbers of the attacks are increasing day by day due to the advent of social media, ever- increasing use of them and most people's presence online for the majority of their time. The types of attacks performed by Internet are called cybercrimes. Cybercrime is not a new concept or term. Joseph Marie Jacquard, a textile manufacturer in France first made a loom in 1820. This device controlled the repetition of the series of the steps in weaving of the series of special

© Springer Nature Singapore Pte Ltd. 2016
L. Batten and G. Li (Eds.): ATIS 2016, CCIS 651, pp. 54–65, 2016.
DOI: 10.1007/978-981-10-2741-3_5

fabrics. Jacquard's employees became afraid of this process and thought their traditional employment and livelihood were at stake. Employees carried out the acts of sabotage to prevent Jacquard from further using of new technology. This is known as the first filed cybercrime [1].

Cyber security refers to safeguarding the information stored in client computers and servers distributed across the world and the transmission of information through the communication infrastructure from cyber-attacks. Thriving use of information technology and social media, and emerging use of web-based Internet computing and applications including cloud, m-Commerce and health informatics have made cyber security to become one of the major and most important issues around the globe. For this reason, it is important to know the contemporary and existing cyber-attacks and their mitigation strategies to develop a security policy for protecting information and communication infrastructures vulnerable to cyber-attacks. Therefore, the recent cyber-attacks and their impacts and mitigation strategies have been presented in this paper.

The paper is organised as follows. Section 2 presents the recent and existing cyber-attacks. The impacts of cyber-attacks and their mitigation strategies are provided in Sects. 3 and 4, respectively. Finally, Sect. 5 concludes the paper.

2 Cyber Attacks

There are many different kinds of cyber-attacks. Figure 1 shows the percentage of cyber-attacks happened worldwide recently in May 2016, which indicates that the most frequently occurring cyber-attacks are malware, Distributed Denial of Service (DDoS), targeted attack, SQL injection (SQLi), defacement, malvertising and others.

Some of the severe and frequently occurring cyber-attacks are described below.

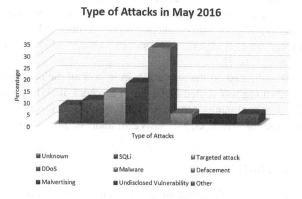

Fig. 1. Types of attacks - May 2016 [2]

2.1 Decrypting RSA with Obsolete and Weakened ENcryption (DROWN) Attack

Transport Layer Security (TLS) is one the main protocols responsible for the security of data transport in modern Internet. TLS and Secure Sockets Layer version 3 (SSLv3) have been the target of a large number of cryptographic attacks in the research community, both on popular implementations and the protocol itself. There have been at least 10 well publicized security vulnerabilities over the past 5 years on different versions of TLS and SSL. Prominent recent examples include attacks on outdated or deliberately weakened encryption in Rivest Cipher (RC)4, Rivest, Shamir, & Adleman (RSA), and Diffie-Hellman, different side channels including Lucky13, Browser Exploit Against SSL/TLS (BEAST), and Padding Oracle On Downgraded Legacy Encryption (POODLE). The latest of which is the DROWN attack. DROWN is a serious vulnerability that affects HTTPS and other services that rely on SSL and TLS. These protocols allow everyone on the Internet to browse the web, use email, shop online, and send instant messages without third-parties being able to read the communication [3–5].

DROWN allows attackers to break the encryption and read or steal sensitive information. Most modern TLS clients do not support SSLv2 at all. Yet in 2016, our Internet-wide scans find that out of 36 million HTTPS servers, 6 million (17 %) support SSLv2. 16 % of the servers allows key reuse. That makes 33 % servers are vulnerable to DROWN attack. If a web server is configured to use SSLv2, and particularly one that's running OpenSSL (even with all SSLv2 ciphers disabled!), you may be vulnerable to a DROWN attack that decrypts many recorded TLS connections made to that box. Most worryingly, the attack does not require the client to ever make an SSLv2 connection itself, and it isn't a downgrade attack. Instead, it relies on the fact that SSLv2 – and particularly the legacy "export" ciphersuites it incorporates – are pure poison, and simply having these active on a server is enough to invalidate the security of all connections made to that device. Any communication between users and the server. This typically includes, but is not limited to, usernames and passwords, credit card numbers, emails, instant messages, and sensitive documents. Under some common scenarios, an attacker can also impersonate a secure website and intercept or change the content the user sees [3, 6, 7].

For each server, we listed all the public IPs in it, and all the open ports in it. Then we used an SSL scanning tool called SSLyze [8] to check if SSLv2 ciphers are supported. The following commands can be used to check if any port in the server has SSLv2 available secsev # sslyze_cli.py – sslv2 Ip address: port (443).

2.2 SQL Injection (SQLi)

SQL injection is type of attack where an attacker injects SQL codes known as malicious playloads into SQL statements during inputting data through a web page. During the execution of a SQL statement, a malicious payload controls a web application's database server. Since an SQL injection vulnerability could possibly affect any website or web application which makes use of an SQL-based database, the vulnerability is one of the oldest, most prevalent and most dangerous of web application vulnerabilities [9]. There are four main subclass of SQLi. They are Classic SQLI, Blind or Inference SQLi,

Database management system specific SQLi and compound SQLi. Compound SQLi in normally combination of SQLi and DDoS or SQLi and unauthorised access or insufficient authentication. According to Open Web Application Security Project (OWASP) SQLI was considered one of the top 10 application vulnerabilities in 2007 and in 2013 SQLI was rated number 1 attack. OWASP is still collecting data for 2016 data to rank top 10 vulnerabilities for 2016 [10]. For a simple example of SQLi, if we consider, a web interface uses the following SQL code to show all records from the table "Users" for a username and password supplied by a user: SELECT * FROM Users WHERE Username = '$username' AND Password = '$password'.

Using a web interface, when username and password field is prompted, a malicious user might enter:

SELECT * FROM Users WHERE Username = '1' OR '1' = '1' AND Password = '1' OR '1' = '1'

By using the above code, attacker has effectively injected a whole OR condition into the authentication process. The condition '1' = '1' is always true, so this SQL query will always result in the authentication process being bypassed.

2.3   Denial of Service Attacks (DoS)

DoS attack is an attempt to make the computer or network resources unavailable for its intended users by interrupting or suspending the services running with the system or

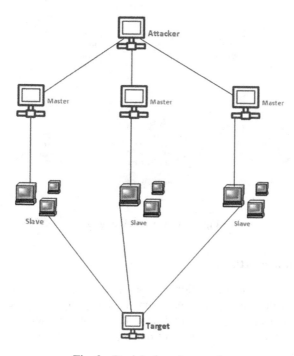

Fig. 2. Denial of service attack

58   A. Chowdhury

the network. In this kind of attack, the attackers trespass into the system by hampering the network to keep the memory resource or system too busy to run the appropriate requests. It also makes the system to decline an authorised user entrance to a machine. Figure 2 shows the basic diagram of Dos attack. Attacker machine runs the client software to initiate the DoS attack. Master machines act as handler and slaves are the compromised machines that help to execute the DoS attacks.

Vehicular ad hoc network (VANET) is one of the prime target of the DoS attacks nowadays. In VANET, the attackers use jamming communication channel, network overloading, and packets dropping to perform DoS attacks [11]. When multiple sources attack a single target to cause denial of service is known as DDoS. In [3], authors reported that with the increase of the number of networks built by bots or machine containing malware increases the number of DDoS attacks mainly in cloud computing environment. According to Digital Trends [12] DDoS attacks increased 7 % from 2015 Quarter 1 to 2015 Quarter 2 and 132 % from 2014 Quarter 2 to 2015 Quarter 2. The DDoS attacks are also happening in lot quicker speed than before. In September 2012 average speed was 1.67 gigabits per second (Gbps) [13] where in 2015 12 mega DDoS attack happened with peak speed of 1,000 Gbps and 50 million packets per second (Mpps). Till quarter two 2016 the peak number of attack was 1,272 on 31st of March [14].

Most recent DoS attack was on Census Website on 09/08/2016. Figure 3 shows one of the error message users were getting during the outage of Census website. Australian Bureau of Statistics advised they had to temporary close the site due to Denial of Service attack. Millions of Australian were unable to submit the census form on time. Census website was down for approximately 43 h [15].

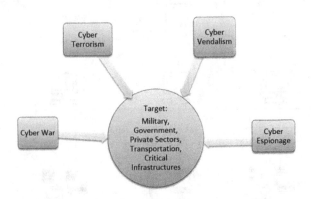

Fig. 3. Cyber-attack targets

2.4   Other Common Attacks

Based on the activities and intention of the cyber attackers, cyber-attacks can be described in four categories – (i) cyber terrorism, (ii) cyber war, (iii) cyber vandalism and (iv) cyber espionage. Figure 3 shows that targets of these attacks are mainly the individual personal, military, government offices, private sectors, transportations and critical infrastructures.

2.4.1   Cyber Terrorism

Cyber terrorism is currently one of the emerging worldwide cyber-attacks. It uses Internet as the medium in place of weapon to do the damage. Its main purpose is to exploit the personal interest or terrorise the government or people for the political, religious or social objective [16]. One of the most recent cyber terrorism attacks was in April 2015. A hacking group called CyberCaliphate attacked Tv5 Monde, a French media outlet. The attack resulted in temporary control of the main website, social media accounts and interruption of 11 TV stations, crippling the company's broadcast capabilities for hours [17].

2.4.2   Cyber War

In this type of attack, one nation targets other nation to damage or destroy the network and obtain an access to the important websites and services or steal information and ruin the economic system. The purpose of the cyber war is to create effects in and through cyberspace in support of a combatant commander's military objectives and to ensure friendly forces freedom of action in cyberspace [18]. The Stuxnet computer worm is an example of cyber war that destroyed centrifuges inside Iran's Natanz uranium enrichment site. This was only one element of a much larger US-prepared cyberattack plan that targeted Iran's air defenses, communications systems, and key parts of its power grid [19].

2.4.3   Cyber Vandalism

Cyber vandalism aims to create destruction or defacement of private and public property in cyber space. Cyber vandals usually perpetrate an attack for personal enjoyment or to increase their stature within a group, club or organization. Some common methods of cyber vandalism are website defacement, denial-of-service attacks, forced system outages and data destruction [16].

2.4.4   Cyber Espionage

This is the practice of spying in cyberspace to gain knowledge about a target. Government intelligent team, large advertising companies and some cyber- criminals spy in personal and organisational online activities to gather information and use that information for their own purposes later on [18]. Between 2007 and 2013, Westinghouse was negotiating the details of a contract with a Chinese company to build four nuclear reactors. From 2010 to 2012, one of the defendants allegedly stole at least 1.4 gigabytes of data from Westinghouse's computers [20].

3   Impact of Cyber Attacks

UK reported that total number of known stolen records were 166,687,282 in April 2016. 55,000,000 voters had their data leaked in the Philippines and 93,424,710 in Mexico. An online site called Beautifulpeople.com suffered a data breach this month, leaking the personal data of 1,100,000 members. The data is already for sale online, including sexual preferences, relationship statuses, income, addresses and more. Unauthorized access refers to obtaining entry or any kind of access without the authorization of the authorised or certified owner. On the other hand, hacking refers to any action concerning breaching into other's computer or network with the purpose of accessing, removing or ruining important data. In 2014 nearly half of the population of USA were victim of hacking with unauthorized access to personal data such as names, credit card information, birthdates and addresses [21]. China has world 41 % of hacking attack traffic followed by USA (10 %), Turkey (4.7 %), Russia (4.3 %), Taiwan (3.7 %) Brazil (3.3 %) Romania (2.8 %), India (2.3 %), Italy (1.6 %), Hungary (1.4 %) [22].

Cyber-crimes cause harm to Citizens, Business, and Government in many ways such as loss of sensitive business information, loss of customer trust, cost of restoration of business, loss of intellectual property and trade secrets etc. In the report of June 2014 taken by Centre for Strategic and International Studies stated that yearly cost to the global economy by the incidents of cyber-crimes is more than $400 billion. Cyber crime affects will gradually increase more and more as business functions are constantly prospering their business online and more of the company's and customers of the world are connected to the internet. In the developed countries cyber crime causes employment rate as researches stated that loss from cyber crime can harm 200,000 American jobs, nearly a third of 1 % fall in the employment. A report of 2013 stated that 3000 companies in US were being hacked as proclaimed by the Government. In 2014, Brazil suffers $1.4 billion from the cyber-attacks since more than 45 % Brazilians are the users of Internet. In 2013, France lost $5.19 million because of cyber-attacks and the recent report stated that France had confronted 19000 cyber-attacks since the terror rampage in 2014 around 91 % percent of the UK business and 93 % households have access to Internet and about £27 billion is calculated cost of the cyber-crimes in UK [18]. Figure 4 shows the sector wise cyber-attacks in 2016. Industrial sector are the main target of the cyber attackers approximately 22 % attacks happened in Industrial sector, then 15 % on finance sector followed by individual computers, financial institution, online services, government sector, adult sites and others.

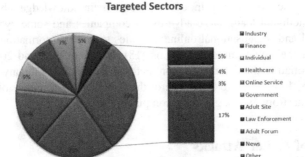

Fig. 4. Sector wise cyber-attacks in May 2016 [2]

4 Mitigation Process

4.1 Mitigation Process for DROWN

To protect or minimise the possibilities of DROWN attacks, server operators need to ensure that their private keys are not used anywhere with server software that allows SSLv2 connections. This includes web servers, SMTP servers, IMAP and POP servers, and any other software that supports SSL/TLS. Disabling SSLv2 can be complicated and depends on the specific server software. If user is using OpenSSL, it needs to be upgraded to the latest version. For an example OpenSSL 1.0.2 users should upgrade to 1.0.2g. OpenSSL 1.0.1 users should upgrade to 1.0.1s. If user is using Microsoft IIS (Windows Server), Support for SSLv2 on the server side is enabled by default only on the OS versions that correspond to IIS 7.0 and IIS 7.5, namely Windows Vista, Windows Server 2008, Windows 7 and Windows Server 2008R2. This support can be disabled in the appropriate SSLv2 subkey for 'Server'. If user is using Network Security Services (NSS), they need to upgrade to NSS versions 3.13. Any version on or after 3.13 has SSLv2 disabled by default [3, 5, 7].

The followings are some commands to patch OpenSSL in different Linux servers [23]:
In CentOS and RedHat server versions 5, 6, 7: # yum update openssl
In SUSE and OpenSUSE servers: # zypper patch
In Ubuntu and Debian servers: # apt-get install – only-upgrade libssl1.0.0 openssl
In Oracle Linux: # yum update openssl
To take protection against DROWN in different Services, the following commands can be used:
In HTTP – Apache: Need to edit the Apache configuration file (/etc/httpd/conf/httpd.conf) as followings: SSLProtocol All - SSLv2 - SSLv3
In HTTP – Nginx: Need to change the Nginx configuration (/etc/nginx/nginx.conf) line from
ssl_protocols SSLv2 SSLv3 TLSv1 TLSv1.1 TLSv1.2; to ssl_protocols TLSv1 TLSv1.1 TLSv1.2;
In SMTP – Exim: Need to edit Exim configuration file (/etc/exim.conf) and changetls_require_ciphers to
ALL:!aNULL:!ADH:!eNULL:!LOW:!EXP:RC4+RSA:+HIGH:+MEDIUM:!SSLv2:!SSLv3
In POP/IMAP – Courier-IMAP/Dovecot: edit mail server configuration file (/etc/dovecot.conf) and change SSL Cipher list to ALL:!aNULL:!ADH:!eNULL:!LOW:!EXP:!RC4+RSA:+HIGH:+MEDIUM:!SSLv2:SSLv3
In FTP – Pure-FTP/Pro-FTP: Edit FTP configuration files (/etc/pure-ftpd.conf, /etc/proftpd/proftpd.conf) and change the TLS Cipher Suite to HIGH:!aNULL:!eNULL:!PSK:!RC4:!MD5:!TLSv1:!SSLv2:!SSLv3

4.2 Basic Precaution Steps

Corporate or individual user needs to deploy antivirus and malicious code checking software for internal or external network. Any suspicious or infected objects suggested by these software should be quarantined and network administrator should be notified for further analysis. In large network environment, a content filtering capability on all external gateways can be deployed to try to prevent attackers delivering malicious code to the common desktop applications (e.g. web browser, email client) used by the user. Where possible, disabling the auto run function will prevent the automatic import of malicious code from any type of removable media. If removable media is introduced, the system should automatically scan it for malicious content. Virus and malware detection software needs to be activated for email clients (e.g. Outlook, Gmail). User needs to make sure that they do not open any email from unknown source without scanning the email [24–26] (Table 1).

Table 1. Other mitigation strategies

Strategy	Description
Using Digital Immune System (DIS)	DIS assists end user (or the anti virus program running on user's system) to report any cyber threat (e.g. virus, Trojan horse, or any malicious software activity) for analysis and repair. Once any new threat is listed or any new solution is found, DIS upload the details so that everyone using DIS can get the benefit.
Software Patching	All applications and software should be patched and updated regularly in every node connected to the network. Any unpatched device in network can create a security hole for the cyber attackers. Operating systems, all applications including antivirus should be updated. Data show that desktop malware infection rates fall by a factor of ten between Windows XP with Service Pack (SP) 3 and Windows 7 64-bit with SP1 (1.09 % and 0.11 %, respectively). This is primarily due to security features such as memory address space randomization (ASLR) and data execution prevention (DEP) [24].
Minimise administrative privileges	Administrative privileges are designed to allow only trusted personnel to configure, manage and monitor computer systems. Accounts with administrative privileges on a system have the ability to make virtually any change to that system and to retrieve almost any information from it. Number of administrative privileged needs to be minimised. If large number of accounts needs to be created in any specific network only user should get access to the software, they require with minimum system right [25].
Multi-factor authentication systems	Using one than one proof of authentication decreases the chance of unauthorised access to any system. There are multiple types of multi-factor authentication system, most commonly used one is two-factor authentication. System can ask user for authentication details from knowledge factor (e.g. password, Personal Identification number, Security questions) or possession factor (e.g. remote token

(Continued)

Table 1. (*Continued*)

Strategy	Description
	for VPN, USB token, Smart Identification Card, Radio-Frequency Identification or wireless tags) or Inherence factor (e.g. finger print, retina scan or voice recognition) [27–29]. In Australia banks are using internet banking password and and Short Message Service authentication for new transfers or international transfers, Mygov website requires multilevel authentication like username, password, sms code and personal security code.
Using Sandbox	Sandbox can be used to monitor and automated dynamic analysis of emails and web contents. Snadbox assists detecting any unusual behaviour of data of any network traffic, software or application.
Using Intrusion Detection/Prevention system	Network based or Host based Intrusion Detection/Prevention System can be used to identify anomalous behaviour of any malicious software (e.g malware, adware or spyware) and anomalous intranet or Internet traffic.
Using Firewall	Firewall provides protection from inbound or malicious and unauthorised traffic. User can set option to reject or deny or block suspicious network traffic using firewall.
Log file monitoring	Automated log monitoring can be used to review and analysis of any successful or failed access request, network traffic information, unauthorised attempts to access external sites and any malicious software installation attempts.
Content filtering	Using content filtering for email and web data will provide protection from getting emails with virus, malware, and adware or keystroke generator. All attachments from new or unknown source from email or web needs to be scanned by antivirus before downloading.
Update and monitor black/block list	Application white listing, email and web content block listing, trusted website list, trusted domain list and any other trusted, blocked, white and vblack list used by the protection software needs to be regularly updated (automated preferred) for protecting the system from recent cyber threats.

5 Conclusion

In recent time, cyber criminals are using different attack methods and adopting modern technology to perform cyber-crimes. Number of cyber-attacks are increasing day by day. These cyber-attacks are not limited to individual or personal computers, attackers are also targeting large corporations, government offices and central banks. Only legal or law enforcement departments will not be able to reduce cyber- crimes effectively unless personal and social awareness about cyber security is widely used. So, this is the duty of the Government, media and IT professionals to educate the people about this critical fields of cyber-world. Regardless the sector responsible for maintaining the security, a common language and lexicon needs to be created so that everyone including end users, professionals, politicians and security vendors understand and can communicate about cyber security issues with each other without anxiety, uncertainty and doubt. For this reason, in this paper, we have reviewed the recent possible cyber-crimes and their impacts and mitigation approaches.

References

1. Clough, J.: Principles of Cybercrime. Cambridge University Press, Cambridge (2015)
2. Passeri, P.: Cyber Attacks StatisticsPaolo Passeri, May 2016. http://www.hackmageddon.com/category/security/cyber-attacks-statistics/. Accessed 07 October 2016
3. Aviram, N., et al.: DROWN: Breaking TLS using SSLv2 (2016). https://www.lemarson.com/public/upload/ressource/filename/DROWN_SSL.pdf. Accessed 08 November 2016
4. Al Fardan, N.J., Paterson, K.G.: Lucky thirteen: breaking the TLS and DTLS record protocols. In: 2013 IEEE Symposium on Security and Privacy (SP). IEEE (2013)
5. Bhargavan, K., Leurent, G.: Transcript collision attacks: breaking authentication in TLS, IKE, and SSH. In: NDSS, February 2016
6. Beattie, D.: The DROWN Attack Vulnerability and Changing Your Server Configuration (2016)
7. Dukhovni, V., Käsper, E.: An OpenSSL User's Guide to DROWN, OpenSSL, Editor (2016)
8. GitHub. Fast and full-featured SSL scanner (2016). https://github.com/iSECPartners/sslyze?_sm_byp=iVVWSrMVJZLN4jMF. Accessed 08 November 2016
9. Chen, P., Huygens, C., Desmet, L., Joosen, W.: Advanced or not? A comparative study of the use of anti-debugging and anti-VM techniques in generic and targeted malware. In: Hoepman, J.-H., Katzenbeisser, S. (eds.) SEC 2016. IFIP AICT, vol. 471, pp. 323–336. Springer, Heidelberg (2016). doi:10.1007/978-3-319-33630-5_22
10. OWASP. Category: OWASP Top Ten Project (2016). https://www.owasp.org/index.php/Category:OWASP_Top_Ten_Project#tab=OWASP_Top_10_for_2013. Accessed 07 October 2016
11. Sharma, P., Singh, A.: A review on detection and prevention techniques of denial of service attack in vanet. Int. J. Adv. Res. Comput. Sci. 6(5) (2015)
12. Keane, J.: DDoS attacks hit record numbers in Q2 2015 (2015). http://www.digitaltrends.com/computing/ddos-attacks-hit-record-numbers-in-q2-2015/. Accessed 07 October 2016
13. Networks, A. DDoS attacks: Understanding the Threat (2013). http://www.slideshare.net/Arbor_Networks/ddos-attacks-understanding-the-threat. Accessed 07 October 2016
14. Lab, K. Kaspersky DDoS Intelligence Report for Q1 2016 (2016). https://securelist.com/analysis/quarterly-malware-reports/74550/kaspersky-ddos-intelligence-report-for-q1-2016/. Accessed 07 October 2016
15. Karp, P.: Census website back online after day of recriminations over 43-hour outage. The Guardian, Australia (2016)
16. Bond, M., et al.: Chip and Skim: cloning EMV cards with the pre-play attack. In: 2014 IEEE Symposium on Security and Privacy. IEEE (2014)
17. CSC. Breaking down the threat of cyber terrorism (2016). http://blogs.csc.com/2016/02/04/breaking-down-the-threat-of-cyber-terrorism/. Accessed 08 November 2016

18. Zolkipli, M.F., Jantan, A.: An approach for malware behavior identification and classification. In: 2011 3rd International Conference on Computer Research and Development (ICCRD). IEEE (2011)
19. Goodin, D.: Massive US-planned cyberattack against Iran went well beyond Stuxnet (2016). http://arstechnica.com/tech-policy/2016/02/massive-us-planned-cyberattack-against-iran-went-well-beyond-stuxnet/. Accessed 08 November 2016
20. Talbot, D.: Cyber-Espionage Nightmare (2015). https://www.technologyreview.com/s/538201/cyber-espionage-nightmare. Accessed 08 November 2016
21. Ajayi, E.F.G.: The Impact of Cyber Crimes on Global Trade and Commerce. Available at SSRN (2016)
22. Milian, M.: Top Ten Hacking Countries (2016). http://www.bloomberg.com/slideshow/2013-04-23/top-ten-hacking-countries.html. Accessed 07 October 2016
23. S, V. How to block DROWN attack – Fix SSL vulnerability in Linux, Apache, Nginx, Exim and other servers (2016). https://bobcares.com/blog/how-to-fix-drown-attack-ssl-vulnerability/. Accessed 08 November 2016
24. Shields, K.: Cybersecurity: recognizing the risk and protecting against attacks. NC Bank. Inst. **19**, 345 (2015)
25. Donaldson, S.E., et al.: Measuring a Cybersecurity Program. In: Enterprise Cybersecurity, pp. 213–229. Springer (2015)
26. Cavelty, M.D., Mauer, V.: Power and Security in the Information Age: Investigating the Role of the State in Cyberspace. Routledge, London (2016)
27. Wang, D., et al.: Preserving privacy for free: efficient and provably secure two-factor authentication scheme with user anonymity. Inf. Sci. **321**, 162–178 (2015)
28. Das, M.L.: Two-factor user authentication in wireless sensor networks. IEEE Trans. Wireless Commun. **8**(3), 1086–1090 (2009)
29. Jin, A.T.B., Ling, D.N.C., Goh, A.: Biohashing: two factor authentication featuring fingerprint data and tokenised random number. Pattern Recogn. **37**(11), 2245–2255 (2004)

Data Security

Evaluating Entropy Sources for True Random Number Generators by Collision Counting

Maciej Skórski[✉]

University of Warsaw, Warszawa, Poland
maciej.skorski@mimuw.edu.pl

Abstract. The general approach to evaluate the quality of entropy sources used in true random number generators is to estimate min-entropy, which is based on estimating frequencies of all possible source outcomes. This method is space inefficient, for example for a source producing 30-bit outputs it needs 30 Gb of storage to get an error smaller than one bit per sample.

We show that for some popular designs estimating min-entropy can be replaced by much more efficient counting the number of collisions between consecutive samples. Namely, we propose an estimator for the collision entropy of a sequence of i.i.d samples $X_1, \ldots, X_n$. The estimator utilizes a simple collision counting technique, and has the following features

- Is memory-efficient (reads samples in a forward-only mode, uses $O(1)$ storage)
- Can be coupled with every min-entropy extractor, losing only extra $\log(1/\epsilon)$ bits.

We implemented our estimator with an iPhone accelerometer as the entropy source, and Toeplitz-matrix based universal hashing as an extractor. The quality of this TRNG was confirmed by applying the NIST tests suite.

1 Introduction

1.1 Randomness in Cryptography

Perfect Randomness. Random numbers are used for many applications, like simulations, sampling, gambling and cryptography. However, depending on an application, the *required quality* changes. Cryptographic applications demand very high quality sequences, where bits are independent and nearly unbiased.

From a cryptographic perspective, a distribution of n bits is considered *truly random* if it is *statistically indistinguishable* (in a very strong sense) from a perfectly random distribution. More precisely, we require the distribution of bits to be at most ϵ-far in the *variational distance*[1] from the uniform distribution over n-bit strings, where

$$\epsilon = 2^{-80}$$

---

[1] Called also the statistical or trace distance.

© Springer Nature Singapore Pte Ltd. 2016
L. Batten and G. Li (Eds.): ATIS 2016, CCIS 651, pp. 69–80, 2016.
DOI: 10.1007/978-981-10-2741-3_6

is the security level recommended nowadays[2]. This means that every test fails with probability $1 - 2^{-80}$ when trying to distinguish the given distribution from uniform[3]. Even with many trials, these bits will be statistically indistinguishable from random, and hence equally good in applications (e.g. as a cryptographic key). The length of $n = 128$ bits is sufficient for modern applications, such as the AES encryption.

Imperfect Sources. In practice, we don't have direct access to truly random bits. Instead, from available sources, we can obtain bits that are *biased but somewhat unpredictable*. These sources are called *weak sources* or simply *entropy sources*. Practical implementations may utilize physical phenomenas like atmospheric noise [Haa], radioactive decay [Wal] or thermal noise [JK99], sensors in mobile devices like the microphone and camera [BKMS09], accelerometer, gyroscope and compass [VSH11,BS], usage patterns of computer devices like mouse, keyboards, hard disk [dRHG+99,DGP07,Zim]. Formally, the unpredictability of a distribution X is measured by so called *min-entropy*. We say that X has at least k bits of min-entropy, if every outcome appears with probability at most 2^{-k}. A more liberal entropy measure, still good for practically used extractors, is collision entropy which bounds the probability that two samples from a given distribution collide. What is important to stress, Shannon entropy widely used in information theory is *not* a good measure of randomness in weak sources. It may be used to as a statistical test of the output uniformity, but when applied to a weak source gives estimates much bigger than min-entropy, leading to overestimating total security. Estimating entropy is of critical importance, as there are examples of real-world attacks based on wrong entropy estimates, for example the case of the Netscape browser [GW96] or the Linux Random Number Generator [KKHD14]. For this reason, works focused on provable security consider the notion of min-entropy as the right security measure [BST03,BKMS09,VSH11,HN09], although sometimes Shannon entropy is being used as a rough estimate [LPR11]. Entropy notions are discussed in Sect. 5.

1.2   True Random Number Generators

The earliest discussion of "weak" random sources was probably due to von Nuemann [vN51]. In recent times, the systematic theory of randomness extractors has been developed, and sufficient and necessary conditions for extracting truly random bits are given in terms of min-entropy (see Lemmas 2 and 3).

True Random Number Generators (as opposed to Pseudo Random Number Generators, PRNGs) utilize a weak physical source to generate random bits. They typically consist [Sun09] of the following components

---

[2] Of course, a different security level for a specific application, if necessary.

[3] Formally, we consider the standard experiment: a sample is generated, either from the given distribution or uniform, and the distinguisher has to guess where it comes from.

- randomness source (weak source)
- harvesting mechanism (gathering data)
- post-processing algorithm (extractor)

This design, with an extra component for estimating the entropy rate is illustrated in Fig. 1.

1.3   Problem Statement

In theory, to construct a good random number generator it suffices to know the min-entropy of the source, choose an appropriate extractor and adjust it's parameters. However, the major issue is that in practice the source entropy is *unknown and hard to estimate*. While there are well-established methods of evaluating outputs of random generators, for example statistical tests batteries like NIST [BRS+10] or DieHard batteries [Mar96], there are no tests for entropy in arbitrary weak sources.

For concreteness, we assume that the entropy source is *memoryless*, that is outputs i.i.d. samples. This assumption is convenient from a theoretical point of view and confirmed empirically [LRSV12, VSH11, BL05, BKMS09]. In certain cases, where so called reset states can be implemented, it has also a solid hardware justification [BL05]. Thus, we assume that our source X produces i.i.d. samples $X_1, X_2, \ldots$ with values in a finite set $\mathcal{X}$. From a good estimator function $\mathsf{Est}(\cdot)$ we require the following features [LRSV12]

(a) Preferably, $\mathsf{Est}(\cdot)$ reads the sequence $X_1, X_2, \ldots, X_m$ in a *forward-only* mode, so that it consumes $O(m)$ time and $O(1)$ space.
(b) The output of $\mathsf{Est}(\cdot)$ approximates the number of extractable bits in the input sequence, at a high confidence level (ideally $1 - \epsilon$)

1.4   Related Works

A naive solution, is to approximate the empirical distribution from samples and plug it into entropy formulas [BST03, VSH11, HN09]. The biggest disadvantage is that it requires a huge number of samples, and cannot be used with smaller number of samples, e.g. when extracting just a few keys[4]

The problem of finding an *online* estimator was raised in [LPR11], however the authors studied only Shannon-entropy estimators (which yield a bad approximation) and gave only asymptotic convergence. A simple on-line estimator for independent bits was proposed in [BL05], though the technique doesn't generalize to higher dimensions.

In this paper, based on these ideas, we propose a collision entropy estimator which fulfils the posed efficiency requirements.

---

[4] However, may be used when extracting a large number of keys for statistical testing.

2   Our Results

2.1   Summary

We present a *collision entropy estimator*, which estimates the collision entropy of the input (i.id. sequence) on the fly. The memory cost is $O(1)$, time is just $n - 1$ comparisons where n is the sequence length. The absolute error is $O(\sqrt{n|\mathcal{X}|}\log(1/\epsilon)$ with probability $1 - \epsilon$, where $\mathcal{X}$ is the set of possible source outputs. An alternative method, discussed in the newest NIST recommendation [TBK+] and used in works focused at provable security [VSH11] is to approximate the probability mass function of the source from samples, and apply the min-entropy formula to empirical frequencies, which is also known as the *plugin estimator*. A comparison with plugin estimators is given in the Table 1. Our method gives a slightly better error estimate but is much more space-efficient. For example, for a source producing 30 bit outputs, evaluating empirical distribution would take more than 30 Gb of memory (as we need 2^{30} bins for frequencies and at least 30 bit of storage for every bin to achieve relevant arithmetic precision), whereas our method needs a constant amount of memory (in this example: 60 bits of storage). See also Appendix A for more details.

Table 1. Accuracy for estimating entropy within n samples. The domain is $\mathcal{X}$ and the confidence $1 - \epsilon$.

Author	Technique	Absolute error	Memory
[TBK+]	Min-Entropy	$\Delta = O\left(\sqrt{n|\mathcal{X}|}\log(|\mathcal{X}|/\epsilon)\right)$	$O(|\mathcal{X}|)$
This paper	Collision-Entropy	$\Delta = O\left(\sqrt{n}\log(|\mathcal{X}|/\epsilon)\right)$	$O(1)$

3   Collision Entropy Estimator

Below we present the pseudocode and convergence results. Note that the function itself is deterministic, it utilizes randomness contained in the input.

The proof of the convergence theorem below is basically an application of the Chernoff Bound coupled with union bounds and can be found in the extended version of this paper, available at eprint.

Theorem(Informal) 1 (Convergence Analysis). *With probability $1 - \epsilon$ we have*

$$\mathbf{H}_2(X_1, \dots, X_n) \gtrsim \mathsf{CollisionEntropyEstimator}(X_1, \dots, X_n)$$

with an absolute error bounded by $O(\sqrt{n|\mathcal{X}|}\log(1/\epsilon))$.

Having established a lower bound on the entropy amount, we can compose our estimator with any min-entropy (or collision-entropy) extractor.

Below a (k, ϵ)-extractor is any function that converts a distribution with k bits of min-entropy into a distribution ϵ-close to uniform. The following result easily follows by applying the last result and converting collision entropy to smooth min-entropy, see Lemma 1.

Algorithm 1. CollisionEntropyEstimator

Data: Samples $x_1, \ldots, x_n \in \mathcal{X}$
Result: An estimate on $\mathbf{H}_2(X_1, \ldots, X_n)$

1 $i \leftarrow 1$
2 $t \leftarrow 0$
    `// count collisions in the sample sequence`
3 **while** $i < n$ **do**
4   **if** $x_{i+1} = x_i$ **then**
5         $t \leftarrow t+1$
6   **end**
7      $i \leftarrow i+1$
8 **end**
    `// estimate the collision probability`
9 $p \leftarrow \frac{t}{n-1}$
    `// estimate the entropy`
10 $k \leftarrow (n-1) \cdot \log(1/p)$
11 **return** k

Theorem(Informal) 2 (Our estimator composed with any min-entropy extractors). *Let* $X_1, \ldots, X_n$ *be i.i.d and let*

$$k = \mathsf{CollisionEntropyEstimator}(X_1, \ldots, X_n) - c\sqrt{n|\mathcal{X}|\log(1/\epsilon)} - \log(1/\epsilon)$$

be the entropy estimate with error (c being an absolute constant), and $\mathrm{Ext}(\cdot, S) : \mathcal{X}^n :\to \{0,1\}^m$ *be any* (k, ϵ)*-extractor with public randomness* S*. Then the extractor output*

$$\mathrm{Ext}((X_1, \ldots, X_n), S)$$

is 2ϵ*-close to the m-bit uniform distribution, on average over* S*.*

3.1 Empirical Evaluation

We tested our estimator on data collected by the i-Phone accelerometer, based on the idea from [VSH11]. See Sect. 5 for details. The design is sketched in Fig. 1.

4 Preliminaries

4.1 Information-Theoretic Divergence Measures

Definition 1 (Variational Distance). *The variational distance of* X_1 *and* X_2 *equals*

$$d_{\mathrm{TV}}((,X)_1, X_2) = \sum_x |\mathbf{P}_{X_1}(x) - \mathbf{P}_{X_2}(x)| \leqslant \epsilon.$$

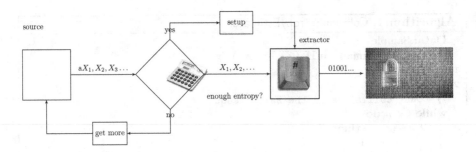

Fig. 1. An overview of our implementation.

4.2   Entropy Notions

Definition 2 (Min-Entropy). *The min-entropy of a random variable X is defined as $\mathbf{H}_\infty(X) = \max_x \log \frac{1}{\mathbf{P}_X(x)}$.*

Definition 3 (Collision-Entropy). *The collision-entropy of a random variable X is defined as $\mathbf{H}_2(X) = -\log\left(\sum_x (\mathbf{P}_X(x))^2\right)$.*

Definition 4 (Shannon-Entropy). *The Shannon-entropy of a random variable X is defined as $\mathbf{H}(X) = -\sum_x \mathbf{P}_X(x) \log \mathbf{P}_X(x)$.*

Definition 5 (Smooth Entropy). *We say that X has k-bits of ϵ-smooth min-entropy if X is ϵ-close to Y such that $\mathbf{H}_\infty(Y) \geqslant k$.*

Lemma 1 (From collision to smooth min-entropy [Cac97]). *Suppose that $\mathbf{H}_2(X) \geqslant k$. Then $\mathbf{H}_\infty^\epsilon \geqslant k - \log(1/\epsilon)$.*

4.3   Extractors

Extractors are functions which process weak sources into distributions that are close (in the information-theoretic sense) to the uniform distribution. In general, they need some amount of auxiliary randomness called *seed*. This argument is passed as an extra argument in the definition.

Definition 6 (Seeded extractors). *A deterministic function* $\mathrm{Ext} : \{0,1\}^n \times \{0,1\}^d \to \{0,1\}^k$ *is a (k,ϵ)-extractor for X if we have*

$$d_{\mathrm{TV}}\left(\mathrm{Ext}((X, U_d), U_d, (U_k, U_d))\right) \leqslant \epsilon$$

Remark 1 (Relaxing weak sources for seeded extractors). *The definition of the weak source can be relaxed at least in two ways:*

(a) X needs to be only close to a distribution with entropy k
(b) The entropy notion can be collision entropy, instead of much more restrictive min-entropy.

Definition 7. *A family* $\mathcal{H}$ *of functions from* n *to* m *is called* universal, *if for a random member* $H \in \mathcal{H}$ *and every* $x, y \in \{0, 1\}^n$ *we have*

$$\Pr[H(x) = H(y)] = 2^{-m}.$$

Lemma 2 (Universal families are good extractors). *Suppose that* $\mathbf{H}_\infty(X) \geqslant k + 2\log(1/\epsilon)$, *or more liberally that* $\mathbf{H}_2(X) \geqslant k + 2\log(1/\epsilon)$. *Let* H *be a random member of the family of hash functions from* n *to* m *bits. For any* $h \in \mathcal{H}$ *define*

$$\mathrm{Ext}(x, h) = h(x)$$

Then we have

$$d_{\mathrm{TV}}\left(\mathrm{Ext}(X, S), S, U_k, S\right) \leqslant \epsilon$$

Lemma 3 (A necessary condition for extracting). *Suppose that* $d_{\mathrm{TV}}\left(\mathrm{Ext}(X, S), S, U_k, S\right) \leqslant \epsilon$ *where* $\mathrm{Ext} = \mathrm{Ext}(x, s)$ *is a* k-*bit output function,* X *is any random variable and* S *is any random variable independent[5] on* X *and* U_k. *Then* X *is* ϵ-*close to a distribution of min-entropy* k.

Remark 2 (Intuition). *The lemma states that if we can extract bits close to be truly random, then the source has to be close to a high-entropy source. Intuitively, this is true because post-processing by an extractors can never add entropy (an auxiliary string is made public).*

5 Empirical Evaluation

In this section we discuss results of the empirical evaluation of a simple TRNG built on an i-Phone accelerometer as a source and our estimator.

5.1 Raw Data

We collected 50 MB of data of accelerometer samples on an i-Phone. This data was collected at the frequency of 50 Hz, when the device was in a stationary state (recent works on generating random numbers based on MEMS sensors [VSH11, BS] show that this gives the worst case estimate).

Every sample contains readings from the x-, y- and z-axes, which are number up to 6 decimal places (see Table 2).

Table 2. A raw data sample (decimal) from the iPhone accelerometer

Timestamp	Accel_X	Accel_Y	Accel_Z
0.023776	0.001297	−0.016479	−1.003845

---

[5] In this lemma S doesn't have to be uniform, although this is typically satisfied for extractors.

Table 3. A raw data sample (binary) from the iPhone accelerometer

Timestamp	Accel_X	Accel_Y	Accel_Z
0.023776	0100010001	1110100001	0101000101

In total, we collected around $1.2 \cdot 10^6$ samples. The frequency of last two digits is more or less uniform, however the distribution of the third digit is heavy biased (see Fig. 2a). For this reason, we use only $d = 10$ last binary digits (see Table 3), which corresponds to $N = 3.6 \cdot 10^7$ raw bits.

5.2   Entropy Estimations

Under the i.i.d assumption, the min-entropy of the empirical distribution was estimated at around $\mathbf{H}_\infty(X) = 18$ bits, and the collision entropy was estimated at around $\mathbf{H}_2(X) = 21$ bits (out of 30)[6]. The frequency distribution for the y-axis is sketched at Fig. 2b, the plots for the x- and z-axes are similar.

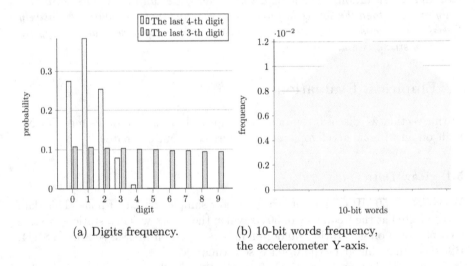

(a) Digits frequency.

(b) 10-bit words frequency, the accelerometer Y-axis.

Fig. 2. Some statistics of the raw data.

5.3   Extractor

Universal Family. As an extractor, we apply a simple family of universal hash functions implemented by Toepltiz matrices. Given m bits of *collision-entropy* $k < m$ on input, this extractor outputs n bits, using an auxiliary string s (seed)

---

[6] Given the huge amount of data, we achieve the confidence level above $1 - \epsilon$, where $\epsilon = 2^{-80}$.

of $d = m + n - 1$ bits. The extractor works as follows: given a seed s, the binary matrix $M(s)$ with m rows and n columns is formulated by "rewinding" an n-bit part of the seed cyclically, which can be described by the formula

$$M(s)_{i,j} = s_{i+j-1}.$$

Then the extractor output $z \in \{0,1\}^n$ on input $y \in \{0,1\}^m$ is defined by

$$\mathsf{Ext}_s(y) = M(s) \cdot y$$

that is $z_i = \sum_{j=1}^n y_j \cdot s_{i+j-1}$ where all the additions and multiplications are understood modulo 2. It can be shown [BST03] that the family $\{M(s)\}_{s \in \{0,1\}^{m+n-1}}$ is universal and hence, by Lemma 2, achieves the security

$$\epsilon = 2^{\frac{k-n}{2}}.$$

Parameters. We chose the parameters as follows:

- Output $n = 128$ bits (standard choice).
- Security level $\epsilon = 2^{-80}$ (standard choice).
- Necessary entropy $k = n + 2\log(1/\epsilon) = 288$ (from the security formula).
- Entropy rate equals 21 bits per 30-bit sample (the empirical evaluation).
- Input consists of $m = 30\lceil\frac{k}{21}\rceil = 420$ bits (given the entropy rate).
- Seed is $d = m + n - 1 = 547$-bit long.

Since the seed s needs to independent from the source, we generated it from an online TRNG [Haa] (based on atmospheric noise).

5.4 Generating Secure Keys

To generate a fresh $n = 128$-bit secure key, we feed the extractor input with consecutive 14 accelerometer binary samples.

Note that extractor can securely reuse the seed multiple times. This only slightly affects the security, as the join distribution of ℓ keys is at most

$$\epsilon' = \ell \cdot \epsilon$$

far from the uniform distribution [BKMS09]. In practice, we set an upper bound on the lifecycle and reseed the extractor from time to time; the number of calls will be much smaller comparing to $\epsilon^{-1} \approx 2^{80}$ so that one seed suffices for a long usage [BKMS09]. In our experiment, we extracted $\ell \approx 10^5$ keys, and the security is still[7] $\epsilon' \approx 2^{-63}$. This theoretical security guarantee was confirmed by evaluating the NIST battery of tests, discussed in the next section.

---

[7] Clearly, we could adjust security parameters to end with an arbitrary security level.

5.5 Evaluation of NIST Tests

We subjected extracted $\ell = 10^5$ keys to the NIST battery of test [BRS+10], using the implementation from [Kra].

Following the NIST recommendations, the dataset was divided into 100 parts and each tests was evaluated 100 times, except Maurer's Universal Test (executed only 10 times as it demands sequences longer than 350,000 bits). For every test, we evaluated *goodness of fit* as follows: the obtained p-values were tested against uniformity by grouping into 10 equal subintervals (see columns C1,..,C10) and applying the chi-square test with 9 degrees of freedom. For every test, the result was positive. Our sequences passed all the rests[8]. The details are presented in Table 4.

Table 4. NIST Tests Results

C1	C2	C3	C4	C5	C6	C7	C8	C9	C10	P-VALUE	PROPORTION	STATISTICAL TEST
5	15	12	7	15	6	5	21	7	7	0.001509	100/100	Frequency
8	11	4	12	9	10	13	12	11	10	0.739918	99/100	BlockFrequency
7	11	11	12	13	11	8	10	3	14	0.401199	99/100	CumulativeSums
5	9	15	15	13	8	4	7	11	13	0.108791	100/100	CumulativeSums
13	12	10	12	9	7	13	12	6	6	0.616305	98/100	Runs
11	13	8	14	12	3	15	12	7	5	0.102526	99/100	LongestRun
12	14	9	10	10	2	12	8	13	10	0.334538	100/100	Rank
5	12	10	10	11	9	13	4	14	12	0.383827	99/100	FFT
9	9	4	13	12	8	12	10	14	9	0.574903	98/100	NonOverlappingTemplate
12	13	11	14	7	8	12	5	11	7	0.514124	99/100	OverlappingTemplate
0	2	2	1	0	2	1	1	0	1	0.739918	10/10	Universal
12	11	7	9	13	12	10	9	9	8	0.946308	97/100	ApproximateEntropy
4	0	1	1	1	1	2	1	1	2	0.213309	13/14	RandomExcursions
9	15	12	8	7	13	11	9	5	11	0.534146	99/100	Serial
6	10	6	11	12	10	14	11	12	8	0.719747	100/100	LinearComplexity

A   Our Estimator Vs Plugin Estimates

Suppose that we want to approximate the empirical frequency of a distribution over $\mathcal{X}$. Let $X_1, \ldots, X_n$ be i.i.d. samples, $x \in \mathcal{X}$ be one fixed word, and $p = \Pr[X = x]$. According to Chernoff Bounds, estimating p from n samples up to a relative error $\sqrt{\frac{3\ln(1/\epsilon)}{np}}$ gives us the confidence $1 - \epsilon$. This is however for one pattern x. To have a guarantee for all patterns x, we need to replace ϵ by $\epsilon/|\mathcal{X}|$ and consider that p can be not bigger than $\frac{1}{|\mathcal{X}|}$. Then, the relative error may be as big as $\delta = \sqrt{\frac{3|\mathcal{X}|\ln(|\mathcal{X}|/\epsilon)}{n}}$. Since the entropy formulas, involve the logarithms

---

[8] For 100 repetitions, the passing threshold is 96.

of p, the relative error of δ yields an absolute error of δ^9. For n samples the total absolute error is

$$\Delta = \sqrt{3n|\mathcal{X}|\ln(|\mathcal{X}|/\epsilon)},$$

and the necessary storage is (assuming that p can be as small as $|\mathcal{X}|^{-1}$)

$$S = |\mathcal{X}| \cdot |\log \delta| > |\mathcal{X}|\log(|\mathcal{X}|) + |\mathcal{X}|\log\log(1/\epsilon)$$

because in order to achieve relative error at most δ, we need $\log(1/delta)$ bits to store every number during computation. Our estimator gives the slightly better error of

$$\Delta = O\left(\sqrt{n|\mathcal{X}|\ln(1/\epsilon)}\right),$$

bits, and the storage $O(\log(|\mathcal{X}|))$.

References

[BKMS09] Bouda, J., Krhovjak, J., Matyas, V., Svenda, P.: Towards true random number generation in mobile environments. In: Jøsang, A., Maseng, T., Knapskog, S.J. (eds.) NordSec 2009. LNCS, vol. 5838, pp. 179–189. Springer, Heidelberg (2009). doi:10.1007/978-3-642-04766-4_13

[BL05] Bucci, M., Luzzi, R.: Design of testable random bit generators. In: Rao, J.R., Sunar, B. (eds.) CHES 2005. LNCS, vol. 3659, pp. 147–156. Springer, Heidelberg (2005). doi:10.1007/11545262_11

[BRS+10] Bassham, III, L.E., Rukhin, A.L., Soto, J., Nechvatal, J.R., Smid, M.E., Barker, E.B., Leigh, S.D., Levenson, M., Vangel, M., Banks, D.L., Heckert, N.A., Dray, J.F., Vo, S.: Sp. 800-22 rev. 1a. a statistical test suite for random and pseudorandom number generators for cryptographic applications, Technical report, Gaithersburg, MD, USA (2010)

[BS] Bedekar, N., Shee, C.: A novel approach to true random number generation in wearable computing environments using mems sensors

[BST03] Barak, B., Shaltiel, R., Tromer, E.: True random number generators secure in a changing environment. In: Walter, C.D., Koç, Ç.K., Paar, C. (eds.) CHES 2003. LNCS, vol. 2779, pp. 166–180. Springer, Heidelberg (2003). doi:10.1007/978-3-540-45238-6_14

[Cac97] Cachin, C.: Smooth entropy and Rényi entropy. In: Fumy, W. (ed.) Advances in Cryptology, EUROCRYPT 1997. LNCS, vol. 1233, pp. 193–208. Springer, Heidelberg (1997). doi:10.1007/3-540-69053-0_14

[DGP07] Dorrendorf, L., Gutterman, Z., Pinkas, B.: Cryptanalysis of the windows random number generator. In: Proceedings of the 14th ACM Conference on Computer and Communications Security, CCS 2007, pp. 476–485. ACM, New York (2007)

[dRHG+99] de Raadt, T., Hallqvist, N., Grabowski, A., Keromytis, A.D., Provos, N.: Cryptography in OpenBSD: an overview. In: Proceedings of the Annual Conference on USENIX Annual Technical Conference, ATEC 1999, p. 33. USENIX Association, Berkeley (1999)

---

[9] We have $\log(p(1 + \delta)) \leqslant \log p + \delta$, for min entropy p is the most likely probability and for collision-entropy p is the collision probability.

[GW96] Goldberg, I., Wagner, D.: Randomness and the netscape browser (1996)

[Haa] Haahr, M.: random.org homepage. Accessed 01 July 2016

[HN09] Halprin, R., Naor, M.: Games for extracting randomness. In: Proceedings of the 5th Symposium on Usable Privacy, Security, SOUPS 2009, pp. 12:1–12:12. ACM, New York (2009)

[JK99] Jun, B., Kocher, P.: The intel random number generator. In: White Paper Prepared for Intel Corporation (1999)

[KKHD14] Kaplan, D., Kedmi, S., Hay, R., Dayan, A.: Attacking the linux PRNG on android: weaknesses in seeding of entropic pools and low boot-time entropy. In: 8th USENIX Workshop on Offensive Technologies (WOOT 14). USENIX Association, San Diego (2014)

[Kra] Krawczyk, P.: A NIST tests implementation. https://github.com/kravietz/nist-sts

[LPR11] Lauradoux, C., Ponge, J., Röck, A.: Online entropy estimation for non-binary sources and applications on iPhone. Rapport de recherche, Inria (2011)

[LRSV12] Lacharme, P., Röck, A., Strubel, V., Videau, M.: The linux pseudorandom number generator revisited, Cryptology ePrint Archive, Report 2012/251 (2012). http://eprint.iacr.org/

[Mar96] Marsaglia, G.: DIEHARD: a battery of tests of randomness. Technical report, Florida State University (1996)

[Sun09] Sunar, B.: True random number generators for cryptography. In: Kaya, K.C. (ed.) Cryptographic Engineering, pp. 55–73. Springer, US, (2009) (English)

[TBK+] Turan, M.S., Barker, E., Kelsey, J., McKay, K.A., Baish, M.L., Boyle, M.:

[vN51] von Neumann, J.: Various techniques used in connection with random digits. J. Res. Nat. Bur. Stand. **12**, 36–38 (1951)

[VSH11] Voris, J., Saxena, N., Halevi, T.: Accelerometers, randomness: perfect together. In: WiSec 2011, pp. 115–126. ACM (2011)

[Wal] Walker, J.: Hotbits homepage. Accessed 01 July 2016

[Zim] Zimmermann, P.: PGP user's guide

Enhancement of Sensor Data Transmission by Inference and Efficient Data Processing

James Jin Kang[✉], Tom H. Luan, and Henry Larkin

School of Information Technology, Deakin University, Burwood, VIC, Australia
{jkang, tom.luan, henry.larkin}@deakin.edu.au

Abstract. When wearable and personal health device and sensors capture data such as heart rate and body temperature for fitness tracking and health services, they simply transfer data without filtering or optimising. This can cause over-loading to the sensors as well as rapid battery consumption when they interact with Internet of Things (IoT) networks, which are expected to increase and demand more health data from device wearers. To solve the problem, this paper proposes to infer sensed data to reduce the data volume, which will affect the bandwidth and battery power reduction that are essential requirements to sensor devices. This is achieved by applying beacon data points after the inferencing of data processing utilising variance rates, which compare the sensed data with adjacent data before and after. This novel approach verifies by experiments that data volume can be saved by up to 99.5 % with a 98.62 % accuracy. Whilst most existing works focus on sensor network improvements such as routing, operation and reading data algorithms, we efficiently reduce data volume to reduce bandwidth and battery power consumption while maintaining accuracy by implementing intelligence and optimisation in sensor devices.

Keywords: Body sensors · mHealth · IoT · Cloud · Big data · Inference · Beacon

1 Introduction

Personal sensors and wearable devices are now prevalent and used to provide health related applications such as fitness tracking and real-time monitoring services, and are also now expected to connect to IoT networks. These demands will cause additional transactions and workloads on wireless personal area networks (WBAN) consisting of sensors and smartphones, which will consequently affect the performance and battery power of devices such as physiological sensors, biomedical sensors, monitoring devices (e.g. heart rate, body temperature, respiratory and glucose monitoring etc.) and wearables. Current sensors do not interact significantly with IoT networks nor have the intelligence to provide data to health networks discretely. Rather, they are passive and simply provide sensed data on a regular basis or on demand due to typical sensors having hardware and size limitations. However, this is now evolving due to the introduction of smartphone and wearable device interactions allowing access to more powerful resources and a greater capacity to provide health information demanded by wellbeing requests. As this is a new area of demand i.e. sensors interacting with IoT

© Springer Nature Singapore Pte Ltd. 2016
L. Batten and G. Li (Eds.): ATIS 2016, CCIS 651, pp. 81–92, 2016.
DOI: 10.1007/978-981-10-2741-3_7

devices which will use health data, there have not been many works done on how to efficiently transfer sensor data to external networks. It is logical to expect and envisage that traffic and transactions of data requests to sensors will be increased greatly by IoT networks as Gartner forecasted that 20.8 billion "things" will be connected by 2020 [1]. To alleviate this problem, we proposed to infer data processing of sensors to reduce transactions from sensors to smartphones and IoT networks [2]. This solution involves inferring to only transmit data if it is significantly different from previous data points captured. Whilst the solution can greatly reduce the number of data to transmit, it may distort the original data and does not properly represent some data such as in short interval sample situations shown in Fig. 10. To solve this problem, we propose to analyse differences between the original and inferred data, and apply beacon data points into the inferred result so that it can represent the original data as closely as possible. There are three aspects used to verify and assess the results:

- Efficiency: ratio of saved (reduced) data volume and actual transmitted data
- Savings: ratio of reduced data and sensed data (%)
- Accuracy: ratio of total value of transmitted data and original data (%)

$$\text{Efficiency Rate(Er)} = \frac{\text{No of Sensed data} - \text{No of Transferred data}}{\text{No of Transferred data}}$$

$$\text{Savings Rate(Sr)} = \frac{\text{No of Sensed data} - \text{No of Transferred data}}{\text{Number of Sensed data}} \times 100$$

$$\text{Accuracy Rate(Ar)} = \frac{\text{Sum of original DPs} - \text{Sum of differences}}{\text{Sum of original DPs}} \times 100$$

2 Related Works

Whilst there are many works on improving sensor networks to process data such as using middleware in a new global sensor network infrastructure [3], improving routing protocols [4–6] or acquisition of reading and modelling the accuracy of the sensor reading using algorithms [7], there are little works performed in trying to minimise the data sampling and transmission from the sensors. Bragg et al. [8] proposes a rein-forcement learning (RL) protocol based queue management and scheduling scheme, which uses data criticality and deadline to determine the scheduling priority in WBAN consisting of sensor devices and a patient data controller (PDC). To optimise the per-formance a packet arrives and placed onto a queue at a PDC, which will be followed by scheduling. Consequently, they try to minimise packet drops using criticality-weighted drop rate. This approach can be further used to incorporate event detection through the use of sensory signatures. If the function of PDC can be implemented within a sensor device, it will be useful to enhance the efficiency of data transmission to smartphones or IoT. However, they do not consider that not every datum has to be transferred if it does not have to be. Where possible, it is unnecessary to send all data consuming bandwidth and power resource if there is a better and effective way such as reducing the volume of original data e.g. sampling 1 in 8000 for voice signaling in PSTN to decode and recover the original voice as in the Nyquist theorem [9]. It is possible to select samples for transfer by inferred algorithms so they can be recovered in the other node without significant distortion. Leu et al. [10] proposes a clustering algorithm for grouping sensor nodes which can increase the energy efficiency of the sensor network, which will cause additional overhead. To solve the issue, they propose a new regional energy aware clustering method using isolated nodes for WSNs, called Regional Energy Aware Clustering with Isolated Nodes (REAC-IN). Like other works in routing, operating and network enhancement, this solution overlooks the cause of the overloading, i.e. data volume increasing in sensor devices.

3   Implementation of Inference System

Variance rates (VR) are used to infer data selection and transmission by comparing the current value with before and after the value to screen out similar data points, and therefore data points which can be saved from transmission. Different VRs can be applied with finer or coarser rates, e.g. 1 % VR is finer than 10 % VR. It can be applied using the formula below.

$$If \ |Vc - Vc1| OR |Vc0 - Vc| > Vc \times Vr,$$

$$then \ Vx = Vc$$

$$Else \ then \ Vx = Nil, \ where \ Vc = current \ value, \ Vc0 = previous \ value, \ Vc1$$
$$= next \ value \ and \ Vx = sampling \ value, \ and \ Vr = variance \ rate$$

When a variance rate has been applied and plotted against the original graph, there are differences between the inferred data graph and the original data graph as shown in Fig. 1. S (Upper) represents the area of gap or distorted portion by the inferred values that are less than the original, whilst S (Lower) represents areas of inferred values that are higher than the original values. The higher the total area of gaps means there is more distortion and therefore it is better to have a lower total area if accuracy is concerned. The formula below depicts the area of upper and lower sides of the inferred graph against the original.

$$Su = \sum_{k=0}^{n} \binom{n}{k} S_n \ where \ S_n = G(S1, \ S2 \ldots, \ Sn),$$

$$Similarly \ S_l = \sum_{k=0}^{n} \binom{n}{k} S_n \ where \ S_n = Y(S1, \ S2 \ldots, \ Sn),$$

Total area of the gaps would be presented as below. A larger value means a 'coarser' and higher VR inference has been used relative to a smaller total area which means that a 'finer' and lower VR value has been applied. When the difference

($Sd = |Su - S_l|$) is larger, that means the result is farther from the average, and therefore the smaller the difference, the better it represents the original trend. However, a smaller difference does not necessarily mean that it always represents the original properly, but can be an indicator of how accurate the inference is to the original along with using the total gaps (S) instead. For example, a small S value as well as a small Sd means it is likely to be closer to the original. Therefore these figures (i.e. S and Sd) can be used to determine how accurate (as below equation) each inference is as the result, whilst savings or reduction of DPs indicate the efficiency. If S = 0, it represents the original data perfectly with no distortion. If Sd = 0, it means the inference represents the mean value of the graph despite not representing the original perfectly.

$$S = Su + S_l$$

$$\text{Accuracy Rate}(\text{Ar}) = \frac{Sum\ of\ original\ DPs - Sum\ of\ differences}{Sum\ of\ original\ DPs} \text{x}100$$

The figure below depicts the upper and lower gaps after inference has been applied.

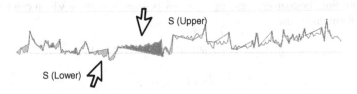

Fig. 1. Differences between the original and inferred value

There is a dilemma when a finer VR is applied to short interval (e.g. every second) samples as short interval data points (DPs) do not fluctuate greatly. For example, heart rate of sleep or resting mode hardly varies by more than 10 points between DPs sensed every second. As the VR compares the current value with adjacent values before and after the current value, it will not take the sample when the DPs being compared fluctuate in a small linear fashion, e.g. rising consecutively from 120, 121, 122, 123, 124 etc. This means that if HR changes from 120 to 150 over 30 s incrementally by 1 BPM per second, the inference will not display the increase to 150 DP at all as each increase in the value is less than the VR threshold specified. To solve this dilemma, a different method should be applied such as adding beacon DPs, which take data at a set frequency regardless of how much it varies in order to maintain representation of the original DPs. When S(upper) is more than 50 %, then the inference has undervalued the original, where the values are measured with the summation of differences against the original values, and accumulated to compare with the differences. In other words, the sampled value is less than the original DP. In the case of 20 % VR in Table 1, the result shows that accuracy (74.6 %) is poor despite savings (98 %) being high. Also it is distorted a lot (26.4 %) against the original graph. Inference level and variance rate can be applied based on design requirements as requestors may have a differing range of what is considered to be an acceptable threshold. Results for body temperature increase reasonably linearly and has a short delay before it drops after exercising. Heart rate fluctuates with a larger range than body temperature. It is also sensed at a higher time frequency, whereas vital signs such as body temperature are sensed on a minute-by-minute basis. Since the nature of sensed data behave differently with their own traits, detailed analysis of data are discussed using the scenarios including;

- Stable and fluctuating cases, e.g. sleep and walk monitoring
- Short and long interval of sampling data
- Fine and coarse inference level

4 Testing and Results

Informed consent from all human subjects were obtained prior to the experiment, and complied with ethical clearance codes such as the Australian 'National Statement on Ethical Conduct in Human Research' [11]. There are two methodologies used to generate and capture test data. These include capturing and exporting sensed data, and transmitting data to requestor networks. Wearables (sensors), Raspberry Pi, PC, Smartphone

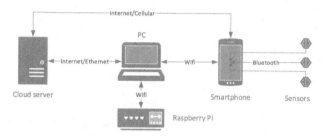

Fig. 2. Test network topology for sensed data capture, transfer and export. Cloud servers are in production network provided by Intel and Fitbit, which collects sensed data via the smartphone and provides export to PC when requested for data processing

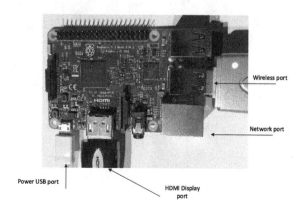

Fig. 3. Raspberry Pi ports configuration

and production servers are used. Testing network topology is depicted in Fig. 2 and Raspberry ports allocation is shown in Fig. 3 including a wireless port for Wi-Fi connection, network port for internet, HDMI port for I/O, and USB port for powering the device. Smartphone interacts with user to display processed data which is exported from the Cloud server. It also collects sensed data from sensors and transfers them to Cloud server, which exports to PC for data processing. These data are used to manipulate and simulate inference algorithms. Sensors include heart rate, body temperature and respiration rate, and Cloud server refers to the actual Fitbit and Basis production servers which collect and export sensed data to smartphones and PC. Raspberry Pi is used to simulate a sensor which transfers data to the PC for data processing.

To obtain and export sensed data from a Fitbit production cloud server which allows developers to export sensed data, API commands are required with a login account specifying data requests details including the timestamp and data ranges. Testing is conducted in two phases, which are simulation and the actual testing using

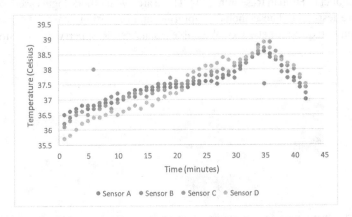

Fig. 4. Sensed data of body temperature simulation

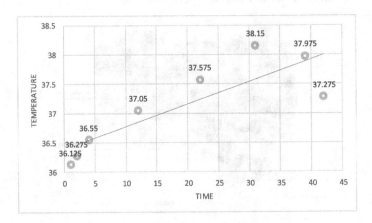

Fig. 5. Result of inferencing (simulation data)

body temperature. In phase 1, body temperature data are created manually and simulated including movements such as resting and exercising. There are four sensors attached on different parts of the body such as the wrist or chest to capture the temperature of the user who initially starts walking and gradually increases to fast walking and running for about 30 min. This is followed by 5 min of slowing down before stopping. The sensors regularly sense every minute and transfer all the sensed data to a smartphone, which results in 168 transmissions as shown in Fig. 4. When the inference algorithm of data optimisation is applied, the number of transmissions is reduced to minimum as pre-defined. Thus, the result in Fig. 5 shows that the number of sensed data are 168 (4 sensors × 42 captures), however these data are inferred and result in 8 transmissions based on the range criteria method. This gives a savings rate of 95.2 %.

In phase 2, actual body temperature is collected during exercise along with various activities and the results show that it varies along with human activity. Detailed testing and results are discussed below. Body temperature shown in Fig. 6 is captured with 45 data points over the exercise period of 40 min on a minute-by-minute basis. After having applied the algorithm, it is inferred with 11 data points, which gives a savings rate of 75.5 %.

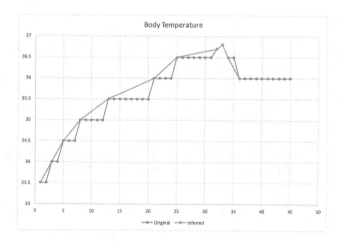

Fig. 6. Body temperature inference result for exercise mode (real data)

Table 1. Data savings for various VR for 24 h samples. S denotes area against the total measurement

Variance rate	0 %	2.5 %	5 %	10 %	20 %
Data points	1420	691	306	146	17
Savings (%)	N/A	51.3	78.5	89.7	98.8
Accuracy (%)	N/A	99.3	97.0	93.7	74.6
S_u: S(upper)	N/A	347 (50 %)	1531 (48.8 %)	2790 (41.8 %)	5125 (19.1 %)
S_l: S(lower)	N/A	347 (50 %)	1608 (51.2 %)	3883 (58.2 %)	21765 (80.9 %)
S: $S_u + S_l$	N/A	694	3139	6673	26890
Accuracy results	N/A	Very Good	Good & Useable	Poor	Unusable

During 24 h, a total of 1420 heart rate data points were sensed and processed for various inference rates including 2.5 %, 5 %, 10 % and 20 % variance rates. Results show that the data points obtained after the inference algorithms have been applied are significantly reduced as shown in Table 1.

5 Discussion

Evaluation approach includes three aspects. Firstly, two test modes and results are discussed including resting (sleeping) and exercising (walking) mode mainly utilising heart rate samples since the nature of data fluctuations and variance are quite different between them. Secondly, short (seconds) and long (minutes) intervals of sensing times are used to analyse gaps and traits of data. Finally fine and coarse inference algorithms are applied to show differences and efficiency of each case.

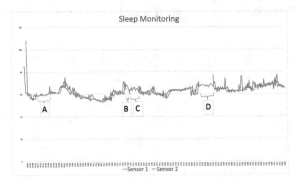

Fig. 7. Sleeping monitoring with multiple sensors on a minute basis showing lost data sections, e.g. Sensor 1 lost (A) and Sensor 2 (B, C & D), which needs to be inferred

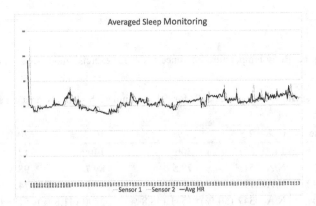

Fig. 8. Averaged sleep monitoring data on a minute basis after inference to fill the gaps from the data loss

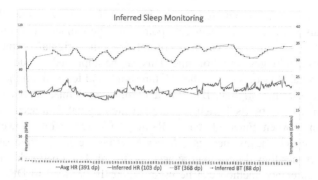

Fig. 9. Inferred HR and BT of sleep monitoring data on a minute basis. Whilst BT represents the original well, HR results show gaps. This can be improved by applying beacons

When capturing data, some sensors may not capture data properly due to an incorrect placement of the device. As shown in Fig. 7 for sleep monitoring data over one night, sensor device 1 did not capture data over the 'A' period, whilst sensor device 2 did not capture during periods of 'B', 'C' and 'D' as labelled on the graph. This may be a potential cause of alarm raising and notification for mHealth services when monitoring in real-time. To avoid the alarm, a sensor can average values from both data as in Fig. 8, which can also be used for inferring process. Having applied a 1 % and 2.5 % of inference rate to reduce the number of transactions for body temperature and heart rate respectively, the volume of data to be transferred reduced by 76 % for BT and 73 % for HR. These results are shown in Fig. 9 and depict HR and BT sensed on a minute basis. BT inference shows better results representing almost identical data as opposed to HR. In other words, savings rate are similar for BT and HR, however accuracy are very different.

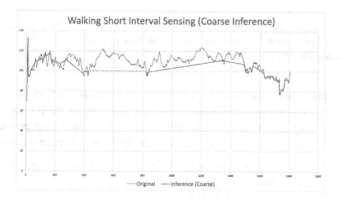

Fig. 10. Short interval with coarse inference (original DP: 1806, inferred DP: 140). Data are distorted a lot without beacons

When sensor data are monitored at short intervals, e.g. every second, the inference system may discard data as adjacent data points may be similar and do not reach the VR threshold. Thus this may cause distortion from the original despite it varying significantly over a longer period of time. This can be improved by adding beacons to transmit data regardless of meeting the VR threshold, and to maintain the inference as close as possible to the original. Beacon data points are defined as once a minute in these experiments and by itself cannot represent the original data accurately as it has 59 s of gaps in between. Finer inference VRs may be more accurate, however it results in more DPs, which means there is a lower Er from the perspective of data transmission. Sometimes they do not require accurate figures but a ballpark only, in which case a coarse inference method can be used. Figure 10 shows 140 DPs out of 1806 resulting in a data reduction of 92.2 %. This may be sufficient enough for a physician to quickly scan HR BPMs during 70 min of exercise as 140 DPs can reasonably represent the original data. However if they require finer and more accurate samples, this cannot be used to represent the original and beacon DPs can be added to improve the accuracy as shown in Fig. 11.

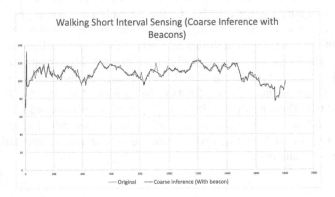

Fig. 11. Short interval with coarse inference and beacon (original DP: 1806, inferred DP: 204). Adding 100 DPs of beacons improve the result with coarse inference reducing approximately 60 % of data comparing to the fine inference

As the results of data reduction with savings rate for each inference scenario show, more data reduction (approximately over 90 %) is achieved in sleep monitoring than during exercise as the sensed values hardly fluctuate over this long period of time. Thus, the steps below can be applied to select the level of inference desired.

- Step1: remove the same data sensed consecutively from the original (BL1).
- Step2: apply coarse inference algorithm
- Step3: apply coarse inference with beacons
- Step4: apply fine inference algorithm
- Step5: apply beacon on fine inference data

Table 2. Summary of Second-by-second Sleep Monitoring

	Original	Beacon	Removed duplication	Fine with beacon	Coarse (3 %)	3 % + beacon
DP	7592	38	1308	107	483	513
Savings (%)		99.5	82.8	98.6	93.6	93.2
Accuracy (%)		95.0	99.0	95.7 %	98.59	98.62

6 Future Research

When sensed data have been transmitted to the requestor networks after having applied inference, it includes personal, private and sensitive content, causing issues related to biometric security and privacy. Threats and attacks can be made including spoofing, in which an attacker presents a falsified biometric trait to the system with the intention of masquerading as another person, and evasion, in which a person attempts to obfuscate or modify a biometric trait to avoid being detected by the system. Evans et al. [12] defines that biometrics is the science of recognizing individuals based on their behavioural and physiological characteristics such as their face, fingerprints, iris, voice, gait, and signature. A typical biometric system may be viewed as a pattern classification system that utilizes advanced signal processing schemes to compare and match biometric data. As this area has been rapidly evolved, it is proposed to utilise physiological data as a novel approach to aid in privacy and security. Everyone has a unique physiological condition, which can be collected and processed to create an individualised biometrics pattern. For example, people who are disabled, inmates, elderly or patients in a hospital will have movement restrictions as compared to commuters and therefore may have less activity such as running or exercising for long periods of time. In this case, physiological data with activity recognition can verify whether the health information of an individual is genuine or modified and injected as an attack. When an individual has a personal health characteristic such as diabetes, obesity, high blood pressure, illness or chronic diseases, it is likely that they have specific data that could be used to analyse and define biometric footprints.

7 Conclusion

Personal sensors are expected to be overloaded by connecting other networks such as IoT, peer-to-peer networks and other sensor networks in addition to the existing mHealth WBAN. We proposed to infer sensed data before transmitting them to the requestor networks in order to reduce data volume and bandwidth to save battery power consumption. To implement, various VRs are used to determine optimal inferencing of data processing such as finer or coarser rates followed by beacon data points to be added to increase the accuracy as high efficiency does not necessarily mean it will represent the original data accurately. By avoiding or removing duplicated data, the accuracy can be up to 99 % which represents the original, and data reduction can be up to 83 % as shown in Table 2. The savings can be improved by applying finer VR to meet the needs from the requestors. To assess the result, we proposed to measure accuracy and efficiency.

References

1. Gartner. http://www.gartner.com/newsroom/id/3165317. Accessed 7 July 2016
2. Kang, J.J., Larkin, H.: Inference of personal sensors in the internet of things. International Journal of Information, Communication Technology and Applications **2**, 1–23 (2016)
3. Aberer, K., Hauswirth, M., Salehi, A.: Infrastructure for data processing in large-scale interconnected sensor networks. In: 2007 International Conference on Mobile Data Management, pp. 198–205 (2007)
4. Sohrabi, K., Gao, J., Ailawadhi, V., Pottie, G.J.: Protocols for self-organization of a wireless sensor network. IEEE Pers. Commun. **7**, 16–27 (2000)
5. Heinzelman, W.R., Chandrakasan, A., Balakrishnan, H.: Energy-efficient communication protocol for wireless microsensor networks. In: Proceedings of the 33rd Annual Hawaii International Conference On System Sciences, vol. 12, pp. 10–pp. IEEE (2000)
6. Manjeshwar, A., Agrawal, D.P.: TEEN: ARouting protocol for enhanced efficiency in wireless sensor networks. In: IPDPS, p. 189 (2001)
7. Osborne, M.A., Roberts, S.J., Rogers, A., Ramchurn, S.D., Jennings, N.R.: Towards real-time information processing of sensor network data using computationally efficient multi-output Gaussian processes. In: Proceedings of the 7th International Conference On Information Processing In Sensor Networks, pp. 109–120. IEEE Computer Society (2008)
8. Bragg, D., Yun, M., Bragg, H., Choi, H.-A.: Intelligent transmission of patient sensor data in wireless hospital networks. In: AMIA Annual Symposium Proceedings, p. 1139. American Medical Informatics Association (2012)
9. Gardiner, C.W.: Handbook of Stochastic Methods. Springer, Berlin (1985)
10. Leu, J.S., Chiang, T.H., Yu, M.C., Su, K.W.: Energy efficient clustering scheme for prolonging the lifetime of wireless sensor network with isolated nodes. IEEE Commun. Lett. **19**, 259–262 (2015)
11. NHMRC: National Statement on Ethical Conduct in Human Research (2007) - Updated May 2015. Australian Government National Health and Medical Research Council (2015)
12. Evans, N., Marcel, S., Ross, A., Teoh, A.B.J.: Biometrics security and privacy protection [from the guest editors]. IEEE Sig. Process. Mag. **32**, 17 (2015)

An Improved EllipticNet Algorithm for Tate Pairing on Weierstrass' Curves, Faster Point Arithmetic and Pairing on Selmer Curves and a Note on Double Scalar Multiplication

Srinivasa Rao Subramanya Rao[✉]

Mathematical Sciences Institute (MSI),
The Australian National University (ANU), Canberra, Australia
srinivasa.subramanya.anu@gmail.com

Abstract. Elliptic Curve point arithmetic is at the heart of all cryptographic algorithms utilizing Elliptic Curves. Pairing based cryptography has been an area of intense research recently. In this context, we

(i) present an improved version of Stange's *Elliptic Net* Algorithm to compute the Tate Pairing,

(ii) present an improved algorithm for Point arithmetic and Pairing on Selmer curves and

(iii) show that *Co-Z* based precomputation algorithms for elliptic curve double scalar multiplication are not necessarily faster than *Conjugate-addition* based precomputation algorithms as claimed in the literature.

Keywords: Elliptic curve cryptography · Point arithmetic · Pairing based cryptography · Tate Pairing · Miller's algorithm · Stange's Elliptic Net algorithm · Selmer curves · Scalar multiplication · Precomputation schemes · Double scalar multiplication · Co-Z addition · Conjugate addition

1 Introduction

Due to smaller key sizes, Elliptic curve cryptography(ECC), independently introduced by Koblitz and Miller 30 years ago, is an attractive alternative to traditional public key algorithms such as RSA, especially in the domain of lightweight applications. Optimized low-cost ECC implementations are crucial for the success of light weight cryptography. Elliptic curve point arithmetic is at the core of most ECC implementations and a speedup of point arithmetic algorithms results in faster ECC implementations.

Pairing based cryptography was first introduced by Joux in his one round Tripartite Diffie-Hellman key exchange scheme [5]. The Weil and the Tate Pairing are two well known examples of pairings which are usually computed using the

© Springer Nature Singapore Pte Ltd. 2016
L. Batten and G. Li (Eds.): ATIS 2016, CCIS 651, pp. 93–105, 2016.
DOI: 10.1007/978-981-10-2741-3_8

well known Miller's algorithm, first described in 1986 and subsequently published in 2004 [15]. In [6], Stange proposed an alternate algorithm to compute the Tate Pairing by using Elliptic Nets which are a generalization of integer sequences satisfying certain properties that were first studied by Ward in [8].

While Miller's algorithm and Stange's Elliptic Net algorithm are both $log(n)$ algorithms, the Elliptic Net algorithm is slower, owing to a difference in the constants, though it is only somewhat slower than an optimized Miller's algorithm, especially at higher embedding degrees [6]. There are numerous papers published on the optimization of Miller's algorithm [2], however, there has hardly been any research published in the literature to optimize Stange's algorithm. This motivates the need to consider optimizations of Stange's algorithm. This paper provides an improved version of Stange's algorithm to compute the Tate Pairing. This improvement may still not make Stange's method faster than that of Miller's yet, but is an improvement worth considering, as Stange's algorithm is the only viable alternative to Miller's algorithm for Pairing computation. This improvement is also applicable to (a) an algorithm due to Kanayama et al. [10] that computes elliptic curve scalar multiplication using an adapted version of Stange's algorithm and (b) an improved version of Kanayama's version due to Chen et al. [1].

In [7], Zhang et al. propose efficient formulae and algorithms for point arithmetic on a new model of Elliptic Curves called "Selmer Curves" They also provide an algorithm for Tate Pairing on these curves. We provide an improved algorithm for point arithmetic and Tate Pairing on Selmer curves.

Recently, new approaches for precomputation that aid in Elliptic curve double scalar multiplication were introduced. In [13], Lin and Zhang construct new algorithms for precomputation of a set of Elliptic Curve points used in Elliptic Curve double scalar multiplication. These algorithms were based on Meloni's *Co-Z* point addition formulae [9] and the authors in [13] conclude that, for any window size, their algorithms using *Co-Z* point addition would cost lesser than Longa and Gebotys' algorithm [12] to achieve the same. Longa and Gebotys' algorithm was based on *Conjugate addition*. In other words, the authors in [13] conclude that *Co-Z* point addition is cheaper than *Conjugate addition*, when it comes to precomputation schemes for double scalar multiplication on elliptic curves. In this paper, we show that this conclusion is not correct.

The rest of the paper is structured as follows: In Sect. 2, we provide an introduction to Stange's Elliptic Net algorithm to compute the Tate Pairing and an improvement to this algorithm. Section 3 provides an introduction to Selmer curves with algorithms for point arithmetic, followed by an improvement of the point addition algorithm and the Tate Pairing on these curves. Section 4 revisits two precomputation schemes that is used to compute elliptic curve double scalar multiplication and further shows that Lin and Zhang's conclusion that their class of algorithms are better than that of Longa and Gebotys' is incorrect.

2 An Improved Version of Stange's Elliptic Net Algorithm to Compute the Tate Pairing

Until recently, Miller's algorithm was the only viable algorithm to compute Pairings. However, in 2006, Stange published an alternative option using Elliptic Nets [6] which are a generalization of elliptic divisibility sequences (integer sequences $h_0, h_1, h_2, ..., h_n$, satisfying the following two properties:

1. For all positive integers $m > n$,

$$h_{m+n}h_{m-n} = h_{m+1}h_{m-1}h_n^2 - h_{n+1}h_{n-1}h_m^2 \qquad (1)$$

2. h_n divides h_m whenever n divides m).

2.1 Stange's Algorithm for Tate Pairing Revisited

Before we outline Stange's algorithm, we must define the Tate Pairing. Let E be an elliptic curve defined over a field L containing the m-th roots of unity, where $m \in \mathbb{Z}^+$. Let $E(L)[m] = \{P \in E(L)|mP = 0\}$ and $mE(L) = \{mP|P \in E(L)\}$. Further let $P \in E(L)[m]$ and $Q \in E(L)/mE(L)$. Since $mP = 0$, there is a rational function f with divisor $div(f_P) = m(P) - m(0)$. If we choose another divisor D_Q defined over L such that $D_Q \sim (Q) - (0)$ and with support disjoint from $div(f_P)$, the Tate Pairing is the mapping

$$T_m : E(L)[m] \times E(L)/mE(L) \to L^*/(L^*)^m \text{ defined by } {}_{Tm}(P,Q) = f_P(D_Q).$$

As stated above, whilst constructing an algorithm to compute the Tate Pairing using Elliptic Nets, Stange provided a theorem useful in constructing the Tate Pairing in her paper [6], which we repeat below for convenience:

Fix a positive $m \in \mathbb{Z}$. Let E be an elliptic curve defined over a finite field L containing the m-th roots of unity. Let $P, Q \in E(L)$, with $[m]P = 0$. Choose $S \in E(L)$ such that $S \notin \{0, Q\}$. Then there exists an Elliptic Net $W : \mathbb{Z}^n \to L$ and $\mathbf{p}, \mathbf{q}, \mathbf{s} \in \mathbb{Z}^n$ such that the quantity

$$T_m(P,Q) = \frac{W(\mathbf{s} + m\mathbf{p} + \mathbf{q})W(\mathbf{s})}{W(\mathbf{s} + m\mathbf{p})W(\mathbf{s} + \mathbf{q})}$$

is exactly the Tate Pairing $T_m =_{Tm} : E(L)[m] \times E(L)/mE(L) \to L^*/(L^*)^m$.

In the above, W is a map $W : A \to R$ satisfying the following recurrence relation for $p, q, r, s \in A$, where R is an integral domain and A is a finitely generated free abelian group.

$$W(p+q+s)W(p-q)W(r+s)W(r)$$
$$+ W(q+r+s)W(q-r)W(p+s)W(p) \qquad (2)$$
$$+ W(r+p+s)W(r-p)W(q+s)W(q) = 0$$

Further Stange provides the following result in [6].

Let E be an elliptic curve defined over a finite field L, m a positive integer, $P \in E(L)[m]$ and $Q \in E(L)$. If W_p is the Elliptic Net associated to E, P, then

$$T_m(P, P) = \frac{W_P(m+2)W_P(1)}{W_P(m+1)W_P(2)}$$

Further if $W_{P,Q}$ is the Elliptic Net associated to E, P, Q, then

$$T_m(P, Q) = \frac{W_{P,Q}(m+1,1)W_{P,Q}(1,0)}{W_{P,Q}(m+1,0)W_{P,Q}(1,1)} \tag{3}$$

Using Shipsey's algorithm [14] for computing terms of an elliptic divisibility sequence and the above theorems, Stange provides a scheme that can be used to compute the Tate Pairing by calculating the terms $W(m,0)$ and $W(m,1)$ of an Elliptic Net. Stange defines a block centered on k to consist of a first vector of eight consecutive terms of the sequence $W(i,0)$ centered on terms $W(k,0)$ and $W(k+1,0)$ and then a second vector of three consecutive terms $W(i,1)$ centered on the term $W(k,1)$. For a block V centered on k, she proposes two algorithms, *Double(V)*, that returns the block centered on $2k$ and *DoubleAdd(V)* that returns the block centered on $2k+1$. While the first vectors of *Double(V)* and *DoubleAdd(V)* are calculated in terms of $W(2,0)$ and the terms of V, using the following instances of (1), where $i = k-1, \ldots, k+3$

$$W(2i-1,0) = W(i+1,0)W(i-1,0)^3 - W(i-2,0)W(i,0)^3 \text{ and} \tag{4}$$
$$xW(2i,0) = (W(i,0)W(i+2,0)W(i-1,0)^2$$
$$- W(i,0)W(i-2,0)W(i+1,0)^2)/W(2,0) \tag{5}$$

the second vectors are computed, in terms of $W(1,1), W(1,1), W(2,1)$ and the terms of V, using the following instances of (2) below:

$$W(2k-1,1) = (W(k+1,1)W(k-1,1)W(k-1,0)^2$$
$$- W(k,0)W(k-2,0)W(k,1)^2)/W(1,1), \tag{6}$$
$$W(2k,1) = W(k-1,1)W(k+1,1)W(k,0)^2$$
$$- W(k-1,0)W(k+1,0)W(k,1)^2, \tag{7}$$
$$W(2k+1,1) = (W(k-1,1)W(k+1,1)W(k+1,0)^2$$
$$- W(k,0)W(k+2,0)W(k,1)2)/W(-1,1), \tag{8}$$
$$W(2k+2,1) = (W(k+1,0)W(k+3,0)W(k,1)^2$$
$$- W(k-1,1)W(k+1,1)W(k+2,0)^2)/W(2,-1). \tag{9}$$

Algorithm 1 below calculates $W(m,1)$ and $W(m,0)$ for any positive integer m.

Algorithm 1. Elliptic Net Algorithm

INPUT: Initial terms $a = W(2,0), b = W(3,0), c = W(4,0), d = W(2,1),$
  $e = W(-1,1), f = W(2,-1), g = W(1,1)$ of an elliptic net satisfying
  $W(1,0) = W(0,1) = 1$ and integer $m = (d_k d_{k-1} \ldots d_0)_2$ with $d_k = 1$
OUTPUT: Elliptic net elements $W(m,0)$ and $W(m,1)$.

1:   $V \leftarrow [[-a, -1, 0, 1, a, b, c, a^3 c - b^3]; [1, g, d]]$
2:   **for** $i = k - 1$ down to 1 **do**
3:       **if** $d_i = 0$ **then**
4:           $V \leftarrow Double(V)$
5:       **else**
6:           $V \leftarrow DoubleAdd(V)$
7:       **end if**
8:   **end for**
9:   **return** $V[0,3], V[1,1]$ //terms $W(m,0)$ and $W(m,1)$ respectively

---

The Tate Pairing is now computed using Eq. 3. If a Weierstrass form elliptic curve E over a finite field $\mathbb{F}_q$ of characteristic not 2 or 3 is given by

$$y^2 = x^3 + Ax + B$$

and points $P = (x_1, y_1)$ and $Q = (x_2, y_2)$ on $E(\mathbb{F}_q)$ with $Q \neq \pm P$, the values of a, b, c, d, e, f, g must be calculated as required inputs for the Elliptic Net Algorithm, which are the terms of the elliptic net associated to E, P, Q. The necessary formulae are given by the functions $\Psi_{m,0}$ called *division polynomials* (see [16, p. 105] and [17, p. 477]). We have

$$W(1,0) = 1, \tag{10}$$

$$W(2,0) = 2y_1, \tag{11}$$

$$W(3,0) = 3x_1^4 + 6Ax_1^2 + 12Bx_1 - A^2, \tag{12}$$

$$W(4,0) = 4y_1(x_1^6 + 5Ax_1^4 + 20Bx_1^3 - 5A^2x_1^2 - 4ABx_1 - 8B^2 - A^3), \tag{13}$$

$$W(0,1) = W(1,1) = 1, \tag{14}$$

$$W(2,1) = 2x_1 + x_2 - \left(\frac{y_2 - y_1}{x_2 - x_1}\right)^2 \tag{15}$$

$$W(-1,1) = x_1 - x_2 \text{ and} \tag{16}$$

$$W(2,-1) = (y_1 + y_2)^2 - (2x_1 + x_2)(x_1 - x_2)^2. \tag{17}$$

If P has order m and if a, b, c, d, e, f, g given by (11)–(17) above, the output of Algorithm 1 can be used to compute the Tate Pairing using Eq. (3) above. Factoring out frequently occurring common subexpressions, Stange provides an optimised version of the Double and DoubleAdd algorithm as follows:

Algorithm 2. Double and DoubleAdd

INPUT: Block V centred at k of an elliptic net satisfying $W(1,0) = W(0,1) = 1$,
       values $\alpha = W(2,0)^{-1}, E = W(-1,1)^{-1}, F = W(2,-1)^{-1}$,
       $G = W(1,1)^{-1}$ and boolean *add*
OUTPUT: Block centered at $2k$ if *add* $== 0$ and centred at $2k+1$ if *add* $== 1$.

---

1. $S \leftarrow [0,0,0,0,0,0]$
2. $P \leftarrow [0,0,0,0,0,0]$
3. $S_0 \leftarrow V[1,1]^2$
4. $P_0 \leftarrow V[1,0]V[1,2]$
5:   **for** $i = 0$ to 5 **do**
6:       $S[i] \leftarrow V[0, i+1]^2$
7:       $P[i] \leftarrow V[0, i]V[0, i+2]$
8:   **end for**
9:   **if** *add* $== 0$ **then**
10:      **for** $i = 1$ to 4 **do**
11:          $V[0, 2i - 2] \leftarrow S[i]P[i+1] - S[i+1]P[i]$
12:          $V[0, 2i - 1] \leftarrow (S[i]P[i+2] - S[i+2]P[i])\alpha$
13:      **end for**
14. $V[1,0] \leftarrow (S_0 P[3] - S[3]P_0)G$
15. $V[1,1] \leftarrow S[3]P_0 - S_0 P[3]$
16. $V[1,2] \leftarrow (S[4]P_0 - S_0 P[4])E$
17: **else**
18:      **for** $i = 1$ to 4 **do**
19:          $V[0, 2i - 2] \leftarrow (S[i]P[i+2] - S[i+2]P[i])\alpha$
20:          $V[0, 2i - 1] \leftarrow S[i+1]P[i+2] - S[i+2]P[i+1]$
21:      **end for**
22. $V[1,0] \leftarrow S[3]P_0 - S_0 P[3]$
23. $V[1,1] \leftarrow (S[4]P_0 - S_0 P[4])E$
24. $V[1,2] \leftarrow (S_0 P[5] - S[5]P_0)F$
25: **end if**
26: **return** V

2.2   Improvement to Stange's Algorithm

Stange calculates the cost of the Double step in the above scheme to be $6S + (6n+26)M + S_n + \frac{3}{2}M_n$, while that of the DoubleAdd steps is $6S + (6n+26)M + S_n + 2M_n$ where M and S are the costs of a multiplication and squaring in $\mathbb{F}_q$ respectively while M_n and S_n are the costs of a multiplication and squaring in $\mathbb{F}_{q^n}$ respectively. Here for the integer m and finite field $\mathbb{F}_q$, embedding degree n is the least integer such that $m|(q^n - 1)$. Usually for the Tate Pairing, a curve defined over $\mathbb{F}_q$ of embedding degree $n > 1$, while $P \in E(\mathbb{F}_q)$ and $Q \in E(\mathbb{F}_{q^n})$.

Now Lines 10–13 of Algorithm 2 costs $4 * 5M = 20M$ while Line 18–21 costs $4 * 5M = 20M$ and can be replaced with the following blocks of code:

Lines 10–13 can be replaced with the following block of code (Block 1):	Lines 18–21 can be replaced with the following block of code (Block 2):
$A \leftarrow (P[1] + P[2])(S[1] - S[2]);$	$A \leftarrow (P[2] + P[3])(S[2] - S[3]);$
$B \leftarrow (P[1] - P[2])(S[1] + S[2]);$	$B \leftarrow (P[2] - P[3])(S[2] + S[3]);$
$C \leftarrow (P[1] + P[3])(S[1] - S[3]);$	$C \leftarrow (P[2] + P[4])(S[2] - S[4]);$
$D \leftarrow (P[1] - P[3])(S[1] + S[3]);$	$D \leftarrow (P[2] - P[4])(S[2] + S[4]);$
$E \leftarrow 2(P[2] - P[3])(S[2] + S[3]);$	$E \leftarrow 2(P[3] - P[4])(S[3] + S[4]);$
$F \leftarrow (P[3] + P[4])(S[3] - S[4]);$	$F \leftarrow (P[4] + P[5])(S[4] - S[5]);$
$G \leftarrow (P[3] - P[4])(S[3] + S[4]);$	$G \leftarrow (P[4] - P[5])(S[4] + S[5]);$
$H \leftarrow (P[3] + P[5])(S[3] - S[5]);$	$H \leftarrow (P[4] + P[6])(S[4] - S[6]);$
$I \leftarrow (P[3] - P[5])(S[3] + S[5]);$	$I \leftarrow (P[4] - P[6])(S[4] + S[6]);$
$J \leftarrow 2(P[4] - P[5])(S[4] + S[5]);$	$J \leftarrow 2(P[5] - P[6])(S[5] + S[6]);$
$V[0,0] \leftarrow (A - B)/2;$	$V[0,0] \leftarrow (S[1]P[3] - S[3]P[1])\alpha;$
$V[0,1] \leftarrow (C - D)\alpha/2;$	$V[0,1] \leftarrow (A - B)/2;$
$V[0,2] \leftarrow ((C + D) - (A + B + E))/2;$	$V[0,2] \leftarrow (C - D)\alpha/2;$
$V[0,3] \leftarrow (S[2]P[4] - S[4]P[2])\alpha;$	$V[0,3] \leftarrow ((C + D) - (A + B + E))/2;$
$V[0,4] \leftarrow (F - G)/2;$	$V[0,4] \leftarrow (S[3]P[5] - S[5]P[3])\alpha;$
$V[0,5] \leftarrow (H - I)\alpha/2;$	$V[0,5] \leftarrow (F - G)/2;$
$V[0,6] \leftarrow ((H + I) - (F + G + J))/2;$	$V[0,6] \leftarrow (H - I)\alpha/2;$
$V[0,7] \leftarrow (S[4]P[6] - S[6]P[4])\alpha;$	$V[0,7] \leftarrow ((H + I) - (F + G + J))/2;$

By inspection, we can see that both Block 1 and Block 2 costs $18M$ each. Thus the cost of the double step in Stange's algorithm can be reduced to $6S + (6n + 24)M + S_n + \frac{3}{2}M_n$, while that of the DoubleAdd step could be reduced to $6S + (6n + 24)M + S_n + 2M_n$, as summarized in the table below.

Tate Pairing algorithm	Double	DoubleAdd
Optimised Millers [11]	$4S + (n + 7)M + S_n + M_n$	$7S + (2n + 19)M + S_n + 2M_n$
Elliptic Net Algorithm [6]	$6S + (6n + 26)M + S_n + \frac{3}{2}M_n$	$6S + (6n + 26)M + S_n + 2M_n$
Improved Elliptic Net Algorithm (this paper)	$6S + (6n + 24)M + S_n + \frac{3}{2}M_n$	$6S + (6n + 24)M + S_n + 2M_n$

Stange's algorithm was adapted by Kanayama et al. to compute Elliptic Curve scalar multiplication [10]. Their Double and DoubleAdd steps costs $26M + 6S$ and this can be reduced to $24M + 6S$ as a result of adapting the optimization to Stange's algorithm presented in this paper. Kanayama's algorithm was then further optimized by Chen et al. in [1] using one of the optimizations outlined by

Stange, which was not utilised by the authors in [10]. Using this optimization and then replacing four multiplications with four squarings in Stange's algorithm, the authors in [10] reduce the cost of the both the Double and DoubleAdd steps in Kanayama's algorithm to $18M + 10S$. Using our optimization in this paper, the cost of the Double and DoubleAdd steps can be reduced to $16M + 10S$ each. These costs are summarized in the table below:

Elliptic Net Algorithm for Scalar Multiplication	Double	DoubleAdd
Kanayama's Algorithm [10]	$26M + 6S$	$26M + 6S$
Improvement due to Chen [1]	$18M + 10S$	$18M + 10S$
Further Improvement (this paper)	$16M + 10S$	$16M + 10S$

3   Selmer Curves

In [7], the authors consider a new model of an elliptic curve called *Selmer Curves* that was so named by Ian Connell [4]. The authors in [7] also provide with explicit point addition and doubling formulae for Selmer curves. Following [4], we provide with the following definition.

Definition: Let K be a field of characteristic $\neq 2$ or 3, a Selmer curve over K is defined by a homogeneous cubic equation of the form $aX^3 + bY^3 = cZ^3$ or in affine coordinates, $ax^3 + by^3 = c$, where $a, b, c \in K$ and $abc = 0$.

3.1   Point Arithmetic on Selmer Curves

Assume $P_1 = (X_1 : Y_1 : Z_1)$, $P_2 = (X_2 : Y_2 : Z_2)$ and let $P_1 + P_2 = P_3 = (X_3 : Y_3 : Z_3)$, then

$$X_3 = X_1 Z_1 Y_2^2 - X_2 Z_2 Y_1^2$$
$$Y_3 = Y_1 Z_1 X_2^2 - Y_2 Z_2 X_1^2$$
$$Z_3 = X_1 Y_1 Z_2^2 - X_2 Y_2 Z_1^2$$

Below, we replicate the algorithm to compute the above formula as provided in [7], which costs $12M$.

$$A = X_1 Y_2; \ B = X_2 Y_1; \ C = Y_1 Z_2; \ D = Y_2 Z_1; \ E = Z_1 X_2; \ F = Z_2 X_1;$$
$$X_3 = AD - BC; \ Y_3 = BE - AF; \ Z_3 = CF - DE.$$

Below we provide a new algorithm for point addition on Selmer Curves:

$$A = X_1 Y_2; \ B = X_2 Y_1; \ C = Y_1 Z_2; \ D = Y_2 Z_1; \ E = Z_1 X_2; \ F = Z_2 X_1;$$
$$G = (B + D)(A - C); \ H = (B - D)(A + C); \ I = (B + F)(A - E);$$
$$J = (B - F)(A + E); \ K = (D - F)(C + E);$$
$$2X_3 = (G - H); \ 2Y_3 = (J - I); \ 2Z_3 = (I + J) - (G + H + 2K)$$

This algorithm costs $11M$, thus saving us $1M$. It should be noted that we have actually computed $2X_3, 2Y_3, 2Z_3$. If $Z_2 = 1$, then the new algorithm costs $9M$.

3.2 Cost of Tate Pairing on Selmer Curves

The authors in [7] use the Miller's algorithm to compute the Tate Pairing on Selmer curves. Using the same notation as in the previous section, the total cost of Miller addition step (ADD) as given in [7] is $M_n + (n + 12)M$, where M_n and M denote multiplication in $\mathbb{F}_{p^n}$ and $\mathbb{F}_p$ respectively. If $Z_2 = 1$ then the authors in [7] show that the cost of mixed Miller addition (mADD) is reduced to $M_n + (n+10)M$. If we use the new algorithm for point addition presented above, then the new total cost of Miller addition step (ADD) is $M_n + (n + 11)M$. If $Z_2 = 1$, then the new cost of mixed Miller addition (mADD) is $M_n + (n+9)M$. The authors in [7] show that Selmer curves are very competitive with the fastest formulae, by comparing the cost of computing the Tate Pairing on other forms of Elliptic curves. They summarize the cost of Tate Pairing computation [7, Table 1] as shown in the table below, whilst not including the common cost $1M_n + nM$ in Miller addition step and $1M_n + 1S + nM$ in Miller doubling step. T_1 is the scenario when $S = 0.8M$ and T_2 is the scenario when $S = M$. As per their analysis, computation of Tate Pairing would be the fastest on Selmer curves in the T_2 scenario. With our new algorithm in this paper, computation of Tate Pairing on Selmer curves would be the fastest under both scenarios, T_1 and T_2.

	DBL	T_1	T_2	mADD	T_1	T_2
$\mathcal{J}$, [18,20]	$1\,m + 11\,s + 1\mathbf{m}_d$	$9.8\,m$	$12\,m$	$6\,m + 6\,s$	$10.8\,m$	$12\,m$
$\mathcal{J}, a = -3$, [18]	$6\,m + 5\,s$	$10\,m$	$11\,m$	$6\,m + 6\,s$	$10.8\,m$	$12\,m$
$\mathcal{J}, a = 0$, [18]	$3\,m + 8\,s$	$9.4\,m$	$11\,m$	$6\,m + 6\,s$	$10.8\,m$	$12\,m$
$\mathcal{P}, a = 0, b = c^2$, [23]	$3\,m + 5\,s$	$7\,m$	$8\,m$	$9\,m + 2\,s + 1\mathbf{m}_d$	$10.6\,m$	$11\,m$
$\mathcal{E}$, [19]	$6\,m + 5\,s$	$10\,m$	$11\,m$	$12\,m$	$12\,m$	$12\,m$
$\mathcal{H}$, [24]	$3\,m + 6\,s + 3\mathbf{m}_d$	$7.8\,m$	$9\,m$	$10\,m$	$10\,m$	$10\,m$
$\mathcal{H}u$, [21]	$11\,m + 6\,s$	$15.8\,m$	$17\,m$	$13\,m$	$13\,m$	$13\,m$
$\mathcal{J}a$, [22]	$4\,m + 8\,s + 1\mathbf{m}_d$	$10.4\,m$	$12\,m$	$16\,m + 1\,s + 4\mathbf{m}_d$	$16.8\,m$	$17\,m$
$\mathcal{S}$, [7]	$5\,m + 3\,s$	$7.4\,m$	$8\,m$	$10\,m$	$10\,m$	$10\,m$
Selmer (this paper)	$5\,m + 3\,s$	$7.4\,m$	$8\,m$	$9\,m$	$9\,m$	$9\,m$

4 Efficient Precomputation of Elliptic Curve Points to Compute $kP + lQ$ in Jacobian Representation $\mathcal{J}$

In [12], Longa and Gebotys provided a new technique to add elliptic curve points with the form $P \pm Q$ and called it *Conjugate Addition* before utilizing it in the generation of precomputed tables of the form $c_i P + d_i Q$ where $c_i, d_i \in \{1, 3 \dots m\}$ which can then be used by various algorithms to compute double scalar multiplication, i.e., $kP + lQ$ where k and l are scalars. In Table 4 of their paper, the cost of computing $3P, 3Q, P + Q, P - Q, 3P + Q, 3P - Q, P + 3Q, P - 3Q, 3P + 3Q$ and $3P - 3Q$ for standard Jacobian coordinates when curve parameter $a = -3$, is provided as $42M + 32S$. In this paper, we improve this to $41M + 31S$, resulting in a saving of $1M + 1S$. The following table shows the scheme that can be utilised: (Refer to [12, Table 1] for the cost break down).

Here MA refers to *Mixed Addition* and CMA refers to *Conjugate Mixed Addition*.

Result	Operation	Cost (when $a = -3$)
$3P, 3Q$	2 Numbers of Mixed Tripling	$(5M + 7S) + (5M + 7S)$
$P \pm Q$	MA(both affine)+CMA	$(4M + 2S) + (1M + 1S)$
$3P \pm Q$	MA(one affine)+CMA	$(7M + 4S) + (1M + 1S)$
$P \pm 3Q$	MA(one affine)+CMA	$(7M + 4S) + (1M + 1S)$
$3P \pm 3Q$	Addition with stored values+CMA	$(9M + 3S) + (1M + 1S)$

Addition of points in Projective coordinates(Weistrass Curves) usually costs $11M + 5S$. But with the square and cube of the Z-coordinate of one of the points available, the point addition cost can be reduced to $(10M + 4S)$. In the above scheme, when $3P + Q$ is computed, both Z_{3P}^2 and Z_{3P}^3 are computed and do not have to be recomputed when $3P + 3Q$ is computed. Further when $P + 3Q$ is computed, Z_{3Q}^2 and Z_{3Q}^3 is computed and thus does not have to be recomputed when $3P + 3Q$ is computed. Thus the new total cost of computing $3P, 3Q, P + Q, P - Q, 3P + Q, 3P - Q, P + 3Q, P - 3Q, 3P + 3Q$ and $3P - 3Q$ for standard Jacobian coordinates can be reduced to $41M + 31S$.

In [13], Lin and Zhang propose to improve upon the cost of Longa and Gebotys' algorithm for precomputation and thus propose new algorithms to compute $c_i P + d_i Q$ where $c_i, d_i \in \{1, 3\}$ and $c_i, d_i \in \{1, 3, 5\}$ and the curve parameter a need not be equal to -3. Their algorithm for $c_i, d_i \in \{1, 3\}$, utilize Co-Z point arithmetic formulae proposed by Meloni in [9] and costs $50M + 36S$. The authors in [13] provide tables to compare costs of their algorithms with that of Longa and Gebotys in [12]. The comparison is provided for curve parameter $a \neq 3$. We reproduce the data in their tables below for our convenience:

Algorithm for $c_i P + d_i Q$	Cost when $c_i, d_i \in \{1, 3\}$	Cost when $c_i, d_i \in \{1, 3, 5\}$
Longa and Gebotys [12]	$56M + 40S$	$129M + 95S$
Lin and Zhang [13]	$50M + 36S$	$98M + 46S$

The authors in [13] also conclude that their scheme becomes more efficient than that of Longa and Gebotys [12], as the *window* size increases. However, this is incorrect because we can structure the Longa and Gebotys' algorithm when $a \neq -3$ and $c_i, d_i \in \{1, 3\}$ (*window*size = 2) as follows:

Thus the total cost of Longa and Gebotys' algorithm when $a \neq -3$ is $43M + 31S$ and thus more efficient than the Lin and Zhang algorithm in [13] which

Result	Operation	Cost (when $a \neq -3$)
$3P, 3Q$	2 Numbers of Mixed Tripling	$(6M + 7S) + (6M + 7S)$
$P \pm Q$	MA(both affine)+CMA	$(4M + 2S) + (1M + 1S)$
$3P \pm Q$	MA(one affine)+CMA	$(7M + 4S) + (1M + 1S)$
$P \pm 3Q$	MA(one affine)+CMA	$(7M + 4S) + (1M + 1S)$
$3P \pm 3Q$	Addition with stored values+CMA	$(9M + 3S) + (1M + 1S)$

costs $50M + 36S$. Moreover, Longa and Gebotys' algorithm computes $3P$ and $3Q$ whereas the algorithm due to Lin and Zhang [13] does not. However, as per the requirements of the algorithm, it is not required to compute $3P$ and $3Q$.

Longa and Gebotys' scheme can be extended when $a \neq -3$ and $c_i, d_i \in \{1, 3, 5\}$ as follows: As suggested in [12], we can start by performing $P \to 2P \to 4P$ and then obtaining $3P$ and $5P$ using $4P \pm P$. Similarly, we can compute $Q \to 2Q \to 4Q$ and then obtain $3Q$ and $5Q$ using $4Q \pm Q$. We structure the complete algorithm as follows:

Result	Operation	Cost (when $a \neq -3$)
$2P$	Doubling (Affine $\to$ Projective)	$(1M + 5S)$
$4P$	Doubling (Projective $\to$ Projective)	$(2M + 8S)$
$4P \pm P$	MA(one affine)+CMA	$(7M + 4S) + (1M + 1S)$
$2Q$	Doubling (Affine $\to$ Projective)	$(1M + 5S)$
$4Q$	Doubling (Projective $\to$ Projective)	$(2M + 8S)$
$4Q \pm Q$	MA(one affine)+CMA	$(7M + 4S) + (1M + 1S)$
$P \pm Q$	MA(both affine)+CMA	$(4M + 2S) + (1M + 1S)$
$3P \pm Q$	MA(one affine)+CMA	$(7M + 4S) + (1M + 1S)$
$P \pm 3Q$	MA(one affine)+CMA	$(7M + 4S) + (1M + 1S)$
$5P \pm Q$	MA(one affine)+CMA	$(7M + 4S) + (1M + 1S)$
$P \pm 5Q$	MA(one affine)+CMA	$(7M + 4S) + (1M + 1S)$
$3P \pm 3Q$	Addition with stored values+CMA	$(9M + 3S) + (1M + 1S)$
$3P \pm 5Q$	Addition with stored values+CMA	$(9M + 3S) + (1M + 1S)$
$5P \pm 3Q$	Addition with stored values+CMA	$(9M + 3S) + (1M + 1S)$
$5P \pm 5Q$	Addition with stored values+CMA	$(9M + 3S) + (1M + 1S)$

Thus the total cost of Longa and Gebotys' algorithm to compute $c_i P + d_i Q$ when $a \neq -3$ and $c_i, d_i \in \{1, 3, 5\}$ is $99M + 75S$. In [13], Lin and Zhang provide an algorithm to do the same with a cost of $98M + 46S$. However, Lin and Zhang's algorithm does not compute $5P \pm Q$ and $P \pm 5Q$ and thus incomplete. Therefore, it may not be appropriate to compare the costs between the two algorithms. If we add the cost of computing $5P \pm Q$ and $P \pm 5Q$ to the cost of the incomplete algorithm of Lin and Zhang, the cost exceeds that of our adaptation of Longa and Gebotys's algorithm shown above. Thus, the use of *Co-Z point arithmetic* based algorithms do not always provide with better performance when compared with those constructed using only *Conjugate addition arithmetic*, atleast not in the two cases studied by Lin and Zhang in [13].

5   Conclusions

In this paper, we provided an improved version of Stange's Elliptic Net algorithm to compute the Tate Pairing. Shipsey's algorithm for Elliptic Divisibility Sequence is an instance of a Binary differential chain. Further research on utilizing Euclidean differential chains [3] may result in faster Elliptic Net algorithms. Further we provided a faster point arithmetic algorithm for Selmer curves resulting in the fastest algorithm for Tate Pairing. Further we showed that the use of Co-Z arithmetic is not always better than Conjugate addition arithmetic.

Acknowledgments. Many thanks to the anonymous reviewers of ATIS 2016 for their valuable feedback.

References

1. Chen, B., Hu, C., Zhao, C.: A note on scalar multiplication using division polynomials. https://eprint.iacr.org/2015/284.pdf
2. Costello, C.: Faster formulas for computing cryptographic pairings. Ph.D. thesis, Queensland University of Technology (2012)
3. Bernstein, D.: Differential addition chains. http://cr.yp.to/ecdh/diffchain-20060219.pdf
4. Connell, I.: Elliptic curve handbook (1999). http://www.math.mcgill.ca/connell
5. Joux, A.: A one round protocol for Tripartite Diffie Hellman. J. Cryptol. **17**(4), 263–276 (2004)
6. Stange, K.E.: The tate pairing via elliptic nets. In: Takagi, T., Okamoto, E., Okamoto, T., Okamoto, T. (eds.) Pairing 2007. LNCS, vol. 4575, pp. 329–348. Springer, Heidelberg (2007). doi:10.1007/978-3-540-73489-5_19
7. Zhang, L., Wang, K., Wang, H., Ye, D.: Another elliptic curve model for faster pairing computation. In: Bao, F., Weng, J. (eds.) ISPEC 2011. LNCS, vol. 6672, pp. 432–446. Springer, Heidelberg (2011). doi:10.1007/978-3-642-21031-0_32
8. Ward, M.: Memoir on elliptic divisibility sequences. Amer. J. Math. **70**, 31–74 (1948)
9. Meloni, N.: New point addition formulae for ECC applications. In: Carlet, C., Sunar, B. (eds.) WAIFI 2007. LNCS, vol. 4547, pp. 189–201. Springer, Heidelberg (2007). doi:10.1007/978-3-540-73074-3_15
10. Kanayama, N., Liu, Y., Okamoto, E., Saito, K., Teruya, T., Uchiyama, S.: Implementation of an Elliptic Curve scalar multiplication method using division polynomials. In: IEICE Trans Fundamentals, vol. E97-A, No. 1 (2014)
11. Koblitz, N., Menezes, A.: Pairing-based cryptography at high security levels. In: Smart, N.P. (ed.) Cryptography and Coding 2005. LNCS, vol. 3796, pp. 13–36. Springer, Heidelberg (2005). doi:10.1007/11586821_2

12. Longa, P., Gebotys, C.: Novel precomputation schemes for Elliptic Curve cryptosystems. https://eprint.iacr.org/2008/256.pdf
13. Lin, Q., Zhang, F.: Efficient precomputation schemes of $kp + lq$. Inf. Process. Lett. **112**(Elsevier B.V.), 462–466 (2012)
14. Shipsey, R.: Elliptic divisibility sequences. Ph.D. thesis, Goldsmith's College, University of London (2000)
15. Miller, V.S.: The Weil Pairing, and its efficient calculation. J. Cryptol. **17**(4), 235–261 (2004)
16. Silverman, J.H.: The Arithmetic of Elliptic Curves. Springer, New York (1992)
17. Silverman, J.H.: Advanced Topics in the Arithmetic of Elliptic Curves. Springer, New York (1994)
18. Arene, C., Lange, T., Naehrig, M., Ritzenthaler, C.: Faster computation of the tate pairing. https://eprint.iacr.org/2009/155.pdf
19. Farashahi, R.R., Joye, M.: Efficient arithmetic on Hessian curves. In: Nguyen, P.Q., Pointcheval, D. (eds.) PKC 2010. LNCS, vol. 6056, pp. 243–260. Springer, Heidelberg (2010). doi:10.1007/978-3-642-13013-7_15
20. Ionica, S., Joux, A.: Another approach to pairing computation in Edwards coordinates. In: Chowdhury, D.R., Rijmen, V., Das, A. (eds.) INDOCRYPT 2008. LNCS, vol. 5365, pp. 400–413. Springer, Heidelberg (2008). doi:10.1007/978-3-540-89754-5_31
21. Joye, M., Tibouchi, M., Vergnaud, D.: Huffs model for elliptic curves. http://eprint.iacr.org/2010/383
22. Zhao, C.A., Zhang, F., Huang, J.: A note on the ate pairing. https://eprint.iacr.org/2007/247.ps
23. Costello, C., Lange, T., Naehrig, M.: Faster pairing computations on curves with high-degree twists. In: Nguyen, P.Q., Pointcheval, D. (eds.) PKC 2010. LNCS, vol. 6056, pp. 224–242. Springer, Heidelberg (2010). doi:10.1007/978-3-642-13013-7_14
24. Gu, H., Gu, D., Xie, W.L.: Efficient pairing computation on elliptic curves in Hessian form. In: Rhee, K.-H., Nyang, D.H. (eds.) ICISC 2010. LNCS, vol. 6829, pp. 169–176. Springer, Heidelberg (2011). doi:10.1007/978-3-642-24209-0_11

Inductive Hierarchical Identity Based Key Agreement with Pre-deployment Interactions (i-H-IB-KA-pdi)

Pinaki Sarkar[1][(✉)] and Morshed Uddin Chowdhury[2]

[1] Department of Computer Science and Automation, IISc,
Bengaluru, Karnataka, India
pinakisark@csa.iisc.ernet.in
[2] School of Information Technology, Deakin University, Burwood, Australia
morshed.chowdhury@deakin.edu.au

Abstract. We propose two hierarchical identity based key agreement schemes with unrestricted number of levels. Our solutions use pre-deployment (encrypted) interactions among ancestors using–(i) purely public key cryptographic techniques and (ii) hybrid of public and symmetric keys. Elegant use of identities based techniques reduces trust (certification) on third parties. Proof of security is based on indistinguishability of keys. Novel use of hybrid technology in our later solution reduces computational complexity and broadens its applicability to networks faced with bandwidth constraints. Compared to prominent works, our designs are better equipped to secure real world hierarchical systems.

Keywords: Hybrid key agreement · Hierarchical networks · Bilinear pairing maps

1 Introduction

Key agreement (KA) is a fundamental functionality for secure communication. Ultimate goal of a KA scheme is to let a pair of users agree on a unique shared key; thus allowing them to use this agreed key(s) for secure communications.

Key agreement may be troublesome for large networks that may well be spread over large geographical region. Practical instances of such networks are military network or internal network of a multi national company (MNC) like Microsoft which has its office all across the world. Yet another example is that of an ad-hoc networks where communications between users is expected to be volatile.

All these network will be well served by a protocol that ensures pair-wise keys for every level. Whereas inter level communications may involve subsets of users to share common keys. For example, for a MNC team leads are responsible for their team member's (child's) performance and interactions (intra and inter). Users above a lead takes collective feedback from these leads. These practical instances are not captured by existing protocols and motivates our key agreement protocols.

© Springer Nature Singapore Pte Ltd. 2016
L. Batten and G. Li (Eds.): ATIS 2016, CCIS 651, pp. 106–114, 2016.
DOI: 10.1007/978-981-10-2741-3_9

1.1   Related Schemes and Their Limitations

Legendary public key protocols like Diffie-Hellmann [3] and RSA [9] use a private key-public key pair and are interactive (post deployment). For proper implementations (to avoid active attacks like man-in-the-middle attack), these pairs are certified by trusted certifying agencies; making their implementations costly.

This led to alternate thoughts of identity-based key agreement (IB-KA) conceptualized by Shamir [11] in 1984, though first such efficient scheme was develop in 2000 by Sakai-Ogishi-Kasahara (SOK) [10]. Their non-interactive pairing based scheme is applicable in distributed scenarios but not in hierarchical environments. Horwitz and Lynn [8] proposed the first hierarchical identity-based cryptosystem that supported *only two levels*. Their key agreement uses a pairing-based scheme at the top level and a polynomial-based key distribution scheme (imitating Blom [2]) is placed at second level. Gennaro et al. [5] cleverly reversed the order in [8] in their first of two proposals, while they used subset based key predistribution scheme of Eschenauer and Glogor [4] (instead of [2]) for their second construction. Underlying polynomial or subset based *symmetric* schemes generally brings in additional key sharing complexity and thereby threshold resilience against node compromise. Resultant hierarchical identity-based key agreement protocols suffers from rapidly increasing threshold value and can support small number of level owing to fast diminishing of keyrings per tier. Another problem is that 'intermediate' users may collude to trace shared key(s) of their ancestors.

Guo et al. [7] attempted a HIBKA protocol using bilinear pairing and claimed that their scheme is resilient against corruption of any number of nodes in hierarchy. Unfortunately, Zhu et al. [12] concretely established that Guo et al.'s scheme is vulnerable against corruption of end-users in the hierarchy. This may be a crucial drawback while implementing many such protocols for tactical networks deployable in real life scenarios like military or MANET applications or in an MNC.

There are certain authenticated key exchange (AKE) or agreement (AKA) protocols that authenticate the identities during exchange of session keys. These schemes were consequences of the pioneering work of Bellare and Rogaway [1] who uses pre-shared symmetric secrets to achieve desired purposes.

1.2   Design Goals and Motivation of Our Work

Through the above literature survey of prominent schemes, we identified certain crucial properties that a key agreement schemes (KAS) should have. They are:

- Identity-based (IB) [11]: to avoid (expensive) certification of third parties. Such protocols allow users to compute their secret keys that will be shared with peers using only their own private key and identity of concerned peer.
- Hierarchical (H) structure [5,6]: decentralizes a network and distributes the load of the (root) PKG to lower level PKGs (i.e. lower level parents).

- Inductive: ensures a scheme must be applicable to networks with unrestricted depth. That is, given positive integers m, l, the scheme should permit key agreement between any user at level m and level l.
- Resilient (in a 'strong sense' [5]): in view of limited physical protection of end devices, the scheme should resilient against compromise of [a] threshold of non-ancestral users in upper levels of hierarchy of concerned (key agreeing) nodes; and, [b] any children joining the network;
- pre-deployment (ancestral) interactions (secure and inexpensive): is considered in our work. We achieve (i) a scheme that uses HIBC [6]; and, (ii) an inexpensive secure communication by use of inductively agreed symmetric key. Ideally, any given pair of users should be able to compute their unique shared secret key(s) without interaction among themselves.

We address these concerns through our i-H-IB-KA-pdi protocols. Finally, both our protocols employ bilinear pairing map like Sakai-Ogishi-Kasahara [10]. We recommend use of our hybrid protocol due to fast efficient implementation of underlying symmetric key cryptosystem;[1] thereby our scheme finds wide-spread applicability. Conducting these (fast) communications among ancestors before a child's deployment slightly deteriorates the communication complexity as compared to non-interactive schemes [5,10]. However resilience is much improved.

2   Definitions: I-H-IB-KA-pdi; Related Concepts

This section is adapted from [6] and recalls adequate background for our work.

1. **ID-Tuple:** ID tuple $(Id_{1_i}, Id_{2_i}, \ldots, Id_{l_i}), l \in \mathbb{Z}_+$ of an user A defines its (hierarchical) position. A's ancestors in the hierarchy tree are root PKG and lower-level PKGs whose ID-tuples are $\{(Id_{1_i}, Id_{2_i}, \ldots, Id_{a_i}) : 1 \leq a < l, i \in \mathbb{Z}_+\}$. For convenience, let E_{l_i} denote the ith user at level l. So that ID-tuples of E_{l_i}'s ancestors at any level a $(1 \leq a \leq l-1)$ are $Id_{1_{i_1}}, Id_{2_{i_2}}, \ldots, Id_{a_{i_a}}$.
2. **Hierarchical Identity-Based Key Agreement (HIBKA):** is a specified by four randomized algorithms: *Root Setup, Lower-level Setup, Extraction* and finally, *Key Agreement (KA)* with consistency check(s). Details in Sect. 3.
3. **Admissible Paring map:** For cyclic groups G, G_T of large prime order $p \approx (160 - 300\ BITS)$, a map $e : G \times G \longmapsto G_T$ is a 'pairing admissible' if it is:
   (a) Non-degenerate map: does not send all pairs in $G \times G$ to identity of G_T.
   (b) Computable: There exists an efficient polynomial time algorithm to compute $e(A, B)$ for any $A, B \in G$.
   (c) Bilinear (multiplicatively): $e(A^x, B^y) = e(A, B)^{xy} \forall A, B \in G, x, y \in \mathbb{Z}_p$.
   (d) Symmetric: $e(A, B) = e(B, A) \forall A, B \in G$ follows from cyclic nature of the group G and bilinear property of the map e.

---

[1] Our hybrid proposal is devoid of user authentication that are not necessary for our pairwise communications, though our purely public key protocol involving HIBC [6] assures so.

4. **Hard problem and computational assumption for security proof:**
Our security proofs are based on the following computational assumptions:
   (a) *Bilinear Diffie-Hellman (BDH)*: Given $g^x, g^y, g^z \in G$ for $x, y, z, r \in_{\Re} \mathbb{Z}_p$, computing $e(g,g)^{abc}$ is hard. Here $g \in G$ is a generator, as usual.
   (b) *Decisional Bilinear Diffie-Hellman (DBDH)*: Given $x, y, z, r \in_{\Re} \mathbb{Z}_p$, it is hard to differentiate $(g^x, g^y, g^z, e(g,g)^{xyz})$ and $(g^x, g^y, g^z, e(g,g)^r)$.

3   Our I-H-IB-KA-pdi Protocols

Inner region key agreement of our hierarchical for any level $a, a > 1$ is a direct (inductive) consequence of SOK protocol. However, inter clusters key agreement is still a major challenge which we try to solve with the help these four protocols:

Root Setup: The root PKG:

1. runs $\mathscr{G}$ on input K to generate groups G, G_T of some (large) prime order p and an admissible pairing $e : G \times G \longmapsto G_T$;
2. chooses an arbitrary generator $g \in G$;
3. picks the master secret key (msk) $s \in_{\Re} \mathbb{Z}_p$ and sets $g_0 = g^s$;
4. chooses cryptographic hash functions $H_1 : \{0,1\} \longmapsto G$ and $H_2 : G_T \longmapsto \{0,1\}^n$ for $n \in \mathbb{Z}_+$. Our security analysis treats H_1 and H_2 as random oracles.

The user identity space is $\mathscr{I} = \{0,1\}^*$. The (eventual agreed) key space is $\mathscr{K} = \{0,1\}^n$. For instance, $n = 128$ in case we desire to implement AES-128 with eventual agreed (symmetric) keys. Public parameters of the system are $pp = (G, G_T, e, g, g^s, H_1, H_2)$. The root PKG's msk is $s \in \mathbb{Z}_p$.

Lower-Level Setup: Entity E_i, i.e., i^{th} would be parent at level $l - 1$:

1. randomly picks a secret $s_l \in_{\Re} \mathbb{Z}_p$ meant for HIBC scheme [6].
2. picks additional secrets t^i meant for key agreement of $E_i's$ children with upper level users and $t_i^j (\neq t^i \neq s_l) \in_{\Re} \mathbb{Z}_p, i, j = 1, 2, \ldots r_l, j \neq i$. We assume that a maximum of $r_l (\in \mathbb{Z}_+)$ many children join under each level $l - 1$ user.
3. securely transmits these t_i^j to existing users at level $l - 1$ using (i) existing HIBC [6] setup, or (ii) agreed symmetric key at parental level $l-1$ by the previous step of this inductive setup. We recommend later process due to faster encryption-decryption owing to application of suitable light weight symmetric key. Of course, a fast hybrid (using public and symmetric cryptosystem) key agreement technique evolves, which is a certain novelty;
4. raises g^{t^i}; securely broadcasts them to existing users at level $i (i \leq l - 1)$ to facilitate their *key agreement* with incomers under E_i.
5. calculates $u_{ij} := t_i^j \cdot t_j^i, j \neq i$ for exponentiation; then loads into each child.

Last four steps are supplemented to HIBC's *lower-level setup* in [6] facilitate key agreement in our protocols. Maximum users at level $a := R_a = r_{a-1} R_{a-1}$, $a \in \mathbb{Z}_+$.

Extraction: Let E_{l_i} be an incoming user(incomer) at level l under i^{th} parent E_i, i.e. $E_{i(l-1)}$ of level $l - 1$. We consider ID-tuple of E_{l_i} to be $Id_{1_{i_1}}, Id_{2_{i_2}}, \ldots,$

Id_{l-1_i}, Id_l (refer to Sect. 2). In case of no confusion, simplified notations may be used for an incomer under a fixed parent E_i at level $l-1$. In the footsteps of HIBC [6], set S_0 to be the identity element of G. Then E_{l_i}'s parent (E_i) at level $l-1$:

1. computes $P_{i_l} = H_1(Id_{1_{i_1}}, Id_{2_{i_2}}, \ldots, Id_{l-1_i}, Id_l) \in G$;
2. sets E_{l_i}'s secret point S_l to be $S_{l-1} \cdot P_{i_l}^{s_{l-1}} = \prod_{a=1}^{l} P_{i_a}^{s_{i-1}}$;
3. exponentiates the additional secrets $P_{i_l}^{t^i}, P_{i_l}^{u_{ij}}, j = 1, 2, \ldots, r_{l-1}, j \neq i$;
4. passes down these secret computed in above step to E_{l_i};
5. gives E_{l_i} the values of $Q_a = g^{s_a}$ for $1 \leq a \leq l-1$. In fact, g^{s_a} of existing user must be provided to E_{l_i} to facilitate key agreement with them. Case 3 of *Key Agreement* protocol (below) exploits these preloaded g^{s_a} to compute eventual shared keys of E_{l_i} and concerned existing user.

Key Agreement: Algorithm consists of three sub-algorithms for distinct cases:

case 1 *both the incomers are under the* same *parent*: This case is similar to the SOK scenario with each level $l-1$ parent playing the role of (lower level) PKG. User E_{l_i} computes $e(P_{i_l}^{s_l}, P_{j_l})$ and user $E_{j_l} = e(P_{i_l}, P_{j_l}^{s_l})$ The agreed key between incomers E_{l_i} and $E_{j_l} = e(P_{i_l}, P_{j_l})^{s_l}$ which shows the correctness.[2]

case 2 *concerned pair of incomers are under the* different *parents*: key agreement in this case is a major outcome of our proposal. Elegant use of our pre-deployment secure communications yield shared secrets (symmetric information u_{ij}). These are exponentiated ($P_{i_l}^{u_{ij}}$) and passed down for computing:
   - $e(P_{i_l}^{u_{ij}}, P_{j_l})$ by an incomer E_{l_i} at level l under i^{th} parent E_i of level $l-1$.
   - $e(P_{j_l}^{u_{ji}}, P_{i_l})$ by another level l incomer E_{j_l} under j^{th} parent E_j.
   - *correctness*: $e(P_{i_l}^{u_{ij}}, P_{j_l}) = e(P_{i_l}, P_{j_l})^{u_{ij}} = e(P_{j_l}^{u_{ji}}, P_{i_l})$ $\because u_{ij} = u_{ji}$.

case 3 *one entity is an existing user and the other an incomer* E_{l_i} *at level* l:
   - the incomer E_{l_i} calculates $e(P_{i_l}^{t^i}, g^{s_a})$ (since it possesses both t^i, g^{s_a}).
   - existing user at level a, $(a \leq l-1)$ similarly calculates $e(P_{i_l}, (g^{t^i})^{s_a})$.
   - *correctness*: $e(P_{i_l}^{t^i}, g^{s_a}) = e(P_{i_l}, g)^{s_a t^i} = e(P_{i_l}, (g^{t^i})^{s_a})$ (tautology).

Remark 1 (Limitation of our HIBKA scheme). Every intermediate users between an incomer at level l and an existing user get to see secrets $g^{s_a}, a < l-1$ meant for key exchange. This implies that they can compute $e(P_{i_l}^{t^i}, g^{s_a})$ in a fashion similar to all its children. Thus the key constructed in case 3 of our *Key Agreement* protocol is known to all intermediate users. This is a potential weakness of our scheme. Of course, level $l-1$ parent E_i of any incomers can compute all keys of its children. However, such scenarios are similar to all prominent schemes like [5,7,10,12] and is useful in assuring escrow, non-repudiation, etc.

---

[2] Replacing s_l by t_i^i makes this case intuitively a special case ($t_j^i = t_i^j$) of our HIBKA proposal. This owes to the fact $s_l, t_i^i \in_{\Re} \mathbb{Z}_p$ are distributed uniformly; special case when $j = i$.

4   Security of Our Scheme

An adversary in our models like most is assumed to be a probabilistic polynomial-time algorithm and controls the communication between each pair of parties. Moreover, the adversary can mount several attacks on communicating parties that include revealing session keys, corrupting a party, etc. After an adversary finishes initial round of queries (i.e. various attacks), a "TEST" query (attack) is send by the adversary on identities of a pair of parties whose keys are being agreed upon. The two parties specified in the "TEST" query are referred to as the target parties. There are certain restriction on this "TEST" query, viz:

1. an adversary cannot mount "TEST" attack on concerned incomers whose keys are being established and their respective parents.
2. an adversary obviously should not mount an attack on a corrupted party.

A challenger $\mathscr{B}$ who controls $BDDH$ parameters responds to this "TEST" query by sending either:

- the secret keyring of the party on which the "TEST" query is made; or
- random strings of same length as any keyring.

The value returned to the adversary has equal probability (1/2) and is called target key. Idea is that an adversary must not be able to distinguish between the above two cases with non-negligible advantage. We formally state and prove our security result based on BDDH problem stated in Sect. 2.

Theorem 1. *Consider G; G_T and e to be two groups of order p and a bilinear pairing that satisfy the BDDH assumption. We model our hash function H_1 as a random oracle. Then our schemes guarantee secure key agreement of:*

- *two incomers at any level against an adversary who can compromise all but these two users and their parents;*
- *an incomer and an existing user against an adversary who can compromise all incomer user other than this one.[3]*

Proof. We prove this result by a reduction from security of our scheme to $BDDH$ assumption. We construct a challenger (algorithm) $\mathscr{B}$ using an adversary $\mathscr{A}$ that can break our scheme with a non-negligible probability. This leads to a contradiction that our challenger can solve an instance of $BDDH$ problem with essentially the same non-negligible advantage. Given an instance of the $BDDH$ problem:p; k; G; G_T; e; g; g^a; g^b; g^c; D; R, where e is a bilinear pairing $e : G \times G \mapsto G_T$, and $D = e(g, g)^{abc}, R = e(g, g)^r$, $\mathscr{B}$'s task is to decide which one among (g, g^a, g^b, g^c, D) and (P, g^a, g^b, g^c, R) is a $BDDH$ tuple. Our challenger $\mathscr{B}$ embeds $BDDH$ input a, b into hash queries and c into "TEST" query issued

---

[3] We shall extend our schemes to be secure against more powerful adversary who can compromise threshold of existing users in extended version of this work.

by $\mathscr{A}$.[4] Setup algorithm and responses to hash, id. compromise and "TEST" queries are below:

Setup algorithm is simulated by challenger $\mathscr{B}$ as follows:

- $\mathscr{B}$ fixes system's public parameters, viz. generator of the group $G(g)$ and the hash function H_1 which is treated as a random oracle controlled by $\mathscr{B}$.
- $\mathscr{B}$ sends the system parameters to adversary $\mathscr{A}$.

Hash queries are smartly used to embed a, b. Challenger $\mathscr{B}$ answers these queries to our adversary $\mathscr{A}$ in arbitrary order as described below:

$H_1(ID_i)$ queries: Challenger $\mathscr{B}$ maintains an initial empty list H_1^{list} with entries of the form (ID_i, h_i). When the oracle H_1 is queried at ID_i by the adversary $\mathscr{A}$, challenger $\mathscr{B}$ responds to this query as follows:

- $\mathscr{B}$ responds with responds with $H_1(ID_i) = h_i$ in case ID_i already appears on the H_1^{list} as the a tuple (ID_i, h_i);
- when ID_i is identity of the parent of first target incomer, $\mathscr{B}$ stores (ID_i, g^a) into the tuple list; responds with $H_1(ID_i) = g^a$;
- there are two cases while embedding b and responding with g^b:
  - first, in case of key agreement between two incomers. Let ID_j be the identity of the parent of second target incomer. Our challenger $\mathscr{B}$ stores (ID_j, g^b) into the tuple list and responds with $H_1(ID_j) = g^b$;
  - second case: for key agreement involving an existing user, ID_j, we consider the same identity ID_j as $c = s_a$ is generates by it. Therefore our challenger $\mathscr{B}$ stores (ID_j, g^b) into the tuple list; responds with $H_1(ID_j) = g^b$;
- or else, our challenger $\mathscr{B}$ randomly selects $r_i \in \mathbb{Z}_p^*$, computes $H_1(ID_i) = h_i = g^{r_i}$, inserts (ID_i, h_i) into the tuple list and responds with $H_1(ID_i) = h_i$.

Compromise identity (ID_s) queries: Challenger $\mathscr{B}$ responds to *identity compromise queries* mounted by our adversary $\mathscr{A}$ in the following manner:

- in case queried on identity of the parent of any target user or is either of the target node, $\mathscr{B}$ aborts the game. This case concerns only parents of key agreeing parties or themselves. Therefore probability of occurrence of such queries (events) is negligible (analysis to be presented in extended version).
- Otherwise, all secret held by user i are returned by $\mathscr{B}$ to $\mathscr{A}$.

A "TEST" query is mounted by an adversary after compromise queries. The game between an adversary and the challenger is as below:

TEST query: Our adversary $\mathscr{A}$ zooms on two identities with restrictions mentioned above and is responded by our challenger $\mathscr{B}$ with a value D as follows:

- $\mathscr{B}$ chooses a bit $b \in \{0, 1\}$ at random;
- if $b = 1$, the real secret key D shared between these two identities is returned; $\mathscr{B}$ computes $D = e(H_1(ID^1), H_1(ID^2))^c$

---

[4] The idea is to embed the secrets c as u_{ij} for the former cases (2) and s_a for the later case (3). The secret key c is unknown to the simulator $\mathscr{B}$.

– otherwise $\mathscr{B}$ returns a randomly sampled value $R = e(H_1(ID^1), H_1(ID^2))^{r_x}$
for identity ID_x generated according to the distribution of the secret key.

Of course $D = e(H_1(ID^1), H_1(ID^2))^c = e(g^a, g^b)^c = e(g, g)^{abc}$ where ID^1, ID^2 are first and second users. Challenger's simulation yields $e(H_1(ID^1)) = g^a$ and $e(H_1(ID^2)) = g^b$, so that the response $D = e(g, g)^{abc} = e(H_1(ID^1), H_1(ID^2))^c$ is the correct key. We find that our challenger $\mathscr{B}$ is able to respond satisfactorily to all simulation queries. So we conclude that this run of $\mathscr{A}$ under $\mathscr{B}$ is identical to its view in a real run against our scheme.

The "TEST" query may be followed by second round compromise queries. After $\mathscr{A}$ finishes the queries, it returns its challenge b' as his/her guess of b. $\mathscr{B}$ outputs this same bit b' as its guess to $BDDH$ problem. We observe that since parent of two identities cannot be queried upon, so challenger $\mathscr{B}$ always responds with r_i in the hash queries; thereby resulting in random keys. This proves the theorem assuring security of our schemes under the restrictions mentioned.

5   Comparison

We present a comparative study of our protocols in terms of security and complexity efficiencies. First we present a comparison among themselves and then, due to page limits, with only prominent works [1, 3–5, 7–10, 12]. A more comprehensive analytical study will be presented in an extended version our work.

Both our protocols uses identity based key exchange like of SOK [10] and pre-deployment interaction. Interactions in our purely public key agreement protocol uses HIBC [6], whereas our hybrid protocol uses inductively derived symmetric keys for pre-deployment encryption decryption. Consequently later protocol has faster implementations than purely public key agreement protocol like ours (previous) and exiting works in identity based key agreement [5, 7, 8, 10, 12]. Moreover, existing protocols either uses purely public key or purely symmetric key techniques–but not an hybrid of both. This is a specialty of our hybrid proposal.

Bellare and Rogaway [1] uses pre-shared symmetric secrets to derive successive session keys and authenticate devices. Our mission is different–we try to establish secret symmetric secrets or keys. In some sense, the eventual share keys resulting out of our schemes can be taken as the pre-shared secret that can be used for their scheme [1]. Moreover, our hybrid design uses these secrets inductively thereby having similar one-time use as [1]; but not successive use.

Use of identity based cryptography [10, 11] in our protocols bypasses the costly requirement of certifications which was prevalent in public key infrastructure schemes that follow footsteps of [3, 9]. This certainly reduces trust on third parties and thereby enhances *security efficiency* of our protocols. Moreover, our schemes involve only pre-deployment secure communication and not post deployment. Most of such computations can be done off-line as opposed to critical on-line computations in (post deployment) interactive schemes based on [3, 9]. Therefore, our protocols outperform such schemes in terms of *complexity efficiency*.

A specialty of our construction is inductive increment in depth of hierarchy. Prominent identity based schemes like Gennaro et al. [5] fail to assure this property. There are attempts in this directions [7] that have been proved futile by [12].

6 Conclusion and Future Prospects of Our Work

Our protocols achieve most design goals described in Sect. 1.2. Clever inductive use of symmetric keys during encryption of randomly generated secrets (t_j^i, t_i^j) after first round using public keys (HIBC [6]) makes our hybrid scheme highly efficient. This paper primarily presents theoretical aspects with some lights on implementation. Further work needs to be done to implement of our protocols. We plan to extend our schemes in future work to secure a hierarchical network under compromise of threshold number of users at ancestral level.

References

1. Bellare, M., Rogaway, P.: Entity authentication and key distribution. In: Stinson, D.R. (ed.) CRYPTO 1993. LNCS, vol. 773, pp. 232–249. Springer, Heidelberg (1994). doi:10.1007/3-540-48329-2_21
2. Blom, R.: An optimal class of symmetric key generation systems. In: Beth, T., Cot, N., Ingemarsson, I. (eds.) EUROCRYPT 1984. LNCS, vol. 209, pp. 335–338. Springer, Heidelberg (1985). doi:10.1007/3-540-39757-4_22
3. Diffie, W., Hellman, M.E.: New directions in cryptography. IEEE Trans. Inf. Theory **22**(6), 644–654 (1976)
4. Eschenauer, L., Gligor, V.D.: A key-management scheme for distributed sensor networks. In: Proceedings of the 9th ACM Conference on Computer and Communications Security, CCS 2002, Washington, DC, USA, 18–22 November 2002, pp. 41–47 (2002)
5. Gennaro, R., Halevi, S., Krawczyk, H., Rabin, T., Reidt, S., Wolthusen, S.D.: Strongly-resilient and non-interactive hierarchical key-agreement in MANETs. In: Jajodia, S., Lopez, J. (eds.) ESORICS 2008. LNCS, vol. 5283, pp. 49–65. Springer, Heidelberg (2008). doi:10.1007/978-3-540-88313-5_4
6. Gentry, C., Silverberg, A.: Hierarchical ID-based cryptography. In: Zheng, Y. (ed.) ASIACRYPT 2002. LNCS, vol. 2501, pp. 548–566. Springer, Heidelberg (2002). doi:10.1007/3-540-36178-2_34
7. Guo, H., Mu, Y., Li, Z., Zhang, X.: An efficient and non-interactive hierarchical key agreement protocol. Comput. Secur. **30**(1), 28–34 (2011)
8. Horwitz, J., Lynn, B.: Toward hierarchical identity-based encryption. In: Knudsen, L.R. (ed.) EUROCRYPT 2002. LNCS, vol. 2332, pp. 466–481. Springer, Heidelberg (2002). doi:10.1007/3-540-46035-7_31
9. Rivest, R.L., Shamir, A., Adleman, L.M.: A method for obtaining digital signatures and public-key cryptosystems. Commun. ACM **21**(2), 120–126 (1978)
10. Sakai, R., Ohgishi, K., Kasahara, M.: Cryptosystems based on pairing. In: Symposium on Cryptography and Information Security SCIS (2000)
11. Shamir, A.: Identity-based cryptosystems and signature schemes. In: Blakley, G.R., Chaum, D. (eds.) CRYPTO 1984. LNCS, vol. 196, pp. 47–53. Springer, Heidelberg (1985). doi:10.1007/3-540-39568-7_5
12. Zhu, G., Xiong, H., Qin, Z.: On the security of an efficient and non-interactive hierarchical key agreement protocol. Wireless Pers. Commun. **74**(2), 883–889 (2014)

Data Privacy

Identity-Based Threshold Encryption on Lattices with Application to Searchable Encryption

Veronika Kuchta[✉] and Olivier Markowitch

Département d'Informatique, Université Libre de Bruxelles, Brussels, Belgium
{veronika.kuchta,olivier.markowitch}@ulb.ac.be

Abstract. As more Internet users are getting interested in using cloud services for storing sensitive data, it motivates the user to encrypt the private data before uploading it to the cloud. There are services which allow an user to conduct searches without revealing anything about the encrypted data. This service is provided by public key encryption with keyword search. Our main contributions is the construction of a lattice-based identity-based threshold decryption (IBTD) that is anonymous and indistinguishable against chosen ciphertext attacks. Furthermore, using the transformation technique from Abdalla et al. [CRYPTO'05] we present the application of our IBTD scheme which can be transformed to a distributed public key encryption with keyword search. The distributed setting allows to split the role of one server into multiple servers in order to distribute the single point of failure. Our construction uses the particularly efficient mathematical construct, called lattices that make our scheme resistant against quantum attacks. We give an efficient construction of a lattice-based IBTD scheme and prove it secure under the hardness of learning with errors (LWE) problem.

1 Introduction

Cloud Computing. Since its invention, cloud computing became an important application for the recent cryptographic community which works on the newest security challenges and provides crucial security protocols for the nowadays common cloud services. Storing data in a cloud system enables users to reduce purchase and maintaining cost of computing and storage tools. These services attract a huge attention from Internet users. When personal and confidential data is outsourced to a cloud server, the customers are especially concerned about privacy and confidentiality of their data. They interested in certain services which guarantee their data will not be watched or accessed by anybody. There are distinct cloud scenarios where cloud service users might be interested in uploading some certain and specific data files, without retrieving the complete data stored in the cloud. In order to provide efficient tasks for aforementioned cloud services, cryptographers develop several protocols we recall in the following paragraphs. Since our main contribution is based on the well-known mathematical construct – lattices – we provide first an overview of lattice-based cryptoschemes and of their significant role in current cryptographic challenges.

© Springer Nature Singapore Pte Ltd. 2016
L. Batten and G. Li (Eds.): ATIS 2016, CCIS 651, pp. 117–129, 2016.
DOI: 10.1007/978-981-10-2741-3_10

Lattice-Based Cryptosystems. Lattice-Based Cryptography represents another topic which attracts a lot of interests from researchers. Cryptographic schemes based on lattices have especially attractive features as stated in [23]. The best attacks of lattice-based schemes require exponential time in security parameter, even for a quantum adversary, where the classic factoring-based cryptographic schemes can be broken in subexponential time or even in polynomial time using quantum algorithms. In contrast to the latter, lattice-based schemes are especially efficient and simple in their implementation. Lattices were introduced to cryptography by Ajtai [5] and became a valuable tool for quantum-resistant cryptography. A deep research has been made in this field: [17,24,27]. Recently, many lattice-based applications have been provided, such as identity-based encryption schemes [3,14,17], public-key encryption [6,25,26], signatures [12,22], attribute-based encryption [13], public-key encryption with keyword search [20]. Miccianchio and Peikert [23] introduced new methods for trapdoor generation which make the constructions simple, efficient and easy in the implementation. We will use their technique in the construction of our scheme.

Identity-Based Threshold Decryption on Lattices. Identity-based encryption scheme represents a useful access control and provides data security in various crucial applications, such as cloud data storage. There is already a construction of an identity-based threshold decryption scheme introduced by Baek and Zheng [7] which is based on a number-theoretic problem and is secure against chosen-plaintext attacks. Later Boneh et al. [9] presented a chosen-ciphertext secure threshold encryption and a threshold version of an IBE scheme due to Boneh and Boyen [8], which is also based on a number-theoretic problem. The first lattice-based identity-based threshold encryption has been presented recently by Singh et al. [28] and was proved indistinguishable against chosen-plaintext attacks. In our work we present the first identity-based threshold decryption scheme which is based on lattices and is secure against chosen-ciphertext attacks. In contrast to [28] we treat the validity checking process for decryption shares implicitly as part of the decryption algorithm Decrypt, whereas in [28] this property was outsourced into a separate verification algorithm, aiming at public verifiability of individual decryption shares. In contrast to the so far known single server IBE schemes [3,4,14], we use in our scheme the more efficient trapdoors, introduced by Micciancio and Peikert [23], which contribute to the secret key generation process. As additional advantage of our scheme in comparison with [28], our security definitions cover anonymity property and robustness which are useful for our application to the searchable encryption as explained below.

Searchable Encryption. With the recent development of cloud storage services, cryptographic encryption became a crucial tool which guarantees that the outsourced data remains encrypted and private such that only those users, who possess valid decryption key are able to retrieve data from the cloud. Boneh et al. [10] introduced the first searchable public key encryption, which provides an important tool for applications in cloud data storage systems.

Many further systems supporting keyword search have been developed to enable users to conduct a search over encrypted data without leaking any information about the encrypted content, distinguished between symmetric encryption [15,18,29]) and public-key encryption (e.g., [10,11,19]) techniques. Searchable encryption applied to the cloud setting allows an user to upload encrypted data together with encrypted keywords for this data and later to conduct a search using special trapdoors for the required keywords.

Our Contribution and Application. Before we can present the crucial application to DPEKS scheme, we begin with introduction of identity-based threshold decryption on lattices and prove its security properties, indistinguishability, anonymity and robustness against chosen ciphertext attacks. Using our IBTD scheme, we construct a DPEKS scheme analogously to the construction of Abdalla et al. [1]. Thus, our scheme is as so-far known the first public-key encryption with keyword search based on lattices, where the role of a cloud server executing the keyword related search operation is distributed among a multiple set of servers. The distributed setting enables to share the only one point of failure of single server constructions among multiple parties, where at least a threshold of all parties is required to collectively complete the search operation. Our presented DPEKS scheme involves different parties. Data owners outsource their encrypted data together with encrypted keywords, called PEKS-ciphertext to the cloud servers. We note that each server stores the same amount of data files. There is a user who generates trapdoor shares on a keyword w which are sent to the N different servers. Upon receiving the search request consisting of trapdoor shares, each server performs the appropriate keyword search using its trapdoor share and outputs test shares to the user. If the user receives at least t-out-of-N valid test shares, she is valid to complete the test operation combining the shares and receiving a positive output 1. The user sends a download request to one of the N server and receives encrypted data. In order to decrypt the documents, she applies decryption algorithm of the underlying encryption scheme.

2   Preliminaries

In this section we recall the main definitions which are significant to our contribution. We shortly review lattices and recall the new trapdoor generation algorithm which was introduced by Micciancio and Peikert [23] ant whose usage allows a more efficient constructions.

Lattices. Let $B = \{b_1, \ldots, b_n\} \subset \mathbb{R}^n$ be a basis of a lattice L which consists of n linearly independent vectors. The $n-$dimensional lattice L is then defined as $L = \sum_{i=1}^{n} \mathbb{Z}b_i$. The i-th minimum of lattice Λ, denoted by $\lambda_i(L)$ is the smallest radius r such that L contains i linearly independent vectors of norms $\leq r$. The norm of vector b_i is defined as $\|b_i\| = \sqrt{\sum_{j=1}^{n} c_{i,j}^2}$, where $c_{i,j}, j \in \{1, \ldots, n\}$ are coefficients of vector b_i. We denote by $\lambda_1^\infty(L)$ the minimum distance measured in the infinity norm, which is defined as $\|b_i\|_\infty := \max(|c_{i,1}|, \ldots, |c_{i,n}|)$. Additionally we recall $\|B\| = \max \|b_i\|$.

Learning With Errors (LWE). The LWE problem, first introduced by Regev [26], relies on the Gaussian error distribution χ, which is given as $\chi = D_{\mathbb{Z},s}$ over integers. The LWE problem instance consists of access to a challenge oracle $\mathcal{O}$, which is either a purely random sampler $\mathcal{O}_r$ or a noisy pseudo-random sampler $\mathcal{O}_s$, with some random secret key $s \in \mathbb{Z}_q^s$. For positive integers n and $q \geq 2$, a vector $s \in \mathbb{Z}_q^n$ and error term $e \leftarrow \chi$, the LWE distribution $A_{s,\chi}$ is sampled over $\mathbb{Z}_q^n \times \mathbb{Z}_q$. Chosen a vector $a \in \mathbb{Z}_q^n$ uniformly at random, it outputs: $(a, t = \langle a, s \rangle + e \mod q) \in \mathbb{Z}_q^n \times \mathbb{Z}_q$. A more detailed description of χ can be found in [26]. The sampling oracles work in the following way:

$\mathcal{O}_s$: outputs samples of the form $(a, t) = (a, as + e) \in \mathbb{Z}_q^n \times \mathbb{Z}_q$, where $s \in \mathbb{Z}_q^n$ is uniformly distributed value across all invocations and $e \in \mathbb{Z}_q$ is a fresh sample from χ.

$\mathcal{O}_r$: outputs truly random samples from $\mathbb{Z}_q^n \times \mathbb{Z}_q$.

Definition 1 (LWE-Problem). *For an integer q, error distribution χ, the goal of $LWE_{q,\chi}$ in n dimensions is to find $s \in \mathbb{Z}_q^n$ with overwhelming probability, given access to any arbitrary $poly(n)$ number of samples from $A_{s,\chi}$ for random s.*

Trapdoor Generation. Micciancio and Peikert [23] defined the new notion or trapdoor and the new method of trapdoor generation, which is simple, efficient and easy to implement. The main results of [23] are formulated in the following theorem:

Definition 2 (TrapGen Algorithm:). *The efficient trapdoor generation algorithm TrapGen proposed in [23] uses a matrix $G \in \mathbb{Z}_q^{n \times w}$ that admits efficient inversion and preimage sampling algorithms. We recall this algorithm in the following algorithm:*

Input: *A matrix $\bar{A} \in \mathbb{Z}_q^{n \times \bar{m}}$ for some $\bar{m} \geq 1$, invertible matrix $H \in \mathbb{Z}_q^{n \times n}$, and a distribution $\mathcal{D}$ over $\mathbb{Z}_q^{\bar{m} \times w}$. (If no particular $\bar{A}, H$ are given as input, then the algorithm may choose them itself, i.e. $\bar{A} \xleftarrow{r} \mathbb{Z}_q^{n \times \bar{m}}$ and $H = I$.*

Output: *A parity-check matrix $A = [\bar{A}|A_1] \in \mathbb{Z}_q^{n \times m}$, where $m = \bar{m} + w$ and trapdoor R with tag H by following steps: (1) Choose $R \xleftarrow{r} \mathbb{Z}_q^{\bar{m} \times w}$ from distribution $\mathcal{D}$. (2) Output $A = [\bar{A}|HG - \bar{A}R] \in \mathbb{Z}_q^{n \times m}$ and trapdoor R.*

Definition 3 (Invert Algorithm:). *For our construction we need to learn how to use the trapdoor from above to solve LWE problem relative to A. As before, we recall the inversion algorithm [23] Invert, which on a given trapdoor R for $A \in \mathbb{Z}_q^{n \times m}$ and an LWE instance $t^t = s^t A + e^t \mod q$ for a short error vector $e \in \mathbb{Z}^m$, recovers s and e.*

Input: *An oracle $\mathcal{O}$ for inverting $g_G(\hat{s}, \hat{e})$ when $\hat{e} \in \mathbb{Z}^w$ is suitably small.*
(1) parity-check matrix $A \in \mathbb{Z}_q^{n \times m}$, (2) G-trapdoor $R \in \mathbb{Z}_q^{\bar{m} \times kn}$ for A with invertible tag $H \in \mathbb{Z}_q^{n \times n}$, (3) $t^t = g_A(s, e) = s^t A + e^t$ for any $s \in \mathbb{Z}_q^n$ and suitably small $e \in \mathbb{Z}^m$.

Output: *The vectors s and e doing the following: (1) Compute $\hat{t}^t = t^t \begin{bmatrix} R \\ I \end{bmatrix}$.*

(2) Get $(\hat{s}, \hat{e}) \leftarrow \mathcal{O}(\hat{t})$. (3) Return $s = H^{-t}\hat{s}$ and $e = t - A^t s$.

3   Identity-Based Threshold Decryption on Lattices

Intuition. In this paragraph we define an identity-based threshold decryption (IBTD) scheme on lattices. Our construction profits from its resistance against quantum attacks while the so far known threshold IBE schemes [7,8,21] are all based on a number theoretical problem. An IBTD scheme consists of the following five algorithms: Setup, KeyDistr, Encrypt, ShareDecrypt, Decrypt. The Setup algorithm generates master public key mpk and master secret key msk. The KeyDistr algorithm takes as input the master secret key and an identity id, extracts the identity-related secret key sk_{id} and distributes it among N servers by computing corresponding secret shares $sk_{id,i}$. The Encrypt algorithm encrypts a message m for a given idenitity id and a public key and outputs a ciphertext C. The ShareDecrypt algorithm computes decryption shares δ_i of a ciphertext using the corresponding secret shares $sk_{id,i}$ of each server $i \in [N]$. The Decrypt algorithm takes t-out-of-N decryption shares and C to compute the message m.

In the following Definition 4 we formalize the IBTD syntax. The syntax of our scheme differs from the already existing ones [7,8] by the role of the decryption algorithm Decrypt, which first includes the validity checking process for decryption shares in contrast to the aforementioned schemes where this property was performed by a separate verification algorithm.

Definition 4 (Identity-Based Threshold Decryption (IBTD)). *An IBTD scheme consists of the following five algorithms:*

Setup$(N, t, 1^\lambda)$: *On input the number of decryption servers N, a threshold parameter t, $(1 \leq t \leq N)$ and a security parameter 1^λ, it outputs a master public key mpk and a master secret key msk.*

KeyDistr(mpk, msk, id, t, N): *On input master keys mpk, msk, identity id, and threshold parameters t, N, it computes secret key sk_{id} on the identity id and its secret shares $\{(i, sk_{id,i})\}_{i \in [N]}$ for servers S_i, where $i \in \{1, \ldots, N\}$.*

Encrypt(mpk, id, m): *On input mpk, an identity id and a message m it outputs a ciphertext C.*

ShareDecrypt$(mpk, (i, sk_{id,i}), C)$: *On input a master public key mpk, secret shares (i, sk_{id_i}) for servers $1 \leq i \leq n$ and ciphertext C, it outputs decryption shares δ_i for $1 \leq i \leq n$.*

Decrypt$(mpk, \{\delta_i\}_{i \in \Omega}, C)$: *On input a master public key mpk, a set of decryption shares $\{\delta_i\}_{i \in \Omega}$, where $|\Omega| \geq t$ and a ciphertext C, it combines t-out-of-n decryption shares to a secret key sk_{id} and computes the decryption of m under sk_{id}, it outputs a message m, or 0.*

In the following game we define IBTD security which combines two properties - *indistinguishability* and *anonymity* against chosen ciphertext attacks.

Security Game: Indistinguishability and Anonymity. The security model of our construction guarantees *indistinguishability* of ciphertexts and recipient *anonymity* against chosen ciphertext attacks. Similar to the security game in (Gentry [16]) we present the chosen ciphertext security via the following game.

Init: The adversary $\mathcal{A}$ chooses a set I of $t-1$ decryptions servers that it wants to corrupt. Let $I = \{i_1, \ldots, i_{t-1}\} \subset \{1, \ldots, N\}$, where N is the number of all involved servers. It outputs a target identity id^*.

Setup: The challenger runs $\mathtt{Setup}(1^\lambda)$ and gives the master public key mpk to the adversary. It keeps the master secret key to itself.

Queries to $\mathcal{O}\mathtt{KeyDistr}(id, i)$: Let **List** be a list containing entries (id, S), where $S := \{(1, sk_{id,1}), \ldots, (N, sk_{id,N})\}$. The challenger checks first if $(id, \cdot) \in$ **List**. If so it returns the corresponding $(i, sk_{id,i})$ to the adversary. Otherwise the challenger responds by running $\mathtt{KeyDistr}$ on id and the index of required secret share i and sends $(i, sk_{id,i})$ to the adversary. We allow an adversary to make adaptive queries, that means, she may issue a query on q_i with knowledge of $q_1, \ldots, q_{i-1}$, but with the only constraint, that $id \neq id^*$.

Queries to $\mathcal{O}\mathtt{Decrypt}(id, C)$: The challenger checks if $(id, \cdot) \in$ **List**. If so, takes t-out-of-N secret key shares and computes $\delta_i \leftarrow \mathtt{ShareDecrypt}(mpk, sk_{id,i}, C)$ for all $i \in [t]$. Taking the t decryption shares it runs $\mathtt{Decrypt}(mpk, \{\delta_i\}_{i \in \Omega}, C)$ and returns either m or 0. If $(id, \cdot) \notin$ **List**, runs $\mathtt{KeyDistr}(mpk, msk, id, t, N)$ to obtain $S :=$ $\{(1, sk_{id,1}), \ldots, (N, sk_{id,N})\}$, takes t-out-of-N secret key shares and runs $\mathtt{ShareDecrypt}(mpk, sk_{id,i}, C)$ to obtain decryption shares $\delta_1, \ldots, \delta_t$. On input these decryption shares and a ciphertext C, runs $\mathtt{Decrypt}$. The challenger sends the result of decryption to $\mathcal{A}$.

Challenge: The adversary outputs identities id_0, id_1 and messages m_0, m_1 on which it wants to be challenged. The challenger picks bits $b, \beta \in \{0, 1\}$ and computes ciphertext $C \leftarrow \mathtt{Encrypt}(mpk, id_b, m_\beta)$. The challenger sends C^* as the challenge to $\mathcal{A}$.

Guess: The adversary outputs a guess $b', \beta' \in \{0, 1\}$. It wins the game if $b = b', \beta = \beta'$.

$\mathcal{A}$'s advantage is given by $\mathbf{Adv}_{\mathcal{A}}^{\mathtt{sIND/ANO-IDTB-CCA}}(\lambda) = |Pr[b = b' \wedge \beta = \beta'] - 1/4|$.

Robustness of an Anonymous IBTD. Abdalla et al. [2] defined robustness of an anonymous encryption. This property describes difficulty to generate a ciphertext which would be valid under two different encryption keys. The authors [2] claimed that an anonymous encryption scheme without robustness would have shortcomings in communication correctness. We describe robustness of IBTD as follows: A sender sends a message to a particular receiver. To hide the receiver's identity, sender anonymously encrypts it using receiver's public key. We can imagine that a sender would like to broadcast the ciphertext to a larger group distinct receivers. As a member of this group each receiver needs to know whether she is the real receiver or not. Since the encryption is anonymous it is impossible to decide just by looking at it. However if the encryption is robust, the decryption procedure allows to decide whether the receiver is the correct one or not. Robustness, denoted by IBTD−ROB−CCA can be achieved by including the encryption key to the ciphertext and checking for this key during the decryption process. In the robustness experiment, the adversary outputs a pair id_0, id_1 and a ciphertext C^*. Adversary wins the game if decryption of C^* using secret keys sk_{id_0}, sk_{id_1} are both non-$\perp$. For more details we refer to Abdalla et al. [2]. In the following definition we formalize IBTD robustness, meaning that the decryption algorithm will output $\perp$ with overwhelming probability if an IBTD ciphertext computed for some id is decrypted using $sk_{id'}$ for $id' \neq id$.

Security Game: Robustness Let $\mathcal{A}_{rob}$ be a probabilistic polynomial-time adversary against the IBTD−ROB−CCA security of the IBTD scheme.

Init: The adversary chooses a set I of $t-1$ decryptions servers that it wants to corrupt. Let **List** be a list comprising (id, S_{id}, I), where $S_{id} := \{(1, sk_{id,1}), \ldots, (N, sk_{id,N})\}$ and $(i, sk_{id,i}) \leftarrow$ KeyDistr(mpk, msk, id, t, N). Initially the list is empty, i.e. **List** $:= \emptyset$, $I = \emptyset$. It outputs a target identity id^*.

Setup: The challenger runs Setup$(1^n, N, t)$, and outputs a master public key mpk and a master secret key msk.

Queries to $\mathcal{O}$KeyDistr(id, i): On input (id, i) check whether $(id, S_{id}, I) \notin$ **List**. If so, run $S_{id} \overset{r}{\leftarrow}$ KeyDistr(mpk, msk, id, t, N), where $S_{id} := \{(1, sk_{id,1}), \ldots, (N, sk_{id,N})\}$, $I \subset [1, N]$. Add (id, S_{id}, I) to **List**, i to I, return $(i, sk_{id,i})$.

Queries to $\mathcal{O}$Decrypt(id, C): On input (id, C) check whether $(id, S_{id}, I) \notin$ **List**. If so, run $S_{id} \overset{r}{\leftarrow}$ KeyDistr(mpk, msk, id, t, N), add (id, S_{id}, I) to **List**. Finally computes decryption shares $\delta_i \overset{r}{\leftarrow}$ ShareDecrypt$(mpk, sk_{id,i}, C)$, $i \in [N]$, $m \leftarrow$ Decrypt$(mpk, \{\delta_i\}_{i \in \Omega}, C)$, where $|\Omega| \geq t$. Output m.

Challenge: $\mathcal{A}_{rob}$ outputs (id_0, id_1, C^*). The challenger takes a master public key mpk and computes ciphertext $C \leftarrow$ Encrypt(mpk, id, m). $\mathcal{A}_{rob}$ outputs id_0, id_1 and a ciphertext C^* on challenge id^*.

Output: (i) If $id_0 = id_1$, challenger returns 0.
(ii) If $(id_0, S_0, I_0) \notin$ **List** or $(id_1, S_1, I_1) \notin$ **List**, it return 0.
(iii) If $|I_0| \geq t$ or $|I_1| \geq t$, then return 0, else compute decryption shares $\delta_{0,i} \overset{r}{\leftarrow}$ ShareDecrypt$(mpk, sk_{id_0,i}, C)$; $m_0 \overset{r}{\leftarrow}$ Decrypt$(mpk, \{\delta_{0,i}\}_{i \in \Omega}, C)$, $\delta_{1,i} \overset{r}{\leftarrow}$ ShareDecrypt$(mpk, sk_{id_1,i}, C)$; $m_1 \overset{r}{\leftarrow}$ Decrypt$(mpk, \{\delta_{1,i}\}_{i \in \Omega}, C)$. If $m_0 \neq \perp$ and $m_1 \neq \perp$ return 1.

An IBTD scheme is robust if $\mathbf{Adv}_{IBTD, \mathcal{A}_{rob}}^{IBTD-ROB-CCA}(1^\lambda)$ is negligible.

3.1 Construction

We present a construction of an identity-based threshold decryption based on lattices. We use the efficient trapdoor generation algorithm proposed in [23].

Setup$(1^\lambda, N, t)$: On input security parameter 1^λ it outputs a master public key $mpk = (A, u) \in \mathbb{Z}_q^{n \times m} \times \mathbb{Z}_q^n$ and master secret key $msk = R \in \mathbb{Z}^{\bar{m} \times w}$.

KeyDistr(mpk, msk, id, t, N): On input master public key $mpk = (A, u)$, where $A \in \mathbb{Z}_q^{n \times m}$ and $u \in \mathbb{Z}_q^n$, a master secret key $msk = R \in \mathbb{Z}^{\bar{m} \times w}$ such that holds

$A = [\bar{A}| - \bar{A}R]$ with random $\bar{A} \xleftarrow{r} \mathbb{Z}_q^{n \times \bar{m}}$ and $m = \bar{m} + w$, generate $H_{id} \in \mathbb{Z}_q^{n \times n}$, which is an invertible matrix that encodes id as presented in [3]. Generate secret key $sk_{id} = (s, e) \in \mathbb{Z}_q^n \times \mathbb{Z}_q^m$ by sampling the preimage of u over a coset of $\Lambda_u^\perp(A_{id})$ via the Invert algorithm from Definition 3. Note that the preimage of u is an id-related secret key $sk_{id} = (s, e) = f_{A_{id}}^{-1}(u)$ with $A_{id} = [\bar{A}|H_{id}G - \bar{A}R]$ $\in \mathbb{Z}_q^{n \times m}$, where $G \in \mathbb{Z}_q^{n \times w}$ as described in ([23], Sect. 5.4), $\bar{A} \in \mathbb{Z}_q^{n \times \bar{m}}$ and $u = s^t A_{id} + e^t$.

The algorithm distributes $sk_{id} = (s, e) \in \mathbb{Z}_q^n \times \mathbb{Z}_q^m$ over $\mathbb{Z}_q$ among N servers using entry-wise secret sharing for additive groups as follows: Choose a set of values $U = \{r_0 = 0, r_1, \dots, r_n\} \in \mathbb{Z}_q$, such that $r_i - r_j$ is invertible in $\mathbb{Z}_q$ for every $i \neq j$. Make U public. Let $s = (s_1, \dots, s_n), e = (e_1, \dots, e_m)$. Then choose n formal polynomials $h_{1,k_1}(x) = \sum_{j=0}^{t-1} h_{1,jk_1} x^j$, $k_1 \in \{1, \dots, n\}$ and m polynomials $h_{2,k_2}(x) = \sum_{j=0}^{t-1} h_{2,jk_2} x^j$, $k_2 \in \{1, \dots, m\}$, where $h_{1,jk_1}, h_{2,jk_2} \in \mathbb{Z}_q$ and $h_{1,0k_1} = s_{k_1}, h_{2,0k_2} = e_{k_2}$ are the n and m secret components of vectors s, e respectively, which are uniformly random and independent. Server i is publicly associated with value $r_i \in \mathbb{Z}_q$, for $i \in [N]$ and N is the number of servers. The corresponding secret share is $sk_{id,i} = (s_i, e_i) = (h_{1,k_1}(r_i), h_{2,k_2}(r_i))$, where $h_{1,k_1}(r_i) = (h_{1,1}(r_i), \dots, h_{1,n}(r_i))$ and $h_{2,k_2}(r_i) = (h_{1,1}(r_i), \dots, h_{2,m}(r_i))$. The algorithm outputs $(i, sk_{id,i})$

Encrypt(mpk, m, id): On input public key A_{id}, u, a message bit b and an identity id, choose $x \leftarrow \mathbb{Z}_q^m$, a vector $\tilde{e} \in \mathbb{Z}^n$ from the Gaussian distribution $D_{\mathbb{Z}^m,c}$ with Gaussian parameter c (s. Appendix), and $\tilde{e} \in \mathbb{Z}_q$. Compute $c_1 = u^t x + \tilde{e} + b\lfloor \frac{q}{2} \rfloor \in \mathbb{Z}_q$ and $c_2 = A_{id} x + \tilde{e} \in \mathbb{Z}_q^n$. Output is a ciphertext $C = (c_1, c_2)$.

ShareDecrypt$(mpk, sk_{id,i}, C)$: On input secret key share $sk_{id,i}$ and a ciphertext C it computes a decryption share $\delta_i = c_1 - c_2^t h_{1,k_1}(r_i) - \|h_{2,k_2}(r_i)\| \in \mathbb{Z}_q$.

Decrypt$(mpk, \{\delta_i\}_{i \in \Omega}, C, \Omega)$: On input t-out-of-n decryption shares, a set Ω with indices $i_1, \dots, i_t$, where $i_j \in [N]$ and a ciphertext $C = (c_1, c_2) \in \mathbb{Z}_q \times \mathbb{Z}_q^n$, compute Lagrange coefficients $\lambda_i = \prod_{j \in \Omega, j \neq i} \frac{-r_j}{r_i - r_j}$ and decrypt the ciphertext by computing $\sum_{i=1}^t \lambda_i \delta_i + c_1 \left(1 - \sum_{i=1}^t \lambda_i\right) \approx b\lfloor \frac{q}{2} \rfloor$.

3.2 Security Reduction

The security of our lattice-based IBTD is based on the lemma from [26]:

Lemma 1. *Let (n, q, χ, m) be such parameters that the $LWE_{n,q,\chi}$ assumption holds. Then for $m = \mathcal{O}(n \log q)$ and $\bar{A}, R$ as provided above, the joint distribution $(\bar{A}, R\bar{A})$ is computationally indistinguishable from uniform over $\mathbb{Z}_q^{n \times \bar{m}} \times \mathbb{Z}_q^{n \times w}$.*

Theorem 1. *Our IBTD scheme is* sIND/ANO $-$ IDTB $-$ CCA *secure under the LWE assumption given in Definition 1.*

Proof. Let $\mathcal{A}$ be an adversary against $\mathtt{sIND/ANO - IDTB - CCA}$ security of IBTD scheme. $\mathcal{A}$ first chooses a set of $t-1$ decryption servers it wants to corrupt. It also announces the identity id^* it wants to be challenged on. We use $\mathcal{A}$ to construct a simulator $\mathcal{B}$ against the LWE problem, where $\mathcal{B}$ plays the role of the challenger. The instance of LWE problem is given as a sampling oracle $\mathcal{O}$. This oracle can be either purely random $\mathcal{O}_r$ or pseudo-random $\mathcal{O}_s$ for some secret $s \in \mathbb{Z}_q^N$. $\mathcal{B}$ queries from his sampling oracle $\mathcal{O}$ and receives for each request i a fresh pair $(\boldsymbol{a}_i, t_i) \in \mathbb{Z}_q^n \times \mathbb{Z}_q$. The challenger $\mathcal{B}$ simulates for $\mathcal{A}$ public parameters (mpk, msk) using upper LWE samples and sends them to $\mathcal{A}$. $\mathcal{B}$ picks random matrices $A, \overset{\bar{r}}{\leftarrow} \mathbb{Z}_q^{n \times \bar{m}}$ and runs $\mathtt{TrapGen}$ algorithm to generate a trapdoor R of A. The challenger also simulates secret key shares of $t-1$ corrupted servers. To do so, $\mathcal{B}$ first picks $2n(t-1)$ random values $\alpha_{1,k}, \ldots, \alpha_{t-1,k}, \beta_{1,k}, \ldots, \beta_{t-1,k} \in \mathbb{Z}_q$, where $k \in [n]$. Let $h_{1,k_1}(x), h_{2,k_2}(x) \in \mathbb{Z}_q[X]$ be $n+m$ polynomials of degree $t-1$ defined so that $h_{1,k_1}(0) = s_{k_1}$, $k_1 \in \{1, \ldots, n\}$ and $h_{2,k_2}(0) = e_{k_2}$, $k_2 \in \{1, \ldots, m\}$, are the k-th secret values of vectors $\boldsymbol{s}, \boldsymbol{e}$ which are simulated by $\mathcal{B}$ using the outputs of $\mathtt{TrapGen}$ algorithm. Further holds $h_{1,k}(r_i) = \alpha_{i,k_1}$ for $k_1 \in \{1, \ldots, n\}$ and $h_{2,k_2}(r_i) = \beta_{i,k_2}$ for $k_2 \in \{1, \ldots, m\}$. $\mathcal{B}$ gives $t-1$ secret shares to $\mathcal{A}$, since they are consistent with the polynomials $h_{1,k_1}(r_i), h_{2,k_2}(r_i)$. The probability that $\mathcal{B}$ matches the same servers as $\mathcal{A}$ is given by $\frac{1}{\binom{N}{t-1}}$.

Key distribution queries: When $\mathcal{A}$ issues up to q_S private key distribution queries on $id \neq id^*$ to the uncorrupted servers, $\mathcal{B}$ simulates them as follows. We assume that $\mathcal{B}$ has control over **List** which consists of entries (id, S), where $S = \{(1, sk_{id,1}), \ldots, (N, sk_{id,N})\}$ encompasses the secret key shares for N servers. Consider a key distribution query to the server i on and identity id. $\mathcal{B}$ first checks if $(id, \cdot) \in$ **List**. If so, the simulator picks the corresponding secret shares $(i, sk_{id,i}), i \in [N]$ and gives it to $\mathcal{A}$. Otherwise, if $(id, \cdot) \notin$ **List**, adversary $\mathcal{B}$ simulates the secret shares as follows: It computes first Lagrange coefficients $\lambda_{j,r_1,k_j}, \ldots, \lambda_{j,r_{t-1},k_j}$ where $j \in [2], k_1 \in [n], k_2 \in [m]$ such that $h_{j,k_j}(r_i) = \lambda_0 h_{j,k_j}(0) + \sum_{l=1}^{t-1} \lambda_l h_{j,k_j}(r_l)$. To simulate an id related secret key it runs $\mathtt{Invert}$ on input a random matrix $A \overset{r}{\leftarrow} \mathbb{Z}_q^{n \times m}$ and the corresponding trapdoor R received upon running $\mathtt{TrapGen}$ algorithm. So $\mathcal{B}$ obtains s_{id} which it can use to compute secret shares $h_{1,k_1}(i), h_{2,k_2}(i)$. $\mathcal{B}$ sends the simulated values to $\mathcal{A}$, and adds the query $(id, \cdot)$ to the **List**.

Decryption queries: When $\mathcal{A}$ issues up to q_D decryption queries on input an id and a ciphertext C, $\mathcal{B}$ first checks if $(id, \cdot) \in$ **List**. If so, it takes t-out-of-n secret shares from this list and computes the decryption shares. Otherwise, if $(id, \cdot) \notin$ **List**, simulator $\mathcal{B}$ first computes secret shares analogously to the computations in the previous simulated key distribution queries. Furthermore, it simulates decryption shares using simulated secret shares $\delta_i = c_1 - c_2^t h_{1,k_1}(r_i) - \|h_{2,k_2}(r_i)\|$. Simulator $\mathcal{B}$ combines t-out-of-N decryption shares using Lagrange coefficients $\lambda_1, \ldots, \lambda_t \in \mathbb{Z}_q$ and outputs either a message or aborts. $\mathcal{B}$ sends the message to $\mathcal{A}$. Adversary $\mathcal{A}$ aborts if the received message is not the same as it received after running the decryption algorithm of IBTD scheme.

Challenge: The adversary $\mathcal{A}$ gives two messages m_0, m_1 and two identities id_0, id_1 to the simulator $\mathcal{B}$. The simulation of the challenge ciphertext also works using as input the entries from the LWE instance. Finally the ciphertext $C(pk, m_b, id_\beta)$, for $b, \beta \in \{0, 1\}$ is sent to $\mathcal{A}$. When the LWE oracle is given by $\mathcal{O}_s$ (i.e. it is pseudo-random), the ciphertext is randomly distributed including some random noise vector which is distributed as Φ_α^n, where the latter notion describes a certain noise distribution over $\mathbb{Z}_q$, as showed in [26]. When $\mathcal{O}$ is given by $\mathcal{O}_r$ then the ciphertext is uniform and independent over $\mathbb{Z}_q^{n'}$, for some n'. Eventually the simulated ciphertext is always uniform in $\mathbb{Z}_q \times \mathbb{Z}_q^n$.

Guess: After issuing additional queries, $\mathcal{A}$ guesses a bit $b', \beta' \in \{0, 1\}$ corresponding to a message index and to an identity index, respectively. The LWE adversary $\mathcal{B}$ outputs its guess as the result of the LWE challenge. Finally, we follow that $\mathcal{B}'$s advantage in solving LWE is at least the same as $\mathcal{A}$'s advantage in distinguishing the ciphertext from a random value, i.e.: $\mathbf{Adv}_\mathcal{B} \geq \frac{1}{q_S q_D \binom{N}{t-1}} \mathbf{Adv}_\mathcal{A}$. $\qquad\square$

Theorem 2 (IBTD Robustness). *Our identity-based threshold decryption scheme from Sect. 3.1 is* IBTD$-$ROB$-$CCA *secure under the hardness of LWE assumption.*

Proof. (Sketch) We show that IBTD$-$ROB$-$CCA property is provided in our IBTD scheme. Let $\mathcal{A}_{rob}$ be an adversary against robustness of IBTD, that is given the public key as input. She can receive at most $t - 1$ secret shares from $\mathcal{O}$KeyDistr. We set $H_{id} = H(id)$ corresponding to an encoding matrix defined in [3] and denoting the encoding of an identity id using $H \in \mathbb{Z}_q^{n \times n}$. The probability of finding two different identities $id_1 \neq id_2$ s.t. $H(id_1) = H(id_2)$ is negligible. As showed in [3] the encoding function $H_{id} : \mathbb{Z}_q^n \to \mathbb{Z}_q^{n \times n}$ has a strong notion of injectivity which means that for two different identities id_1, id_2 the difference of the outputs $H(id_1)$ and $H(id_2)$ is never singular, i.e. $\det(H(id_1) - H(id_2)) \neq 0$. $\qquad\square$

4   Application to Distributed Searchable Encryption

In this section we apply our IBTD scheme for the construction of a distributed public key encryption with keyword search on lattices (DPEKS). We follow the idea from Abdalla et al. [1] in order to transform our anonymous IBTD scheme into a consistent and secure DPEKS scheme. A distributed public key encryption with keyword search scheme was also defined in [21]. It consists of five algorithms, Setup, PEKS, ShareTrpd, ShareTest, Test. The setup algorithm Setup of DPEKS is equal to the same algorithm of our IBTD scheme while the master public and master secret keys are set equal to the public and secret key of DPEKS, respectively. Further we obtain ShareTrpd algorithm from the KeyDistr algorithm of IBTD scheme by setting the identity equal to the keyword of DPEKS. The output of ShareTrpd is a trapdoor share, which is equal to the secret shares of IBTD. The encryption of a plaintext under identity id in IBTD corresponds to the PEKS ciphertext on a keyword w of DPEKS. Analogously we transform ShareDecrypt algorithm of IBTD into ShareTest algorithm of DPEKS, where the output of DPEKS is a test share τ_i corresponding to the decryption share in a IBTD scheme. Finally the Test algorithm of DPEKS is derived from the Decrypt algorithm, where the input of Test consists of PEKS ciphertext Φ that consists of C of IBTD and a bit string $R \xleftarrow{r} \{0,1\}^k$, $\Phi = (C, R)$.

In order to make the application intelligible, we observe a cloud scenario as showed in Fig. 1, which allows data owner to upload encrypted data together with encrypted keywords to a multiple number of cloud servers, such that an authorized user can outsource particular search operations and download data upon a successful cloud search.

In order to enable the search operation without revealing any information of the data, the user creates trapdoors, which hide keywords and sends the generated trapdoor shares to the N cloud servers. We assume existence of a trusted party which generates these trapdoor shares for an user upon receiving a trapdoor generation request. The search operation allows an user to find out whether the stored

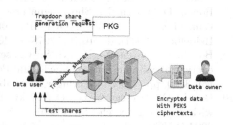

Fig. 1. DPEKS in cloud setting

encrypted data contains the required keyword she is looking for or not. If the search result has a positive outcome, upon sending a download request to one of the cloud servers, the user can easily download the needed files, and decrypt them with the decryption algorithm of the underlying encryption scheme.

5   Conclusion

In this paper we have motivated and presented a solution for the problem of distributing the role of a single server among a certain number of servers and provided a crucial application to the cloud storage setting. We first introduced an identity-based threshold decryption scheme which is based on lattices and defined its security properties. We also presented its security proof and finally provided the syntax of a distributed public key encryption with keyword search with application to the cloud setting.

References

1. Abdalla, M., Bellare, M., Catalano, D., Kiltz, E., Kohno, T., Lange, T., Malone-Lee, J., Neven, G., Pailier, P., Shi, H.: Searchable encryption revisited: Consistency properties, relation to anonymous ibe and extensions. J. Cryptol. **21**, 350–391 (2008)
2. Abdalla, M., Bellare, M., Neven, G.: Robust encryption. In: Micciancio, D. (ed.) TCC 2010. LNCS, vol. 5978, pp. 480–497. Springer, Heidelberg (2010). doi:10.1007/978-3-642-11799-2_28

3. Agrawal, S., Boneh, D., Boyen, X.: Efficient lattice (H)IBE in the standard model. In: Gilbert, H. (ed.) EUROCRYPT 2010. LNCS, vol. 6110, pp. 553–572. Springer, Heidelberg (2010). doi:10.1007/978-3-642-13190-5_28

4. Agrawal, S., Boneh, D., Boyen, X.: Lattice basis delegation in fixed dimension and shorter-ciphertext hierarchical IBE. In: Rabin, T. (ed.) CRYPTO 2010. LNCS, vol. 6223, pp. 98–115. Springer, Heidelberg (2010). doi:10.1007/978-3-642-14623-7_6

5. Ajtai, M.: Generating hard instances of lattice problems (extended abstract). In: STOC 1996, pp. 99–108. ACM (1996)

6. Ajtai, M., Dwork, C.: A public-key cryptosystem with worst-case/average-case equivalence. In: STOC 1997, pp. 284–293. ACM (1997)

7. Baek, J., Zheng, Y.: Identity-based threshold decryption. In: Bao, F., Deng, R., Zhou, J. (eds.) PKC 2004. LNCS, vol. 2947, pp. 262–276. Springer, Heidelberg (2004). doi:10.1007/978-3-540-24632-9_19

8. Boneh, D., Boyen, X.: Short signatures without random oracles. In: Cachin, C., Camenisch, J.L. (eds.) EUROCRYPT 2004. LNCS, vol. 3027, pp. 56–73. Springer, Heidelberg (2004). doi:10.1007/978-3-540-24676-3_4

9. Boneh, D., Boyen, X., Halevi, S.: Chosen ciphertext secure public key threshold encryption without random oracles. In: Pointcheval, D. (ed.) CT-RSA 2006. LNCS, vol. 3860, pp. 226–243. Springer, Heidelberg (2006). doi:10.1007/11605805_15

10. Boneh, D., Crescenzo, G., Ostrovsky, R., Persiano, G.: Public key encryption with keyword search. In: Cachin, C., Camenisch, J.L. (eds.) EUROCRYPT 2004. LNCS, vol. 3027, pp. 506–522. Springer, Heidelberg (2004). doi:10.1007/978-3-540-24676-3_30

11. Boneh, D., Waters, B.: Conjunctive, subset, and range queries on encrypted data. In: Vadhan, S.P. (ed.) TCC 2007. LNCS, vol. 4392, pp. 535–554. Springer, Heidelberg (2007). doi:10.1007/978-3-540-70936-7_29

12. Boyen, X.: Lattice mixing and vanishing trapdoors: a framework for fully secure short signatures and more. In: Nguyen, P.Q., Pointcheval, D. (eds.) PKC 2010. LNCS, vol. 6056, pp. 499–517. Springer, Heidelberg (2010). doi:10.1007/978-3-642-13013-7_29

13. Boyen, X.: Attribute-based functional encryption on lattices. In: Sahai, A. (ed.) TCC 2013. LNCS, vol. 7785, pp. 122–142. Springer, Heidelberg (2013). doi:10.1007/978-3-642-36594-2_8

14. Cash, D., Hofheinz, D., Kiltz, E., Peikert, C.: Bonsai trees, or how to delegate a lattice basis. In: Gilbert, H. (ed.) EUROCRYPT 2010. LNCS, vol. 6110, pp. 523–552. Springer, Heidelberg (2010). doi:10.1007/978-3-642-13190-5_27

15. Chang, Y.-C., Mitzenmacher, M.: Privacy preserving keyword searches on remote encrypted data. In: Ioannidis, J., Keromytis, A., Yung, M. (eds.) ACNS 2005. LNCS, vol. 3531, pp. 442–455. Springer, Heidelberg (2005). doi:10.1007/11496137_30

16. Gentry, C.: Practical identity-based encryption without random oracles. In: Vaudenay, S. (ed.) EUROCRYPT 2006. LNCS, vol. 4004, pp. 445–464. Springer, Heidelberg (2006). doi:10.1007/11761679_27

17. Gentry, C., Peikert, C., Vaikuntanathan, V.: Trapdoors for hard lattices and new cryptographic constructions. In: STOC 2008, pp. 197–206. ACM (2008)

18. Goh, E.: Secure indexes. IACR Cryptology ePrint Archive, 2003: 216 (2003)

19. Golle, P., Staddon, J., Waters, B.: Secure conjunctive keyword search over encrypted data. In: Jakobsson, M., Yung, M., Zhou, J. (eds.) ACNS 2004. LNCS, vol. 3089, pp. 31–45. Springer, Heidelberg (2004). doi:10.1007/978-3-540-24852-1_3

20. Hou, C., Liu, F., Bai, H., Ren, L.: Public-key encryption with keyword search from lattice. In: P2P, Parallel, Grid, Cloud and Internet Computing (2013)

21. Kuchta, V., Manulis, M.: Public key encryption with distributed keyword search. In: Yung, M., Zhang, J., Yang, Z. (eds.) INTRUST 2015. LNCS, vol. 9565, pp. 62–83. Springer, Heidelberg (2016). doi:10.1007/978-3-319-31550-8_5

22. Lyubashevsky, V.: Lattice signatures without trapdoors. In: Pointcheval, D., Johansson, T. (eds.) EUROCRYPT 2012. LNCS, vol. 7237, pp. 738–755. Springer, Heidelberg (2012). doi:10.1007/978-3-642-29011-4_43

23. Micciancio, D., Peikert, C.: Trapdoors for lattices: simpler, tighter, faster, smaller. In: Pointcheval, D., Johansson, T. (eds.) EUROCRYPT 2012. LNCS, vol. 7237, pp. 700–718. Springer, Heidelberg (2012). doi:10.1007/978-3-642-29011-4_41

24. Peikert, C.: Public-key cryptosystems from the worst-case shortest vector problem: extended abstract. In: STOC 2009, pp. 333–342. ACM (2009)

25. Regev, O.: New lattice based cryptographic constructions. In: STOC 2003, pp. 407–416. ACM (2003)

26. Regev, O.: On lattices, learning with errors, random linear codes and cryptography. In: STOC 2005, pp. 84–93. ACM (2005)

27. Regev, O.: Lattice-based cryptography. In: Dwork, C. (ed.) CRYPTO 2006. LNCS, vol. 4117, pp. 131–141. Springer, Heidelberg (2006). doi:10.1007/11818175_8

28. Singh, K., Rangan, C.P., Banerjee, A.K.: Lattice-based identity-based resplittable threshold public key encryption scheme. Int. J. Comput. Math. 93(2), 289–307 (2016)

29. Liesdonk, P., Sedghi, S., Doumen, J., Hartel, P., Jonker, W.: Computationally efficient searchable symmetric encryption. In: Jonker, W., Petković, M. (eds.) SDM 2010. LNCS, vol. 6358, pp. 87–100. Springer, Heidelberg (2010). doi:10.1007/978-3-642-15546-8_7

Recursive M-ORAM: A Matrix ORAM
for Clients with Constrained Storage Space

Karin Sumongkayothin[1,5(✉)], Steven Gordon[4], Atsuko Miyaji[1,2,3],
Chunhua Su[3], and Komwut Wipusitwarakun[5]

[1] Japan Advance Institute of Science and Technology (JAIST), Nomi, Japan
s1420209@jaist.ac.jp
[2] Japan Science and Technology Agency (JST) CREST, Tokyo, Japan
[3] Graduate School of Engineering, Osaka University, Suita, Japan
[4] School of Engineering and Technology, Central Queensland University,
Rockhampton, Australia
[5] Sirindhorn International Institute of Technology, Thammasat University (SIIT),
Pathum Thani, Thailand

Abstract. Although oblivious RAM (ORAM) can hide a client's access
pattern from an untrusted server, bandwidth and local storage requirements can be excessive. Path ORAM, Matrix ORAM and other schemes
can greatly bandwidth cost, but on devices with constrained storage
space they require too much local storage. We design a recursive version
of Matrix ORAM, where data addresses are stored on the server instead
of client, and are recursively accessed with revealing important information. We analyse our algorithm and show it keeps bandwidth, client
storage and computational overhead each to $O(\log N)$.

1 Introduction

A major limitation of clouding computing is privacy: the client may reveal valuable information to the server operator when uploading data, downloading data
and performing operations on the server. Although necessary for data confidentiality, encrypting data before uploading to the server is not sufficient for
privacy. It has been shown that even with encryption the sequence of server
storage locations read/written by the client can reveal valuable information to
the server [7,9]. Oblivious RAM [4] is one technique that can be used to hide
this information from the server. It does this using a combination of several
approaches: re-encrypting data before uploading again; uploading the same data
to different locations on the server; and uploading/downloading multiple blocks
of data from the server every time the client wants to access a single block of
data. The result is that, from the server's perspective, the clients access pattern
is indistinguishable from a series of random accesses.

Many different ORAM algorithms have been designed [6,10,12,13,15].
Despite all offering privacy, they make trade-offs in performance, where a key
metric is bandwidth cost. Downloading/uploading multiple blocks in order to
access just a single block leads to significant bandwidth cost. Schemes such as

© Springer Nature Singapore Pte Ltd. 2016
L. Batten and G. Li (Eds.): ATIS 2016, CCIS 651, pp. 130–141, 2016.
DOI: 10.1007/978-981-10-2741-3_11

Path ORAM [13] and M-ORAM [6] aim to minimize bandwidth cost. However that comes at the expense of increased storage space on clients and/or computational overheads. In particular, both Path ORAM and M-ORAM store a position map on the client which records the addresses of each data item on the server. This has $O(N)$ client storage requirements, where N is the maximum number of data blocks on the server. A general technique to reduce the storage requirements (at the expense of increased bandwidth cost) is recursion: store the position map on the server in ORAM, and a second, smaller position map to that is stored on the client. While Path ORAM has a recursive construction designed and analyzed in [13], only an outline of the recursive construction for M-ORAM is given in [6]. In this paper we present a detailed design of *Recursive M-ORAM (RM-ORAM)*, and provide performance and security analysis of this new ORAM construction.

1.1   Related Work

There have many many ORAM algorithms proposed, differing mainly on the server storage structure (hierarchical [1–3,5,8,10,14–16], tree [11–13,17], matrix [6]) and trade-offs of bandwidth and storage. Some of these algorithms also define a recursive construction to reduce client storage space.

The first ORAM algorithm [4] was a hierarchical based construction. While the client storage space required was constant, it requires significant bandwidth consumption as well as complex computations. Several ORAM constructions were introduced to try to reduce those costs [1–3,5,8,10–12,14–17]. However, these hierarchical based constructions still require computationally expensive operations, such as oblivious shuffling and background eviction.

Path ORAM [13] is a binary-tree based ORAM construction which uses much simpler operation and $\log N$ bandwidth cost to achieve the desired security properties. This was a significant advancement over hierarchical ORAMs. However Path ORAM requires increase client storage to contain a position map and local stash. To reduce this extra storage, a recursion technique is applied. The recursion technique was introduced in [15] to reduce the number of elements that have to be stored on the client. By using this technique, Path ORAM can reduces the client's storage space requirement from $O(N)$ to $O(\log N) \cdot \omega(1)$ while the bandwidth cost is increased from $O(\log N)$ to $O(\log^2 N)$ respectively.

Unlike any existing schemes, M-ORAM [6] is built upon a matrix data structure for server storage which can achieve $O(1)$ bandwidth cost. However M-ORAM requires N blocks of position map on the client, giving $O(N)$ storage space requirement. [6] outlines an idea for a recursive construction of M-ORAM, but lacks details and analysis. The difference in the storage structure used by M-ORAM and Path ORAM means the recursive design for Path ORAM is not suitable for M-ORAM. Hence we present a detailed design and analysis of a recursive construction for M-ORAM.

1.2   Contribution and Paper Organization

This paper proposes Recursive M-ORAM (RM-ORAM), a recursive version of M-ORAM [6]. Our contributions are:

1. Detailed design of RM-ORAM storage structures and access operations.
2. An ORAM that can achieve $O(\log N)$ bandwidth cost, as well as requiring $O(\log N)$ client storage space.
3. A recursive model different from existing models (e.g. used in Recursive Path ORAM), and in particular tailored for M-ORAM.
4. Performance and security analysis of RM-ORAM.

The rest of the paper is organized as follows. Section 2 overviews the general recursive algorithm used in ORAM constructions. Then the concept of RM-ORAM is provided in Sect. 3, with detailed design of the storage given in Sect. 4 and access operations in Sect. 5. In Sect. 6 we compare the performance of RM-ORAM with other schemes and the security issues are discussed in Sect. 7. Finally, we give a conclusion in Sect. 8.

2   General Concept of Recursive ORAM Construction

ORAM schemes typically have the following components: logical organization of storage on the server (e.g. hierarchy, tree, matrix), referred to as the *ORAM*; permanent storage on the client to keep track of addresses of data on the server (often called a *position map*); temporary storage on the client for processing downloaded data blocks before they are uploaded again (also called a *stash*); and an algorithm that triggers a series of accesses (downloads/uploads) to the server to obtain a single data block of interest, but such that the server sees those accesses as random (and thereby not being able to identify the desired data block). A major limitation of ORAM is performance. Accessing multiple blocks on the server in order to access only one data block of interest leads to significant bandwidth cost. Also, storing large amounts of data on the client, in particular the permanent position map, goes against the goal of cloud computing. To overcome this latter performance problem, the position map can also be stored on the server using ORAM, with a second, smaller position map used on the client to access the original position map. Hence a recursive ORAM construction is obtained. The general concept of recursive ORAM will be explained with the aid of Fig. 1. Initially the focus is on explaining the steps, without considering security properties (which will be discussed later).

There are three important storage structures in a recursive ORAM, as shown in Fig. 1: *ORAM* contains the actual blocks of data and is stored on the server; a position map (*Pos*) contains addresses of the data in ORAM or addresses of the next position map; and a temporary buffer on the client contains downloaded information for processing. When the client wants to retrieve a data block from ORAM, it starts by looking for the address in *Pos#0* which is stored on the client. The address points to a block in *Pos#1* (which is stored on the server),

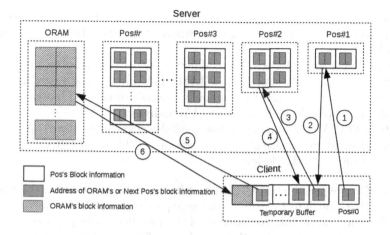

Fig. 1. General recursive operation for ORAM

which the client downloads to the temporary buffer. That downloaded block contains m addresses, with the address of interest pointing to a block in $Pos\#2$, which is then downloaded. This continues until the block from $Pos\#r$ is downloaded, which contains the address of the data block of interest in ORAM, which is then downloaded.

In summary, a recursive ORAM stores a small position map on the client, with each block containing m addresses, and then recursively accesses position maps in the server until the data of interest is obtained. The drawback is extra bandwidth cost (accesses to the server): with N data blocks in the ORAM, the recursive operation will take $\lceil \log_m N \rceil$ rounds to cover every address of data block in ORAM (where each round requires communications between client and server). The next section provides a specific design of a recursive construction for M-ORAM.

3 Recursive M-ORAM Construction

The general recursive construction in the previous section can be implemented differently depending on the underlying ORAM construction. The Path ORAM recursive construction uses one position map ORAM ($PosORAM$) for each level of recursion. A PosORAM stores m addresses per data block, where these addresses point to either the data ORAM or another PosORAM. Each access from client to server (to either data ORAM or a PosORAM) is performed using the normal Path ORAM access operations (e.g. download a path, then upload a path). The model of recursive ORAM used with Path ORAM cannot be applied directly to M-ORAM. There are three main reasons:

1. Path ORAM and M-ORAM use different methods to specify the address of a data block. In Path ORAM, the leaf-ID is used to identify the path which

contains the data block of interest. On the other hand, M-ORAM uses row and column to address the exact location of the data block of interest in ORAM.

2. Path ORAM and M-ORAM use different algorithms for assigning a new address for accessed data. Path ORAM randomly assigns a new leaf-ID to access data, while M-ORAM randomly selects downloaded blocks from the stash to be uploaded to existing ORAM addresses.

3. In Path ORAM, the number of downloaded blocks during access operation is varied depend on the size of ORAM structure. While in M-ORAM, it is fixed and can be set by the designer.

Therefore we propose RM-ORAM that integrates all position map blocks (i.e. from *Pos#1* through to *Pos#r*) into a single position map ORAM (*PosORAM*). This allows for controlling the number of downloaded blocks per access request independent of the size of the ORAM (a key performance feature of M-ORAM). Also, by having a single PosORAM, the server will be unable to distinguish blocks from different recursion levels (a key security property of M-ORAM).

Two key design issues with ORAM are the data structures and the operations for accessing data. In Sect. 4 we describe the server and client storage structures used by RM-ORAM while the operations will be described in Sect. 5.

4   RM-ORAM Storage

The RM-ORAM storage architecture is illustrated in Fig. 2. The server contains two logical data structures: (data) ORAM to store the N data blocks and PosORAM to store multiple position maps (with a total of N' blocks). Both ORAMs use the format of M-ORAM: the physical addresses of server storage are mapped to the set of logical addresses in the matrix format, x and y (rows and columns).

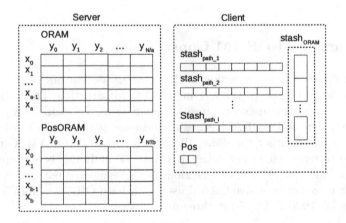

Fig. 2. RM-ORAM storage

The height of the ORAM and PosORAM matrices are a and b, respectively. Note that the block of ORAM and PosORAM are not necessarily the same size.

Similar to M-ORAM, the RM-ORAM client uses stash buffers to temporarily store downloaded blocks. While M-ORAM uses one stash for each row in ORAM, RM-ORAM uses a separate stash buffer to contain the blocks in each path that leads to the downloaded blocks in ORAM. The use of these stashes is explained in Sect. 5. In addition, the RM-ORAM client includes a position map, $Pos\#0$, which stores the addresses for the next position map on the server (i.e. $Pos\#1$) as illustrated in Fig. 3. The next section explains how these storage structures are used in various RM-ORAM operations.

5   RM-ORAM Operation

When a client wants to access (upload or download) a data block from the server, with M-ORAM it must read (download) multiple blocks from the server and then write (upload) mutiple blocks to the server. The set of blocks read/written is designed such that the desired block is accessed but the server cannot distinguish a sequence of accesses from a random sequence of accesses. In brief, with M-ORAM the client reads one block from each row in the ORAM matrix, where the columns are chosen randomly except: for the row that contains the data block of interest, and some columns must be the same as the previous access operation. After the H blocks are read, they are randomly spread into stashes on the client, and then the write operation takes (potentially different) blocks from the stashes and writes them to the same entries of the server storage matrix.

For RM-ORAM there are also read and write operations (see Fig. 4), but with substantial differences from M-ORAM to ensure the security properties are maintained. Section 5.1 describes the read operation while Sect. 5.2 describes the write operation.

5.1   Read Operation

Consider RM-ORAM where the server has N data blocks, r levels of recursion will be used and each Pos block contains m addresses. Each data block has a unique ID, ID_n where $n \in N$. Suppose the client wants to access data block ID_i (also referred to as the block of interest or real data). Initially the client checks if the block ID_i is in a stash on the client. If so, reading or updating of the data is performed locally; there is no communication with the server. If not, the client consecutively reads multiple blocks from the server, where one among them is the block which can lead to the data of interest in the ORAM. The reading of blocks is performed in rounds where the number of rounds equals the levels of recursion.

Let $Pos\#r$ be the Pos that is accessed in round $\#r$. At the round $\#r$, there are m^r of $Pos\#r$, called $Pos_i\#r$. Each $Pos_i\#r$ is mapped to the range of data $\{ID_{1+(N(j+(mi)))/(m^{(r+1)})}, ID_{N(j+(mi)+1)/(m^{(r+1)})}\}$ where $0 \leq j \leq m - 1$ and $0 \leq i \leq m^r - 1$. For security purposes which will be analyzed in Sect. 7, in

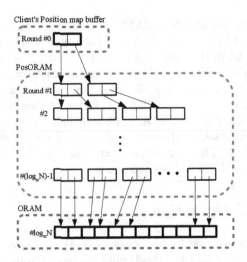

Fig. 3. Relation of Pos blocks from each level of recursion

addition to the block of interest the client needs to select $H - 1$ other data blocks, and o of those must be from the previous access operation. That is, 1 block is that of interest, $H - (o + 1)$ blocks are randomly selected, and o blocks are selected from the previous operation. In total the client access H blocks, creating H different paths of accessing the Pos from round #1 to round #r. Of the H blocks downloaded, γ blocks must remain in $stash_{ORAM}$ after completing the write operation. γ is chosen uniformly at random where $1 < \gamma < o$. This γ will be considered the old blocks for the next operation.

Initially, in round #0, the client reads from the locally stored $Pos\#0$, which returns an address in PosORAM pointing to a block of $Pos\#1$. In round #1 the client reads from the (server stored) $Pos\#1$ obtaining an address pointing to $Pos\#2$, and so on. After $\log_m(N) - 1$ rounds the address to the data block of interest in ORAM is obtained. Finally, the client accesses the (data) ORAM to obtain the block of interest. After the final round, H data blocks are retrieved.

The dummy content (see Sect. 5.2) is discarded, and the rest are stored in $stash_{ORAM}$. The content of ID_i will be updated if necessary then the write operation is started. Note that the accesses to PosORAM follow the normal M-ORAM procedure, as do the accesses to (data) ORAM.

5.2   Write Operation

After a read operation, the downloaded blocks will be uploaded back to the server. The locations that have been accessed during the read operation are randomly assigned to every block, and the information (address) in the blocks of $stash_{path}$ are updated to coincide with the new address. The client saves the ID of all downloaded data to the *history list*. This list will be used for selecting o old blocks during the next read operation, and it is overwritten every write

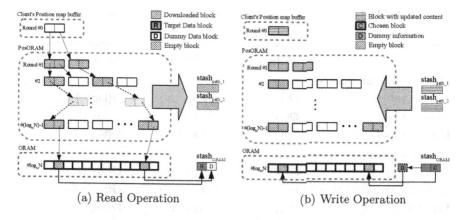

(a) Read Operation   (b) Write Operation

Fig. 4. RM-ORAM access request operation

operation. Suppose there are H data blocks that have been downloaded and stored in $stash_{ORAM}$. The γ blocks where $\gamma < H$ will be selected to remain on the client and be counted as the old blocks for next access operation. Then the dummy content will be uploaded rather than theirs real content. The remaining $H - \gamma$ blocks will be uploaded with their original content but encrypted with a new secret key. At this state, all blocks in the $stash_{path}$ and the chosen blocks in the $stash_{ORAM}$ will be uploaded to the server according to their new address.

6   Performance Analysis

A key aim of RM-ORAM when used in constrained devices is to balance the communication overhead, the client's storage overhead and the client's processing overhead. This section discusses each performance metric for RM-ORAM, and compares against other ORAM schemes which the results are per Table 1.

6.1   RM-ORAM Communication Overhead

During an access operation, the client needs to download H different paths to retrieve the data of interest. There are N blocks in ORAM with each block containing B bytes, and N' blocks in PosORAM with each blocking containing B' bytes. Let each position map, Pos, contain m addresses. Hence, the client must perform $\log_m N$ recursions to retrieve the block of interest. Therefore the total bandwidth cost for a single access operation is:

$$\text{Bandwidth} = 2(BH + B'(\log_m N - 1)) = O(\log_m N)$$

6.2   RM-ORAM Client's Storage Overhead

The client has several fixed size items to store: position map of size *pos* bytes, a history list of size *hist* bytes, and the stash used for ORAM which contains

Table 1. Performance comparison of different ORAM schemes

Scheme	Client storage (#Block)	Bandwidth cost (#Block)	Computational overhead
Hierarchical Structure			
GO-ORAM [4]	$O(1)$	$O(\log^3 N)$	$O(\log^3(N))$
SSS-ORAM [15]	$O(N)$	$O(\log N)$	$O(\log^2(N))$
Recurisve SSS-ORAM [15]	$O(\sqrt{N})$	$O(\log^2 N)$	$O(\log^2(N))$
Tree Structure			
Tree-ORAM [12]	$O(N)$	$O(\log^2 N)$	$O(\log^3(N))$
Recursive Tree-ORAM [12]	$O(1)$	$O(\log^3 N)$	$O(\log^3(N))$
Path ORAM [13]	$O(N)$	$O(\log N)$	$O(\log^2(N)/\log(\chi))$
Recursive Path ORAM [13]	$O(\log N) \cdot \omega(1)$	$O(\log^2 N)$	$O(\log^2(N)/\log(\chi))$
Matrix Structure			
M-ORAM	$O(N)$	$O(1)$	$O(1)$
Recursive M-ORAM	$O(\log N)$	$O(\log N)$	$O(\log N)$

$H \times B$ bytes. The only variable sized data structure is the stash for the path, $stash_{path}$, which varies according to the number of recursions. Therefore the total client storage is:

$$\text{Storage} = pos + HB + hist + HB'(\log_m N - 1) = O(\log_m N)$$

6.3 RM-ORAM Client's Computational Overhead

The main operations to be performed in RM-ORAM, and their costs, are:

- **Random number generation:** We suppose that the random number generator which is used in our construction is efficient. Therefore it has cost $O(1)$.
- **Searching ID in $stash_{ORAM}$ during read operation:** A cost $O(1)$ because $stash_{ORAM}$ has a constant size.
- **Randomly assign the new address to the Pos block:** This operation causes the client to randomly select the new address for $H \log_m N$ blocks. Therefore, it has cost $O \log_m N$.
- **Updating the address in Pos blocks:** This operation causes the client to access $H \log_m N$ blocks for updating their content. Therefore, it has cost $O \log_m N$.
- **Randomly choose some blocks to remain in $stash_{ORAM}$:.** The range of random numbers is bounded by $o - 1$, where o is some constant number that less than H. Therefore, it has cost $O(1)$.
- **Randomly choose new blocks during read operation:** The range of random numbers is bounded by $H - o$, where o and H are constant. Therefore, it has cost $O(1)$.

The total computational cost is the sum of the above operations, which gives:

$$Computational\ Overhead = O(\log_m N)$$

7   Security Analysis

7.1   Security Requirements

The security requirements of ORAM are:

1. The server cannot observe the relationship between data and its address.
2. The server cannot distinguish between updated and non-updated information that is rewritten to the server.
3. Two sequences of accesses to the server of the same length are computationally indistinguishable.

To show that RM-ORAM meets the requirements, we consider a series of access requests to the server as:

$$AssessRequest = (pos_i(ID_i)), pos_{i-1}(ID_{i-1}), \ldots, pos_1(ID_1))$$

where for data item ID_j, $pos_j(ID_j)$ is the set of block positions for retrieving ID_j where $j \in \{1, 2, \ldots, i\}$. Each block of information is encrypted, and ID_j maybe ID_k where $j \neq k$ and $j, k \in i$.

7.2   Random Re-Encryption

Every data block downloaded from the server with RM-ORAM is decrypted, and will be encrypted with a different key before being uploaded again. Therefore even if downloaded data is not modified before uploading, the server cannot identify that it is the same data being uploaded (recall multiple blocks are uploaded with M-ORAM). With this random re-encryption, the server cannot distinguish between updated and non-updated information, nor observe the relationship between data and its address.

7.3   Indistinguishable Access Pattern

The indistinguishable access pattern consists of two factors which are server cannot identify what data is written to which location, and the client's request sequence is no difference from random binary string from the server's point of view. After download operation, the set of addresses that has been accessed will be randomly arranged and distributed to the blocks within the stashes. Suppose the block size of $PosORAM$ and $ORAM$ is difference, and there are $H(\log_m N - 1)$ addresses of $PosORAM$ and H addresses of $ORAM$ have been accessed during the operation. The $H(\log_m N - 1)$ and H addresses are randomly assigned without duplication to the blocks in $stash_{path}$ and $stash_{ORAM}$ respectively. Therefore the number of ways to assign the address is $H! + H(\log_m N - 1)!$.

Hence, the probability that the same pattern of access request will be sent to the server is:

$$\Pr(pos_j(dataID_j)) = \frac{1}{H! + H(\log_m N - 1)!}, \text{ where } j \in \{1, 2, \dots, i\}.$$

Suppose the client do access operation i times and $j < k \in \{1, 2, \dots, i\}$. When the $pos_j(ID_j)$ is revealed to the server, it will be randomly remapped to the new position. Therefore the $pos_j(ID_j)$ is statically independent from $pos_k(ID_k)$, even though $ID_j = ID_k$. As Bayes rule, we can describe the statistically independent of series of access sequence as :

$$\prod_{j=1}^{i} \Pr(pos_j(ID_j)) = (H! + H(\log_m N - 1)!)^{-i}$$

By fact that H must be greater than 1 and $log_m N$ is grater or equal to 1, it shows the series of access request is computationally indistinguishable from a random sequence of bit string.

8   Conclusion

RM-ORAM is a recursive ORAM built on top of M-ORAM. While M-ORAM achieves excellent bandwidth cost, RM-ORAM aims to use the same principles as M-ORAM but to reduce the client storage requirement by storing position maps recursively on the server. This results in an increase in bandwidth cost compared to M-ORAM. RM-ORAM maintains the key security properties of ORAM. This paper also quantified the bandwidth cost, client storage and computational overhead of RM-ORAM. Future work will provide theoretical and practical comparison to other ORAM schemes.

References

1. Boneh, D., Mazieres, D., Popa, R.A.: Remote oblivious storage: making oblivious RAM practical. Tech. rep. MIT-CSAIL-TR-2011-018, Massachusetts Institute of Technology, March 2011. http://hdl.handle.net/1721.1/62006
2. Dautrich, J., Stefanov, E., Shi, E.: Burst ORAM: minimizing ORAM response times for bursty access patterns. In: Proceedings of the 23rd USENIX Security Symposium, San Diego, CA, pp. 749–764, August 2014
3. Gentry, C., Goldman, K.A., Halevi, S., Julta, C., Raykova, M., Wichs, D.: Optimizing ORAM and using it efficiently for secure computation. In: Cristofaro, E., Wright, M. (eds.) PETS 2013. LNCS, vol. 7981, pp. 1–18. Springer, Heidelberg (2013). doi:10.1007/978-3-642-39077-7_1
4. Goldreich, O., Ostrovsky, R.: Software protection and simulation on oblivious RAMs. J. ACM **43**(3), 431–473 (1996)
5. Goodrich, M.T., Mitzenmacher, M., Ohrimenko, O., Tamassia, R.: Privacy-preserving group data access via stateless oblivious RAM simulation. In: Proceedings of the ACM-SIAM Symposium on Discrete Algorithms, Kyoto, Japan, pp. 157–167, January 2012

6. Gordon, S., Miyaji, A., Su, C., Sumongkayothin, K.: A matrix based ORAM: design, implementation and experimental analysis. IEICE Trans. Inf. Syst. **E99–D**(8), 2044–2055 (2016)

7. Islam, M.S., Kuzu, M., Kantarcioglu, M.: Access pattern disclosure on searchable encryption: ramification, attack and mitigation. In: Proceedings of the 19th Annual Network & Distributed System Security Symposium, San Diego, CA, February 2012

8. Karvelas, N.P., Peter, A., Katzenbeisser, S., Biedermann, S.: Efficient privacy-preserving big data processing through proxy-assisted ORAM. Proc. IACR Cryptology ePrint Archive 2014, 72 (2014)

9. Liu, C., Zhu, L., Wang, M., Tan, Y.: Search pattern leakage in searchable encryption: attacks and new construction. Inf. Sci. Int. J. **265**, 176–188 (2014)

10. Pinkas, B., Reinman, T.: Oblivious RAM revisited. In: Proceedings of the 30th Annual Cryptology Conference, Santa Barbara, CA, pp. 502–519, August 2010

11. Ren, L., Fletcher, C.W., Yu, X., Kwon, A., van Dijk, M., Devadas, S.: Unified oblivious-RAM: Improving recursive ORAM with locality and pseudorandomness. Proc. IACR Cryptology ePrint Archive 2014, 205 (2014)

12. Shi, E., Chan, T.-H.H., Stefanov, E., Li, M.: Oblivious RAM with $O((\log N)^3)$ worst-case cost. In: Lee, D.H., Wang, X. (eds.) ASIACRYPT 2011. LNCS, vol. 7073, pp. 197–214. Springer, Heidelberg (2011). doi:10.1007/978-3-642-25385-0_11

13. Stefanov, E., van Dijk, M., Shi, E., Fletcher, C.W., Ren, L., Yu, X., Devadas, S.: Path ORAM: an extremely simple oblivious RAM protocol. In: Proceedings of the ACM SIGSAC Conference on Computer and Communications Security, Berlin, Germany, pp. 299–310, November 2013

14. Stefanov, E., Shi, E.: Oblivistore: high performance oblivious cloud storage. In: Proceedings of the IEEE Symposium on Security and Privacy, Berkeley, CA, pp. 253–267, May 2013

15. Stefanov, E., Shi, E., Song, D.X.: Towards practical oblivious RAM. In: Proceedings of the 19th Annual Network & Distributed System Security Symposium, The Internet Society, San Diego, CA, USA, February 2012

16. Williams, P., Sion, R., Tomescu, A.: PrivateFS: a parallel oblivious file system. In: Proceedings of the ACM Conference on Computer and Communications Security, New York, NY, pp. 977–988, October 2012

17. Zhang, J., Ma, Q., Zhang, W., Qiao, D.: KT-ORAM: A Bandwidth-efficient ORAM Built on K-ary Tree of PIR Nodes. Proc. IACR Cryptology ePrint Archive 2014, 624 (2014)

False Signal Injection Attack Detection of Cyber Physical Systems by Event-Triggered Distributed Filtering over Sensor Networks

Yufeng Lin[1]([⊠]), Biplob Ray[1], Dennis Jarvis[1], and Jia Wang[2]

[1] Centre for Intelligent Systems, CQUniversity, Rockhampton, QLD 4702, Australia
{y.lin,b.ray,d.jarvis}@cqu.edu.au
[2] College of Mathematics and Computer Science, Fuzhou University, Fuzhou, China
j.wang@fzu.edu.cn

Abstract. This paper is concerned with false signal injection attack detection mechanism using a novel distributed event-triggered filtering for cyber physical systems over sensor networks. By the Internet of Things, the classic physical systems are transformed to the networked cyber physical systems, which are built with a large number of distributed networked sensors. In order to save the precious network resources, a novel distributed event-triggered strategy is proposed. Under this strategy, to generate the localized residual signals, the event-triggered distributed fault detection filters are proposed. By Lyapunov- Krasovskii functional theory, the distributed fault detection filtering problem can be formulated as stability and an H_∞ performance of the residual system. Furthermore, a sufficient condition is derived such that the resultant residual system is stable while the transmission of the sampled data is reduced. Based on this condition, the codesign method of the fault detection filters and the transmission strategy is proposed. An illustrative example is given to show the effectiveness of the proposed method.

Keywords: False signal injection attack · Security · Fault-detection · Event-triggering · Sensor networks

1 Introduction

Recent advancements of creating automated and intelligent systems require computing systems, sensor networks, industrial automation systems, and critical infrastructures to work together [1]. This integration of sensors, actuators and computing systems with tradition physical systems creates cyber physical systems. At the same time, the Internet of Things (IoT) brings the idea of networking cyber physical systems to utilizing the communication network resources efficiently and smartly. This kind of systems have been applied in wide fields such as transportation networks, power generation and distribution networks. The rise

This work was supported in part by the Nature Science Foundation of Fujian Province under Grant 2016J05156, China.

L. Batten and G. Li (Eds.): ATIS 2016, CCIS 651, pp. 142–153, 2016.
DOI: 10.1007/978-981-10-2741-3_12

of cyber physical systems raises the concern about cyber-attacks as they are more widely accessible than traditional ones. However, the existing traditional security solutions are not feasible to protect these systems from cyber-attacks. Furthermore, attacks on these systems may create devastative effects to other connected systems. For example, a large scale attacks on a Self-Driving Car network can disrupt transportation systems of an entire nation for long period of time. Recently, this issue has attracted attention of many scientists to model different attack scenarios [2,3]. However, because of the stealthiness of these attacks, system operators often have little knowledge about them until severe physical damage has already occurred. The false signal injection (FSI) attacks inject malicious signal to control systems using distributed sensor nodes, and mislead the system to unsafe states and cause system disruption. The detection of FSI attacks is challenging because the detector typically needs to understand physical semantics of the sensor and/or control data being monitored. To address the challenge, there is growing momentum to apply existing control system fault detectors, designed based on understood physical semantics of the data, against FSI attacks [4,5]. Examples of simplistic fault-like attacks include: set a signal to its maximum or minimum [2], inject ramps, surges, and random noises [4,6]. In addition, traditional security measures may not work well for cyber physical systems and most of the possible attacks on cyber physical systems are not presently known, which is the first motivation of this study.

With the rapid development of network technologies, several practical systems are physically distributed, such as traffic networks, smart grids [7]. At the same time, under the recent advancements in hardware and wireless communication technologies, sensor networks have been widely applied in infrastructure security, intelligent traffic systems and space exploration [8,9]. In sensor networks, a variety of sensors are usually distributed scatteredly and work cooperatively through networks and are often battery operated with limited energy resources and capabilities to sense, gather, process data. In addition, the network bandwidth is also limited for data transmission among sensors. In order to use the network resources effectively, event-triggered control schemes have been proposed in the published literature to mitigate the need for unnecessary data transmission while preserving desired system performance [10,11]. Furthermore, it should be pointed out that in the traditional fault detector model, all the measurement outputs are sampled by one sensor and sent in a single packet to the fault detector, however, due to the complexity of the cyber physical systems, such an assumption may not be held in practical situations [12]. Hence, a distributed fault detection algorithm for sensor network-based cyber physical systems are demanded. To the best of the authors knowledge, there is no systematic result that addresses the distributed event-triggered fault detection filtering for cyber physical systems over sensor networks, which is the second motivation of the current study.

In this paper, we aim to investigate distributed fault detection of a broad class of false signal injection (FSI) attacks over mobile sensor networks in which data transmission of each sensor is triggered by a well defined event. Each sensor is capable to determine whether the sampled data should be broadcasted to its neighbors. Then each sensor gathers the measurements from itself and all neighboring sensors and transmits the sampled data to the distributed fault detectors through the communication network. Under this event-triggered scheme, the precious communication resources can be saved significantly. In this paper, the event-triggered distributed fault detection filters are proposed as the localized residual generators. By employing Lyapunov-Krasovskii functional method, the event-triggered distributed fault detection filters are designed such that the overall residual system is asymptotically stable with a prescribed disturbance attenuation level. Then the fault detection filters and the parameters of the event-triggered scheme can be codesigned, provided that a set of linear matrix inequalities are satisfied. Finally, a quarter-car suspension model is given to show the effectiveness of the proposed method.

2   System Modeling and Problem Statement

Consider the following plant

$$
\begin{cases}
\dot{x}(t) = Ax(t) + Bw(t) + Ef(t) \\
x(t_0) = \phi_0,
\end{cases}
\tag{1}
$$

The measurement outputs transmitted over a sensor network are in the form of

$$
y_i(t) = C_i x(t), \quad i \in \Omega = \{1, 2, \ldots, N\}
\tag{2}
$$

where $x(t) \in \mathbb{R}^n$ is the state vector; $w(t) \in \mathbb{R}^p$ is the disturbance noise belonging to $\mathcal{L}_2$; $f(t) \in \mathbb{R}^r$ is the fault to be detected; $y_i(t) \in \mathbb{R}^s$ is the measurement output received by the sensor i from the plant; ϕ_0 is the initial state. A, B, E, C_i and D_i, $i \in S$ are known as constant matrices of appropriate dimensions.

2.1   A Novel Event-Triggered Scheme

Assume that there is a communication network between the sensor nodes and the distributed fault detection filters as shown in Fig. 1.

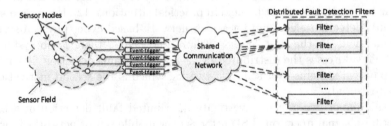

Fig. 1. Event-triggered Distributed Fault Detection Filters over Sensor Networks

In order to efficiently utilise the precious network resources, a novel event-triggered scheme is proposed by employing distributed event-generators. When the measurement signal $\tilde{y}_i(t)$ gathered from the sensor i and its neighbors j is transmitted to the distributed fault detection filter i through the sensor network i, a novel event-triggered scheme is proposed to choose the necessary packet data. The distributed measurement output $y_j(t)$ is first sampled at the time instants sh ($s = 1, 2, \cdots$) with $h > 0$ being a given sampling period. Then the sampled signal with its time stamp is encapsulated into a data packet. Whether or not a data packet is transmitted to the filter closely depends on a predefined event-triggered condition. Only those data packets violate the predefined event-triggered condition are transmitted through a communication channel. In this communication scheme, the distributed event-generator j is introduced to select necessary data packets. In the event-generator j, there is a register to store the latest transmitted data packet $(t_k^j, y_j(t_k^j))$ and a logical comparator to check if the current data packet should be transmitted. In the logical comparator, we introduce a judgement function $\chi_j(t_k^j h)$ to select the sampled measurement output $y_j(t_k^j h)$ as

$$\chi_j(s_k h) = \psi_j^T(s_k h)\Omega_j\psi_j(s_k h) - \lambda y_j^T(t_k^j h)\Omega_j y_j(t_k^j h) \tag{3}$$

$$\psi(s_k h) := y_j(s_k h) - y_j(t_k^j h), \quad l = 1, 2, \cdots \tag{4}$$

where $s_k = t_k^j h + \sum_{l=1}^{s} h$ is the current sampling instant; $\lambda > 0$ is a threshold parameter; $\Omega_j > 0$ are weighting matrices to be determined. For sensor j, the mechanism of the event-generator j is as follows: If the current data packet $(s_k h, y_j(s_k h))$ satisfies $\chi_j(s_k h) < 0$, the processor discards this data packet right away; otherwise, set $t_{k+1}^j h = t_k^j h + h$ and the register updates its store with the data packet $(t_{k+1}^j h, y_j(t_{k+1}^j h))$. At the same time, the processor j immediately releases this data packet; The logic ZOH keeps the data received at $t_k h + \tau(t_k h)$ available until the new data arrives at $t_{k+1} h + \tau(t_{k+1} h)$, where $\tau(t_k h)$ is the communication network induced delay. The release time sequence that indicates when those necessary data packets are released to the communication channel can be given by $t_1^j h, t_2^j h, \cdots, t_k^j h, \cdots$ with $t_k^j h < t_{k+1}^j h$. In fact, when data packets carry signals with little fluctuating compared with its previous transmitted ones, it is definitely a waste of communication resources to transmit them through a communication channel. Therefore, under the proposed event-triggered scheme, the communication resources can be utilised efficiently compared with the time-triggered scheme.

2.2   The Sensing Topology

In this section, we introduce some basic graph theory notions for the following analysis. The directed graph $\mathcal{G} = (\mathcal{S}, \mathcal{E}, \mathcal{W})$ represents the sensing topology of the sensor network, where $\mathcal{S}$, $\mathcal{E} \subseteq \mathcal{S} \times \mathcal{S}$, $\mathcal{W} = [w_{ij}] \in \mathbb{R}^{N \times N}$ are an index set of N sensor nodes; the edge set of paired sensor nodes and the weighted adjacency matrix, respectively. An edge of $\mathcal{G}$ is denoted by (i, j). The adjacency elements w_{ij} associated with the edges of the graph are positive, i.e., $w_{ij} > 0 \Longleftrightarrow (i,j) \in \mathcal{E}$. The set of neighbors of node i plus the node itself is denoted by $\mathcal{N}_i = \{j \in \mathcal{S} : (i,j) \in \mathcal{E}\}$. After the measurement output j surrounding the sensor i is triggered by the event-generator j, the sensor i is then gathered the information i from itself and its neighboring nodes $j \in \mathcal{N}^i$. Then the selected data will be transmitted to the distributed fault detection filter i. Based on the above analysis, the information collected by sensor node i is given by

$$\tilde{y}_i(t_k h) = \sum_{j \in \mathcal{N}^i} a^{ij} y_j(t_k h) \tag{5}$$

where $t_k h = \min\{t_k^j h\}$. The holding zone of the logic ZOH $[t_k h + \tau(t_k h), t_{k+1} h + \tau(t_{k+1} h)]$ can be divided in to $\bigcup_{l=0}^{n-1} \Theta_k^l$ where $\Theta_k^l = t_k^l h + \tau(t_k^l h), t_k^{l+1} h + \tau(t_k^{l+1} h)]$ with $n = t_{k+1} h - t_k h$. By introducing an artificial time delay $\eta(t) = t - t_k^l h$, $t \in \Theta_k^l$, one obtains that

$$y_i(t_k h) = y_i(t - \eta(t)) - \psi_i(s_k h) \tag{6}$$

where $\eta(t)$ is piecewise-linear with the derivative $\dot{\eta}(t) = 1$. In order to keep the right order of the $y_i(t_k h)$, assume that $\eta_m \leq \eta(t) \leq \eta_M < \infty$ for $t \neq t_k^l h + \tau(t_k^l h)$ with $\eta_m = \min\{\tau(t_k^l h)\}$, $\eta_M = h + \max\{\tau(t_k^l h)\}$. Then $\tilde{y}_i(t_k h)$ can be rewritten as

$$\tilde{y}_i(t_k h) = \sum_{j \in \mathcal{N}^i} a^{ij} y_j(t_k h) = \sum_{j \in \mathcal{N}^i} a^{ij}(y_j(t - \eta(t)) - \psi_j(s_k h)), \quad t \in \Theta_j^l. \tag{7}$$

2.3   Event-Triggered Fault Detection Filters

In this section, the event-triggered fault detection filters are proposed to generate the localized residual signals. The mechanism of the fault detection procedure is as follows. Firstly, when a false signal injection attack has been detected, a residual signal is generated by a localized residual generator to express the information of the fault of the plant under the attack; Secondly, an evaluator, including an evaluation function, a prescribed threshold, and a decision logic, is constructed to evaluate the residual signal. When the evaluation function has a value greater than the threshold, an alarm under the false signal injection attack is given.

The distributed fault detection filters to generate the localized residual are proposed as

$$\begin{cases} \dot{\hat{x}}_i(t) = \hat{A}_i \hat{x}_i(t) + \hat{B}_i \tilde{y}_i(t_k h), \ \hat{x}_i(0) = 0, i \in \Omega \\ r_i(t) = \hat{C}_i \hat{x}_i(t), t \in \Theta_i^l \end{cases} \tag{8}$$

where $\hat{x}_i(t) \in \mathbb{R}^x$ is the state estimate of the distributed fault detection filter i; $\tilde{y}_i(t_k h)$ is the input of the distributed fault detection filter; $r_i(t) \in \mathbb{R}^r$ is the residual signal that is compatible with the fault vector $f(t)$; the matrices $\hat{A}_i$, $\hat{B}_i$ and $\hat{C}_i$ are parameters of the distributed fault detection filter to be determined.

To detect the occurrence of the fault as attack occurred, one should construct a suitable localized residual evaluation function $J_i(t)$ which is in the form as

$$J_i(t) = (\int_0^t r_i^T(s)r_i(s)ds)^{\frac{1}{2}} \tag{9}$$

The residual evaluation function threshold J_{th}^i can be chosen as

$$J_{th}^i(t) = \sup_{w(t) \in \mathcal{L}_2, f(t)=0} J_i(t) \tag{10}$$

Then the false signal injection attack detection alarm is

$$\begin{cases} J_i(t) > J_{th}^i, with\ faults \\ J_i(t) \leq J_{th}^i, without\ faults \end{cases} \tag{11}$$

Based on the alarm of faults under the attack, some measures can be taken to guarantee the safety of the cyber-physical systems in network environments.

2.4   Modelling the Whole Framework

For the convenience, define a localized residual error signal as

$$g_i(t) = r_i(t) - f(t) \tag{12}$$

Denote $\bar{\hat{x}}(t) = col_N\{\hat{x}_i(t)\}$, $\bar{x}(t) = col_N\{x(t)\}$, $d(t) = col_N\{w(t), vec_N\{v(s_kh)\}, f(t)\}$, $r(t) = col_N\{g_i(t)\}$, $\xi(t) = col_2\{\bar{x}(t), \bar{\hat{x}}(t)\}$, $\bar{A} = diag_N\{A\}$, $\bar{B} = col_N\{B\}$, $\bar{E} = col_N\{E\}$, $\bar{I} = col_N\{I\}$, $\bar{C} = col_N\{C\}$, $\hat{\bar{A}} = diag_N\{\hat{A}_j\}$, $\hat{\bar{B}} = diag_N\{\hat{B}_j\}$, $\hat{\bar{C}} = diag_N\{\hat{C}_j\}$, $\bar{\psi}(s_kh) = col_N\{\psi_j(s_kh)\}$. Then, by substituting (7) into (8) and combining (1), we obtain the following augmented residual system

$$\begin{cases} \dot{\xi}(t) = \tilde{A}\xi(t) + \sum_{j=1}^N \tilde{F}\xi(s_kh) + \sum_{j=1}^N \tilde{B}\bar{\psi}(s_kh) + \tilde{E}d(t) \\ g(t) = \tilde{C}\xi(t) + \tilde{H}d(t) \end{cases} \tag{13}$$

where $\tilde{A} = \begin{bmatrix} \bar{A} & 0 \\ 0 & \hat{\bar{A}} \end{bmatrix}$, $\tilde{F} = \begin{bmatrix} 0 & 0 \\ \hat{\bar{B}}(A \otimes I)\bar{C} & 0 \end{bmatrix}$, $\tilde{B} = \begin{bmatrix} 0 \\ -\hat{\bar{B}}(A \otimes I) \end{bmatrix}$, $\tilde{E} = \begin{bmatrix} \bar{B} & \bar{E} \\ 0 & 0 \end{bmatrix}$, $\tilde{C} = \begin{bmatrix} 0 & \hat{\bar{C}} \end{bmatrix}$, $\tilde{H} = \begin{bmatrix} 0 & -\bar{I} \end{bmatrix}$.

From the above discussion, one can see that the residual system (13) reveals the difference between the residual signal and the fault under FSI attacks. The minimized effect of the disturbance can be measured by the H_∞ norm. Therefore, the distributed fault detection filtering problem can be transformed to an H_∞-optimization problem. **The event-triggered distributed fault detection filtering problem** to be addressed in this paper is formulated as: for given scalars η_m, η_M and λ, design suitable distributed filters and event-triggered weighting matrices $\Omega_i > 0$ such that i) the residual system (13) with $d(t) \equiv 0$ is asymptotically stable; and ii) the residual system (13) is satisfied the H_∞ norm $\|g(t)\|_{\mathcal{L}_2} < \gamma\|\{d(t)\}\|_{\mathcal{L}_2}$ for any nonzero $w(t) \in \mathcal{L}_2[0, \infty)$ under the zero initial condition.

3   Event-Triggered Distributed Fault Detection Filtering Performance Analysis

In this section, a residual system performance analysis criterion for the resultant residual system (13) is proposed.

Theorem 1. *Given positive scalars η_m, η_M, λ and the parameters $\hat{A}_i$, $\hat{B}_i$ and $\hat{C}_i$, the resultant residual system (13) is stable with a prescribed disturbance attenuation level γ, if there exist symmetric positive definite matrices P, Q_j, R_j, $j = 1, 2$ and Ω of appropriate dimensions such that*

$$\begin{bmatrix} \Sigma_{11} & \Sigma_{12} & \Sigma_{13} \\ \star & \Sigma_{22} & \Sigma_{23} \\ \star & \star & \Sigma_{33} \end{bmatrix} < 0, \tag{14}$$

where

$$\Sigma_{11} = \begin{bmatrix} \Psi_{11} & H^T R_1 & P\tilde{F} \\ \star & \Psi_{22} & R_2 \\ \star & \star & -2R_2 + \lambda H^T \bar{C}^T \Omega \bar{C} H \end{bmatrix},$$

$$\Psi_{11} = P\tilde{A} + \tilde{A}^T P + H^T Q_1 H - H^T R_1 H, \Psi_{22} = Q_2 - Q_1 - R_1 - R_2,$$

$$\Sigma_{22} = diag\{-Q_2 - R_2, -\Omega, -\gamma I\},$$

$$\Sigma_{12} = \begin{bmatrix} 0 & P\tilde{B} & P\tilde{E} \\ 0 & 0 & 0 \\ R_2 & 0 & 0 \end{bmatrix}, \tilde{F} = \sum_{j=1}^{N} \begin{bmatrix} 0 & 0 \\ \hat{B}(A \otimes I)\bar{C} & 0 \end{bmatrix}, \tilde{B} = \sum_{j=1}^{N} \begin{bmatrix} 0 \\ -\hat{B}(A \otimes I) \end{bmatrix},$$

$$\Sigma_{13} = \begin{bmatrix} \eta_m \tilde{A}^T H^T R_1 & \bar{\eta} \tilde{A}^T H^T R_2 & \bar{C}^T \\ 0 & 0 & 0 \\ \eta_m \tilde{F}^T H^T R_1 & \bar{\eta} \tilde{F}^T H^T R_2 & 0 \end{bmatrix}, \Sigma_{23} = \begin{bmatrix} 0 & 0 & 0 \\ \eta_m \tilde{B}^T H^T R_1 & \bar{\eta} \tilde{B}^T H^T R_2 & 0 \\ 0 & 0 & 0 \\ \eta_m \tilde{E}^T H^T R_1 & \bar{\eta} \tilde{E}^T H^T R_2 & \tilde{H}^T \end{bmatrix},$$

$$\Sigma_{33} = diag\{-R_1, -R_2, -\gamma I\}, \bar{\eta} = \eta_M - \eta_m, \tilde{A} = diag\{\bar{A}, \hat{A}\},$$

$$\tilde{E} = \begin{bmatrix} \bar{B} & \bar{E} \\ 0 & 0 \end{bmatrix}, \tilde{C} = \begin{bmatrix} 0 & \hat{C} \end{bmatrix}, \tilde{H} = \begin{bmatrix} 0 & -\bar{I} \end{bmatrix}, \Omega = diag_N\{\Omega_j\}.$$

Proof. The proof is omitted due to page limitation.

4   Event-Triggered Distributed Fault Detection Filters Design

In this section, based on Theorem 1, the following theorem provides a sufficient condition on the existence of the distributed fault detection filters such that the residual system (13) stable with a prescribed disturbance attenuation performance.

Theorem 2. *Given positive scalars η_m, η_M, λ, the resultant residual system (13) is stable with a prescribed disturbance attenuation level γ, if there exist symmetric positive definite matrices P, Q_j, R_j, W, $j = 1, 2$ and Ω of appropriate dimensions such that*

$$\begin{bmatrix} \tilde{\Sigma}_{11} & \tilde{\Sigma}_{12} & \tilde{\Sigma}_{13} & \tilde{\Sigma}_{14} \\ \star & \tilde{\Sigma}_{22} & 0 & 0 \\ \star & \star & \tilde{\Sigma}_{33} & \tilde{\Sigma}_{34} \\ \star & \star & \star & \tilde{\Sigma}_{44} \end{bmatrix} < 0, \tag{15}$$

where

$$\tilde{\Sigma}_{11} = \begin{bmatrix} P_1 \bar{A} + Q_1 - R_1 \ A_f + \bar{A}^T W^T \\ \star & A_f + A_f^T \end{bmatrix}, \tilde{\Sigma}_{12} = \begin{bmatrix} R_1 \sum_1^N B_f (A \otimes I)\bar{C} \ 0 \\ 0 \ \sum_1^N B_f (A \otimes I)\bar{C} \ 0 \end{bmatrix},$$

$$\tilde{\Sigma}_{13} = \begin{bmatrix} -\sum_1^N B_f (A \otimes I) \ P_1 \bar{B} \ P_1 \bar{E} \\ -\sum_1^N B_f (A \otimes I) \ W\bar{B} \ W\bar{E} \end{bmatrix}, \tilde{\Sigma}_{14} = \begin{bmatrix} \eta_m \bar{A}^T R_1 \ \bar{\eta} \bar{A}^T R_2 \ 0 \\ 0 \ 0 \ C_f^T \end{bmatrix},$$

$$\tilde{\Sigma}_{22} = \begin{bmatrix} Q_2 - Q_1 - R_1 - R_2 & R_2 & 0 \\ \star & -2R_2 + \lambda H^T \bar{C}^T \Omega \bar{C} H & R_2 \\ \star & \star & -Q_2 - R_2 \end{bmatrix}$$

$$\tilde{\Sigma}_{33} = diag\{-\Omega, -\gamma I, -\gamma I\}, \tilde{\Sigma}_{44} = diag\{-R_1, -R_2, -\gamma I\},$$

$$\tilde{\Sigma}_{34} = \begin{bmatrix} 0 & 0 & 0 \\ \eta_m \bar{B}^T R_1 & \bar{\eta} \bar{B}^T R_2 & 0 \\ \eta_m \bar{E}^T R_1 & \bar{\eta} \bar{E}^T R_2 & -\bar{I} \end{bmatrix}.$$

Moreover, if the above conditions are feasible, the parameters of the distributed filters are given as

$$\hat{A} = A_f W^{-1}, \hat{B} = B_f, \hat{C} = C_f W^{-1}. \tag{16}$$

Proof. The proof is omitted due to page limitation.

5   An Illustrative Example

A quarter-car suspension model, as depicted in Fig. 2, is provided to show the effectiveness of the proposed fault detection filter design method. The sprung mass m_s denotes the car chassis; the unsprung mass m_u represents the wheel assembly; the spring k_s is the stiffness and the damper c_s represents the damping of the uncontrolled suspension that is placed between the car body and the wheel assembly; the spring k_t serves to the model of the compressibility of the pneumatic tire. The variables x_s, x_u and x_r are the displacements of the car body, the wheel and the road disturbance input, respectively. The ideal dynamic equations for the sprung and unsprung masses of the quarter-car model are described as

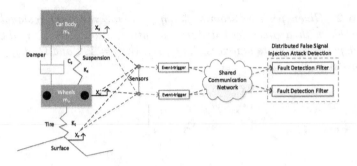

Fig. 2. The quarter-car suspension over a sensor network

$$\begin{cases} m_s\ddot{x}_s(t) + C_s(\dot{x}_s - \dot{x}_u(t)) + k_s(x_s(t) - x_u(t)) = 0, \\ m_u\ddot{x}_u(t) + C_s(\dot{x}_u - \dot{x}_s(t)) + k_s(x_u(t) - x_s(t)) + k_t(x_u(t) - x_r(t)) = 0. \end{cases} \quad (17)$$

Denote $x_1(t) = x_s(t) - x_u(t)$, $x_2(t) = x_u(t) - x_r(t)$, $x_3 = \dot{x}_s(t)$ and $x_4(t) = \dot{x}_u(t)$, where $x_1(t)$, $x_2(t)$, $x_3(t)$, $x_4(t)$ are the suspension deflection, the tire deflection, the sprung mass speed, and the unsprung mass speed, respectively. Then the quarter-car suspension model can be represented as

$$\dot{x}(t) = Ax(t) + Bw(t) \quad (18)$$

with

$$A = \begin{bmatrix} 0 & 0 & 1 & -1 \\ 0 & 0 & 0 & 1 \\ -\frac{k_s}{m_s} & 0 & -\frac{c_s}{m_s} & \frac{c_s}{m_s} \\ \frac{k_s}{m_u} & -\frac{k_u}{m_u} & \frac{c_s}{m_u} & -\frac{c_s}{m_u} \end{bmatrix}, B = \begin{bmatrix} 0 \\ -2\pi q_0\sqrt{G_0 v_0} \\ 0 \\ 0 \end{bmatrix}.$$

The parameters in the quarter-car model matrices are chosen as: $m_s = 973$ kg, $k_s = 42720$ N/m, $c_s = 3000$ Ns/m, $k_u = 101115$ N/m, $m_u = 114$ kg, $G_0 = 512 \times 10^{-6}$ m^3, $q_0 = 0.1$ m^{-1} and $v_0 = 12.5$ m/s. Assume two nodes are deployed in the sensor field. The sensing topology of the considered sensor network is characterized by a directed graph $\mathcal{G} = (\mathcal{S}, \mathcal{E}, \mathcal{W})$, with set of nodes $(\mathcal{S} = 1, 2)$, set of edges $\mathcal{E} = \{(1,1), (1,2), (2,2)\}$, and the set adjacency matrices $\mathcal{W} = [w^{ij}]_{2 \times 2}$ where adjacency elements $w^{ij} = 1$ when $(i, j) \in \mathcal{E}$; otherwise $w^{ij} = 0$. The measurement output matrices are given by $C_1 = \begin{bmatrix} 0 & 0 & 0 & 0.005 \end{bmatrix}$, $C_2 = \begin{bmatrix} 0 & 0.1 & 0 & 0 \end{bmatrix}$. The objective is to design desired distributed fault detection filters in the form of (8) over the sensor network to detect the fault induced by the attack of the sprung mass speed x_3 by using the measurement of the unsprung mass speed $x_4(t)$ or the tire deflection $x_2(t)$ on different sensor nodes.

Firstly, choose $h = 0.1$ s and network induced delays are lower and upper bounded by $\tau_m = 0.02$ s and $\tau_M = 0.06$ s, respectively. With the H_∞ disturbance attenuation performances level $\gamma = 1.5$, by the proposed event-triggered scheme, for $\lambda = 0.8$, applying Theorem 2, the corresponding parameters of the distributed fault detection filters are given as

$$
A_{f1} = \begin{bmatrix} -5.7331 & 11.5864 & 5.8085 & -342.2602 \\ 13.2871 & -29.1706 & 101.1032 & 666.2046 \\ -1.4728 & 0.9710 & -1.1373 & -2.9456 \\ 1.1982 & -1.1999 & -2.1269 & -7.7911 \end{bmatrix}, B_{f1} = \begin{bmatrix} 72.8 \\ -206.8 \\ -5591.5 \\ -771.2 \end{bmatrix},
$$

$$
C_{f1} = \begin{bmatrix} 0.0321 & 0.7601 & -6.1392 & 1.5599 \end{bmatrix},
$$

$$
A_{f2} = \begin{bmatrix} -5.7008 & 11.5769 & 5.7689 & -341.6595 \\ 13.2345 & -29.1426 & 101.8555 & 665.8959 \\ -1.4709 & 0.9720 & -1.1590 & -2.9319 \\ 1.1970 & -1.2039 & -2.1425 & -7.7845 \end{bmatrix}, B_{f2} = \begin{bmatrix} -45.6 \\ 129.1 \\ 3494.7 \\ 482.0 \end{bmatrix},
$$

$$
C_{f2} = \begin{bmatrix} 0.0379 & 0.7551 & -6.1687 & 1.6797 \end{bmatrix}.
$$

Consider the case of an isolated bump in an otherwise smooth road surface, the corresponding disturbance input signal is taken as: $w(t) = \frac{0.1\sin^2(t - \tau(t))}{(0.5 + t^2)}$. To further illustrate the effectiveness of the designed distributed fault detection filers, we assume that the fault signal induced by FSI attacks is simulated as

$$
f(t) = \begin{cases} 0.6, t \in [0.3s, 0.5s) \\ 0, \quad otherwise. \end{cases} \tag{19}
$$

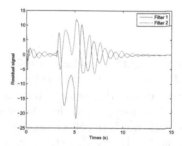

Fig. 3. The residual responses $r(t)$ with $f(t)$ over sensor networks

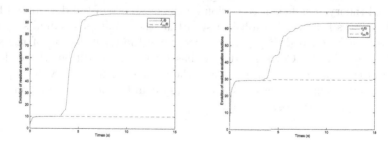

Fig. 4. The residual evaluation function responses $J(t)$ with and without $f(t)$

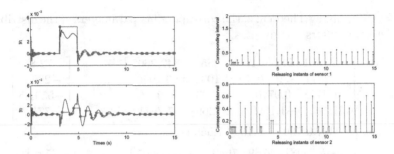

Fig. 5. The measurement outputs $y(t)$, releasing instants and intervals

Taking an initial condition as $x_0 = \begin{bmatrix} 0.02 & -0.02 & 0.02 & -0.02 \end{bmatrix}$, with the sampling period $h = 0.1$ s, the residual signals $r_i(t)$ under time sequences are depicted in Fig. 3. The residual evaluation functions $J_i(t)$ with fault and without fault $J_{th}^i(t)$, $i \in S$ are shown in Fig. 4. From Fig. 4, the simulation results show that the fault $f(t)$ can be detected in 0.16 s for the residual signal $r_1(t)$ and 0.19 s for the residual signal $r_2(t)$ after the occurrence of the fault induced by FSI attacks at 3 s. Associated with the above distributed fault detection filters, the measurement outputs trajectories of the physical plant and the transmission instants and the release intervals are shown in Fig. 5. From Fig. 5, it is clear to see the residual signals can reflect the fault in time while the utilization of the communication network is reduced, which verifies the effectiveness of the derived results.

6   Conclusions

The problem of event-triggered distributed false signal injection attack detection filtering of cyber physical systems over sensor networks has been investigated. A novel distributed discrete event-triggered strategy is proposed to select the necessary sampled data to be transmitted so that the precious network resources can be saved. Each sensor node needs to collect measurement outputs both from itself and all neighboring nodes. Under this strategy, to generate the localized residual signals, the event-triggered distributed fault detection filters have been proposed as localized residual signal generators. Based on Lyapunov-Krasovskii functional theory, a sufficient condition on the existence of the distributed fault detection filters has been established such that the resultant residual system is stable with a prescribed H_∞ performance while the transmission of the sampled data is reduced. Correspondingly, based on this condition, the codesign method of the fault detection filters and the transmission strategy is proposed. Finally, a continuous quarter-car suspension system has been given to verify the effectiveness of the proposed results.

References

1. Pasqualetti, F., Dorfler, F., Bullo, F.: Control-theoretic methods for cyberphysical security: geometric principles for optimal cross-layer resilient control systems. IEEE Contr. Syst. **35**(1), 110–127 (2015)
2. Langner, R.: Stuxnet: dissecting a cyberwarfare weapon. IEEE Secur. Priv. **9**(3), 49–51 (2011)
3. Kwon, C., Liu, W., Hwang, I.: Security analysis for cyber-physical systems against stealthy deception attacks. In: The Proceedings of the 2013 American Control Conference, Washington, DC, pp. 3344–3349 (2013)
4. Amin, S., Litrico, X., Sastry, S.S., Bayen, A.M.: Cyber security of water SCADA systems Part II: attack detection using enhanced hydrodynamic models. IEEE Trans. Contr. Syst. Techn. **21**(5), 1679–1693 (2013)
5. Sridhar, S., Govindarasu, M.: Model-based attack detection and mitigation for automatic generation control. IEEE Trans. Smart Grid **5**(2), 580–591 (2014)
6. Eyisi, E., Koutsoukos, X.: Energy-based attack detection in networked control systems. In: HiCoNS, pp. 115–124 (2014)
7. Ge, X., Han, Q.-L.: Distributed fault detection over sensor networks with Markovian switching topologies. Int. J. Gen. Syst. **43**(3–4), 305–318 (2014)
8. Shen, B., Wang, Z., Hung, Y.: Distributed H_∞-consesus filtering in sensor networks with multiple missing measurements: the finite-horizon case. Automatica **46**(10), 1682–1688 (2010)
9. Milln, P., Orihuela, L., Vivas, C., Rubio, F.: Distributed consensus-based estimation considering network induced delays and dropouts. Automatica **48**(10), 2726–2729 (2012)
10. Lin, Y., Han, Q.-L., Yang, F., Jarvis, D.: Event-triggered H_∞ filtering for networked systems based on network dynamics. In: The Proceedings of the 39th Annual Conference of the IEEE Industrial Electronics Society, pp. 5638–5643 (2013)
11. Ding, L., Guo, G.: Distributed event-triggered H_∞ consensus filtering in sensor networks. Sig. Process. **108**, 365–375 (2015)
12. Ferrari, R., Parisini, T., Polycarpou, M.: Distributed fault detection and isolation of largescale discrete-time nonlinear systems: an adaptive approximation approach. IEEE Trans. Autom. Control **57**(2), 275–290 (2012)

Mobile Money in the Australasian Region - A Technical Security Perspective

Swathi Parasa[1] and Lynn Margaret Batten[2(✉)]

[1] HCL Australia Services Pty. Ltd., Sydney, Australia
sswathi.tarini@hotmail.com
[2] Deakin University, Geelong, Australia
lynn.batten@deakin.edu.au

Abstract. While mobile money originated in Africa, its success has led to a spread around the world. This paper is the first to focus specifically on its uptake in the region of Australasia; we give a brief description of the current situation of mobile money usage in each of eight countries within this region. Despite the convenience of mobile money systems, their underlying technologies are susceptible to many threats associated with insecure Wi-Fi communication. We detail such threats and discuss possible countermeasures.

Keywords: Mobile money · Australasia · Vulnerabilities

1 Introduction

For centuries, traditional banking required individuals to be physically present at banks for depositing or withdrawing funds and making payments. However with the advent of ATMs in the 1970s, developing a few years later into home use of computers and the Internet, it became easy to perform banking activities from anywhere in the world and at any time. Pioneered in Kenya [1] in about 2007, mobile money systems leveraged the ubiquity of cellular networks through smart phones to encourage access to banking facilities world-wide. In developing countries, mobile money systems have become an affordable and easily accessible option for individuals; none-the-less, there are many people in developed countries who do not have a bank account and who benefit from the use of mobile money technologies. Furthermore, mobile optimized websites and applications (APPs) offer almost every service that a physical bank offers, encouraging millions of people, even those with traditional bank accounts, to use mobile money systems. In 2013, the president of the World Bank Group set a goal of 'universal financial access by 2020' [2; p. 24]. And according to a research report from Javelin Strategy & Research, mobile money systems usage went up by 63 percent between the years 2007 and 2011 [3].

Despite, and because of, its convenience, mobile banking has brought with it many emerging threats from unsecure Wi-Fi, mobile malware and third party APPs. We detail such vulnerabilities and associated threats in Sect. 3 and discuss possible countermeasures in Sect. 4.

L. Batten and G. Li (Eds.): ATIS 2016, CCIS 651, pp. 154–162, 2016.
DOI: 10.1007/978-981-10-2741-3_13

Key Enablers of a Mobile Money System

In order to design and implement a successful mobile money system, many elements need to be analysed and an understanding of what is meant by 'successful' is required. The figure on page 9 of [1] depicts the key drivers that are required to enable a successful mobile money system. These include economic drivers related to the capacity of the market, as well as regulations needed to prevent fraud and money laundering; a great deal has been written about these issues and we do not focus on them here. Also included are the risks of sending money through small devices, and the infrastructure and communications technologies required to do this; our focus is on this technology.

While mobile money originated in Africa, it has affected the Australasian region in significant ways. In this report, we present several mobile money systems used in Australasian countries and move on to analyse the inherent security problems associated with these systems, most of which rely on wireless technologies. We show that sending money through small devices in the context of the available infrastructure and communications technologies used is fraught with dangers; but we also make recommendations in order for users to gain some control of the security of their mobile financial systems.

The contributions of this paper are:

- A survey of types of mobile money systems used in 9 countries in the Australasia region;
- A description of the known vulnerabilities in these systems;
- References to counter-measures needed to mitigate these vulnerabilities.

2 Mobile Money Systems in the Australasia Region

We now focus on various mobile money systems that are popular in the region and we examine these country by country. Table 1 lists those countries we consider along with some of the mobile money systems they use.

Table 1. Summary of the most popular mobile money systems by country

Country	Mobile money systems in use
India	Airtel money, MoneyOnMobile, OxigenWallet
Philippines	GCash, SMART money, SMART padala
Australia and New Zealand	MPay, Tap & Go
Japan	Osaifu-Keitai
China	Alipay
Taiwan	Pi Wallet and Raspberry Pi
Malaysia	M-Money, AirCash
Indonesia	TCash

2.1   Mobile Money Systems in India

According to the Bank of India, around 41 % of the Indian population is unbanked and only 59 % of adults have bank accounts with around 45 % of total deposits contributed by the top six metropolitan areas in the country [4]. This indicates that financial exclusion may be due to low income levels, unemployment, lack of access to banking facilities and lower literacy rates. Technology is the only solution to financial inclusion that has the capability to reduce the costs and increase approachability to all classes of people. Recently mobile money systems have become the most favourable channel for financial inclusion [5].

2.2   Mobile Money Systems in the Philippines

The Philippines was one of the earliest adopters of mobile money systems and has achieved a considerable amount of success when compared to other countries in Asia. Its mobile penetration matches that of upper middle income countries. The broad success of mobile money systems there may be attributed to the high literacy levels of the population alongside relatively low incomes. Filipinos send hundreds of millions of SMS's per day, earning them the title of 'Text message capital' [6].

The first Mobile money system was launched in 2000 by Smart in collaboration with the large Bank D'Oro, upgraded to a preloaded SIM card in 2003, followed by Smart padala released in 2004 which enabled customers to accomplish national and international money transfers (http://smart.com.ph). Globe telecom entered the mobile money market in the year 2004 with its wallet called GCash operating like a portable ATM allowing users to make payments, remittances and money transfers without the use of prepaid cards. G-Cash has enlarged its network by offering loan disbursements and repayment services to rural banks [7].

By the year 2006, 2.5 million people used Smart mobile money services for paying utility bills, payroll credit and receipt of international remittances [8; p. 5]. Entering the market in 2008, **Sun Cellular**, a wholly-owned subsidiary of Digitel, is one of the Philippines' leading mobile telecommunications companies, attracting 7 million new subscribers; subsequently, the penetration rate of mobiles reached 82 % in the year 2009, with around 65 million mobile phone users. Globe and Smart communications now occupy the major share of the mobile market in the country.

2.3   Mobile Money Systems in Australia and New Zealand

When compared to other developing nations, there is less focus on the development of mobile money systems in Australia and New Zealand. Nevertheless, the facility of paying bills using a mobile money system connected with a bank account has been available for many years with MPay and BPay. Such systems specialise in micro-payments through a combination of contactless technology, POS terminal solutions and payment processing gateways.

Some financial institutions have implemented trials to assess the likelihood of success of more pervasive mobile money systems. In 2008, NAB, Telstra and Visa collaborated to launch a trial version of Australia's first mobile money system that allows users to download NAB's credit card software application onto any phone with Telstra's SIM card. In Australia, Commonwealth bank's Tap and Pay option is now available for debit cards to be used with Android phones and iPhone; in New Zealand, this facility has been rolled out by Mastercard. The systems require that the user have a valid bank account. Tap and Pay is enabled through Near-Field-Communication (NFC) technology and allows users to make purchases or perform transactions at any contactless terminal, whether at home or overseas.

2.4   Mobile Money Systems in Japan

Osaifu-Keitai (Japanese for Wallet Mobile) launched by NTT DOCOMO in 2004, is also based on NFC and was built using Sony's contactless chip "Felica". It allows mobile phones to be used by scanning any phone terminal against the NFC reader. Initially there was a reluctance among Japanese people in adopting this system as NFC compatible mobile handsets were required, but with strategic alliances, DOCOMO installed read/write terminals at various proprietorships. By 2011, around 65 % of mobile money users used Osaifu-Keitai with NFC compatible handsets, and around 1.4 million merchants across Japan accept payments through credit card and Osaifu-Keitai [9; p. 1]. Beneficial features of Osaifu Keitai include speed, ease of use, an online top-up facility, promotional coupons and the ability to make overseas payments. Also, Osaifu-Keitai complies with the guidelines released by GSMA for mobile payments.

2.5   Mobile Money Systems in China

At the end of 2014, over 70 million people in rural areas still lived below the poverty line (http://www.worldbank.org/en/country/china/overview). China's strategy to enable financial inclusion includes a mix of banks, financial institutions, infrastructure, e-commerce groups and social networks. By January 2016, China was the world's largest e-commerce market, an achievement enabled by its access to mobile money. Alipay, established in 2004 [10], is the clear winner in online payment services in China, with version 9.0 being released in early June 2015. But Tencent, one of the largest Internet companies in the world, launched competitor Tenpay in 2005 which has become very popular in the mobile gaming market.

2.6   Mobile Money Systems in Taiwan

In Taiwan, cash payments remain the most popular payment method. In fact "Electronic payments represent only 25.8 % of personal consumption expenditure in Taiwan, far below other Asian markets such as Hong Kong (64.5 %), China (55.9 %), South Korea (54.8 %) and Singapore (53.0 %)" according to Visa's statistics [11]. When compared to other countries, Taiwan has lagged. Its first mobile payment system Pi mobile wallet was launched by PChome in the year 2015. The Pi wallet set-up consists of a device called Raspberry Pi with removable SD cards attached to a host device with USB or HDMI cables; users can shop virtually by scanning corresponding QR codes or making small financial transfers with the device (e.g. https://en.wikipedia.org/wiki/Raspberry_Pi).

2.7 Mobile Money Systems in Malaysia

Cash also remains a popular method of payment in Malaysia [12; Chap. 5], but the use of mobile money systems has grown since 2007 with current services mainly focusing on bill payments and mobile banking. Four mobile operators have launched mobile payment services: Maxis was the first, launched in 2007; this was followed by products by Celcom, Digi and U Mobile.

2.8 Mobile Money Systems in Indonesia

Indonesia is the fourth largest country in the world, with a 2015 population of 259 million (http://www.internetworldstats.com/stats8.htm) of whom 34 % were not using any form of electronic communication (computers or mobile devices), even though these were available to 90 % of the population [13]. Affordability and lack of awareness were cited as being the biggest barriers [13; p. 11], while the lack of websites available in the local language also plays a key role [13; Fig. 4].

Since 2007, transactions per day have risen from IDR5 billion to IDR30 trillion in 2016 (https://www.techinasia.com/17-emoney-options-indonesia). Most forms of mobile money used are pre-paid bank cards, but in March 2016, Bank Negara Indonesia introduced a tap and pay card (https://www.techinasia.com/17-emoney-options-indonesia) similar to those used in Australia and New Zealand.

Despite the unawareness of mobile money in the population, in 2007 Telkomsel rolled out the e-wallet TCash, which now has 15 million registered users. In 2016, XL Axiata, Telkomsel, and Indosat, the three big Indonesian telcos, provide emoney services in the form of e-wallets. To encourage user growth, all three companies agreed to allow their users to transfer cash to each other even though they are competitors.

3 Vulnerabilities in Mobile Money Systems

Several vulnerabilities have been found in mobile money systems (e.g. In [14–17]). We divide them into four main categories and give examples of mobile money systems with each vulnerability.

3.1 Authentication of Sender and Receiver

When sending money, it is critical that the intended recipient receive it; it is also important that the recipient knows from whom it came. Authentication techniques such as certificates and digital signatures provide such guarantees.

MPay does not properly ensure that it is communicating with the correct endpoint. This can result in message modification, replay attacks and denial of service.

M-Money relies on improper enforcement of message integrity during transmission over the communication channel.

3.2 Data Integrity

Messages about financial transfers need to be protected from changes (e.g. increasing amounts, changing the account number). Data integrity can be achieved by encrypting the data.

G-Cash. In this system, data is not encrypted between end points.
MoneyOnMobile does not attempt to secure data in transmission.
Oxigen Wallet does not use SSL/TLS cryptographic protocols to protect data from changes in transit.

3.3 Poor Protocol Implementation

While all the appropriate pieces of the needed security can be to hand, the final implementation of them may be done poorly, making them attack targets.

Oxigen Wallet uses a poorly implemented version of the known encryption algorithm blowfish. Requests for secure keys are unauthenticated putting all transactions at risk.

Osaifu-Keitai has poor security software upgrade implementation on an open source operating system such as Android (e.g. [9]).

3.4 Malfunctions and Overlooked Attack Vectors

Some mobile money systems are prone to malfunctions, and some are badly constructed, leaving attack vectors for criminals.

G-Cash. In this system, outgoing SMS messages save the pin in the user's mobile phone's outbox; if the device is lost, any attacker can easily access the pin.

Osaifu-Keitai. Malfunctions and software upgrades have led to tampering with the device and loss or alteration to data, as well as leakage of private information.

Alipay. The software company Trend Micro discovered vulnerabilities in the Alipay Software Development Kit v. 1.0 that can be exploited for phishing attacks (http://blog. trendmicro.com/trendlabs-security-intelligence), explaining that the original Alipay wallet can be replaced by a malicious APP which can obtain payment details from the user. Attackers can use malicious APPs to intercept sensitive information between the mobile payment application and its clients.

Pi Wallet. One recently discovered vulnerability is due to the absence of a hardware random generator in Raspberry Pi 2, restricting the secure keys generated to known ones [18]. Moreover, in a recent discovery, the updated version Raspberry Pi 2 crashes when exposed to intense bursts of light produced by Xenon or laser pointers [19].

TCash. When a user taps a smart phone, a hacker can use the NFC tag to instruct an APP on the smart phone to redirect to a web page that contains an exploit for a weakness in a browser. This gives the attacker access to the user's smart phone to monitor payment transactions, key strokes, make phone calls, send SMSs and steal sensitive data [20].

4   Countermeasures

Any mobile financial service runs the risk of supporting money laundering and terrorist financing because of its features of anonymity, speed and general lack of oversight. Mitigation techniques to help prevent fraud and money laundering are presented in the table on pages 7 to 15 of [21] and in the report [22]. In this section, we focus on mitigation of technical difficulties, some of which were identified in the previous section.

As stated in the report by Javelin Research [3]: "Authentication measures uniquely suited to mobile devices such as biometrics, device fingerprinting, mobile location, and in-APP authentication can provide protection against current and developing fraud schemes such as mobile remote-access Trojans and business email compromise. … offering strong mobile authentication is crucial to financial institutions in both pre-venting their customers from suffering fraud losses and in providing (them) reasonable security measures under the Uniform Commercial Code for protection against litigation."

Recommendations: Our recommendations are aimed at mobile money system designers, telecommunications and Internet Service Providers as well as to users:

- To prevent communications being diverted to false entities or being accepted from false entities, it is important to have *authentication of both user and application by a trusted third party.*
- To prevent loss of secure key data, *PINs should be saved in secured memory and stored in encrypted form.* In addition, *two forms of authentication* should secure the most important communications, such as money transfers.
- Strong cryptographic protocols providing *end-to-end communication encryption* should be used, along with SMS message authentication. *SSL/TLS protocols* should be established across communication channels.

References

1. Dharmapalan, J., Lonergan, N., Price, K., Pilorge, P.: Mobile Money: An Overview for Global Telecommunications Operators, 44 pages. Ernst & Young Global Ltd. (2009)
2. Coere, B., Walliser, J.: Payment aspects of financial inclusion. Consultative Report by the Committee on Payments and Market Infrastructures, World Bank Group. Published by the Bank for International Settlements and World Bank Group (2015)
3. Pascual, A., Moeser, M., Marchini, K.: Mobile Authentication in Small Business Banking, November 2015. https://www.javelinstrategy.com/coverage-area/mobile-authentication-small-business-banking
4. Rajan, M.S.S.: Replication of Financial Inclusion: Opportunities and Challenges – Indian Bank Experience. Publication of the Bank of India, 7 pages (2007)
5. Niyogi, A., Niyogi, S.: Mobile Money for Unbanked in India. Int. J. Finan. Policy Anal. **4** (2), 26–35 (2012)
6. Bankable Frontier Associates (2010). Mobile Money Regulation in the Philippines, Paper presented to Seminar on Regulating Branchless Banking, Windsor, pp. 1–15. http://www. afiglobal.org/sites/default/files/mobile%20money%20regulation%20in%20the% 20philippines.pdf. Retrieved July 2016
7. Flores-Roux, E., Mariscal, J.: The development of mobile money systems. Centro de Investigación y Docencia Económicas, División de Administración Pública (Centre for Economic Research and Teaching, Division of Public Administration), Number 256, 38 pages (2011)
8. Chatain, P.: Integrity in mobile phone financial services: measures for mitigating risks from money laundering and terrorist financing. No. 146. World Bank Publications (2008)
9. Miura, N., Hoshino, J., Hirose, J., Fukuzono, T.: Credit Services for the Osaifu-Keitai Mobile Payment System On Open OS Terminals. NTT DOCOMO Tech. J. **13**(2), 43–48 (2011)
10. Chuen, D.L.K., Teo, E.G.: Emergence of FinTech and the LASIC principles. In 'Who will disrupt the disruptors?'. J. Finan. Perspect. **V1**, 24–36 (2015)
11. FocusTaiwan: Electronic payment usage remains low in Taiwan: Visa Taiwan (update), June 2014. http://focustaiwan.tw/search/201406300017.aspx?q=cash%20payments%20
12. Mohammad, A.: The Development of E-Payments and Challenges in Malaysia. In the Development of E-payments and Challenges for Central Banks in the SEACEN Countries edited by Seng, V., Chap. 5, pp. 123–157. The SEACEN Centre (2008)
13. Lucese, B.: Connected Society: Consumer Barriers to mobile Internet adoption in Asia. Report produced by Global Mobile Communications Asia, 24 pages. http://www.gsma.com/ mobilefordevelopment/wp-content/uploads/2016/06/Consumer-Barriers-to-Mobile-Internet-Adoption-in-Asia.pdf
14. Reaves, B., Scaife, N., Bates, N., Traynor, P., Butler, K.: Mo(Bile) money, Mo(Bile) problems: analysis of branchless banking applications in the developing world. In: Proceedings of the 24th USENIX Security Symposium, Washington, DC, pp. 17–32. USENIX, August 2015
15. Moonsamy, V., Batten, L., Shore, M.: Can smartphone users turn off tracking service settings? In: Proceedings of International Conference on Advances in Mobile Computing & Multimedia, 9 pages. ACM (2013)
16. Rahulamathavan, Y., Moonsamy, V., Batten, L., Shunliang, S., Rajarajan, M.: An analysis of tracking settings in blackberry 10 and windows phone 8 smartphones. In: Susilo, W., Mu, Y. (eds.) ACISP 2014. LNCS, vol. 8544, pp. 430–437. Springer, Heidelberg (2014)

17. Batten, L.M., Moonsamy, V., Alazab, M.: Smartphone applications, malware and data theft. In: Senthilkumar, M., et al. (eds.) Computational Intelligence, Cyber Security and Computational Models. AISC, vol. 412, pp. 15–24. Springer, Singapore (2016)
18. Singh, M.: Raspberry Pi Mini Computers Vulnerable to Attacks, Company Acknowledges, December 2015. http://gadgets.ndtv.com/laptops/news/raspberry-pi-mini-computers-vulnerable-to-attacks-company-acknowledges-772661. Retrieved July 2016
19. Goodin, D.: Just-released Raspberry Pi 2 can be DoSed by bright flashes of light (2015). http://arstechnica.com/security/2015/02/just-released-raspberry-pi-2-can-be-dosed-by-bright-flashes-of-light/. Retrieved July 2016
20. Tung, L.: Hackers can bank on NFC (2012). http://www.smh.com.au/it-pro/security-it/hackers-can-bank-on-nfc-20120808-23tdt.html. Retrieved July 2016
21. Lake, A.J.: Risk management in Mobile Money: Observed risks and proposed mitigants for mobile money operators. Report of the International Finance Corporation, World Bank Group, 22 pages (2013)
22. Chatain, P., Zerzan, A., Noor, W., Dannaoui, N., de Koker, L.: Protecting Mobile Money against Financial Crimes. Publication of the World Bank, vol. 1(1), pp. 1–195 (2011). http://www.globalinitiative.net/download/financial-crime/global/World%20Bank%20-%20Protecting%20Mobile%20Money%20against%20Financial%20Crimes.pdf. Retrieved July 2016

Author Index

Printed in the United States
By Bookmasters